Frommer

G000038583

irreverent

guide to

Chicago

other titles in the

irreverent guide

series

Frommer's®

irreverent
guide to
Chicago

2nd Edition

By
Dan Santow
and
Todd Savage

A BALLIETT & FITZGERALD BOOK
MACMILLAN • USA

a disclaimer

Prices fluctuate in the course of time, and travel information changes under the impact of the varied and volatile factors that influence the travel industry. Neither the author nor the publisher can be held responsible for the experiences of readers while traveling. Readers are invited to write to the publisher with ideas, comments, and suggestions for future editions.

about the authors

Dan Santow was a senior editor at *Chicago* magazine and an on-air correspondent for the city's Fox network news. After *Chicago*, Santow was a producer for "The Oprah Winfrey Show" and a staffwriter for *People*. He is currently the managing editor of the National Travel division of Rand McNally.

Todd Savage is a freelance writer and researcher based in Chicago who has contributed to *Chicago* magazine, *Chicago Tribune*, *Chicago Reader*, *Town and Country*, and *Outside*.

Balliett & Fitzgerald, Inc.

Editorial director: Will Balliett / Line editor: Holly Hughes / Executive editor: Tom Dyja / Managing editor: Rachel Aydt / Production editor: Maria Fernandez / Associate editor: Vijay Balakrishnan

MACMILLAN TRAVEL

A Simon & Schuster Macmillan Company
1633 Broadway
New York, NY 10019

Find us online at www.frommers.com

ISBN 0-02-862572-2
ISSN 1085-4797

Macmillan Travel Art director: Michele Laseau
Interior design contributed to by Tsang Seymour Design Studio

what's so irreverent?

It's up to you.

You can buy a traditional guidebook with its fluff, its promotional hype, its let's-find-something-nice-to-say-about-everything point of view. Or you can buy an Irreverent guide.

What the Irreverents give you is the lowdown, the inside story. They have nothing to sell but the truth, which includes a balance of good and bad. They praise, they trash, they weigh, and leave the final decisions up to you. No tourist board, no chamber of commerce will ever recommend them.

Our writers are insiders, who feel passionate about the cities they live in, and have strong opinions they want to share with you. They take a special pleasure leading you where other guides fear to tread.

How irreverent are they? One of our authors insisted on writing under a pseudonym. "I couldn't show my face in town again if I used my own name," she told me. "My friends would never speak to me." Such is the price of honesty. She, like you, should know she'll always have a friend at Frommer's.

Warm regards,

Michael Spring

Michael Spring
Publisher

contents

DIVERSIONS

THE INDEX

An A to Z list of venues, with vital statistics

HOTLINES & OTHER BASICS 194

introduction

In Yiddish to "schmy" means to walk around, window shop, stop for a cup of coffee and maybe a tuna club, window shop some more, stop and have another cup of coffee, maybe a nice piece of carrot cake... you buy a little here, a little there. You check out everyone else schmying around and try to decide if they're wearing Anne Klein or Calvin Klein, whether their fur is real or fake. You go into fancy stores and five-and-dimes. You schmy.

Half the fun of visiting Chicago is schmying around, checking out the neighborhoods—itineraries and agendas be damned. To get to know the people, the architecture, the parks, you have to be willing to explore (on foot if possible, though this is a driving town).

The first thing that will strike you is Lake Michigan, so immense you can't see across to Indiana or Michigan (much to the surprise of many who've never been here). The lake is always east, and the city faces that way. Early this century, the great architect Louis Sullivan wrote, "Chicago can pull itself down and rebuild itself in a generation, if it will... a dream born of the incomparable lake..." Nearly 80 years later, as new towers cast shadows over his creations, his words are still true. The water—and the open sky above—give Chicagoans room to breathe, room to think, room to hope. Stand on Oak Street Beach, a backdrop of high-rises and hotels behind you, and stare out at the vastness. Sit on the rocks at Belmont Harbor and watch the sailboats gracefully lope across the horizon on an early summer morning. It will clear your head for sure, maybe even calm your soul.

Turn away from the vastness, and you'll learn that Chicago is a city of neighborhoods: The Loop, Lincoln Park, Hyde Park, Lake View, Andersonville, Ravenswood Manor—the list could fill a page (now more than ever, as old-time neighborhoods get carved up and renamed to give developers and other real estate sharks a new sales handle). But just a list of names would be meaningless. Canaryville sounds quaint, doesn't it? Well, it's not; it's a tough Irish enclave. Streeterville is a lumpy moniker, right? Well, it's the ritzy neighborhood where Oprah Winfrey lives.

It was in these neighborhoods that the city's successive waves of immigrants hunkered down and tried to recreate their homeland in the face of the next influx. The neighborhood known as Pilsen, for instance, began as an immigrant Czech area, but starting in the 1950s, Mexicans moved in, and today its main drag, 18th Street, is lined with Mexican diners, taquerias, and music shops blaring salsa. Rogers Park still has kosher delis, bakeries, and butchers with window signs in Hebrew, but in the past decade it's been infiltrated by East Indian restaurants, sari shops (mysteriously, they also often sell small appliances), and video stores trafficking in Indian films. Wicker Park, touted by many as the successor to Seattle's grunge scene, was once a well-to-do German neighborhood.

The South and West Sides were prime destinations for the great black migration earlier in this century, explaining why Chicago has contributed so much to African-American culture. This is the home of the Nation of Islam, Johnson Publications *(Ebony* and *Jet)*, Oprah's Harpo Productions, the late *Native Son* novelist Richard Wright, and the blues of Muddy Waters and Howlin' Wolf. This is also the home of grinding poverty and some of the most notoriously crime-ridden housing projects in the country, as anyone who's read Alex Kotlowitz's sobering bestseller *There Are No Children Here*, or who's seen the 1994 documentary *Hoop Dreams*, knows. Though long reputed to be America's most segregated big city, the races here seem to have reached a détente, as the popularity of Mayor Richard Daley the younger has, in Harold Washington's wake, spread across racial lines and Michael Jordan and Oprah Winfrey serve as role models for kids of all colors. The increasing Hispanic population forms the other third of the racial balance here, its visibility and power growing accordingly.

Chicago has the variety you'd expect in America's third largest city—rich ditzy socialites, yuppie advertising copywriters, drug dealers, 21-year-old Porsche-driving millionaire commodity traders, dowdy gay men and lipstick lesbians, jetsetters, Tibetan refugees, Pakistani taxi drivers, grocery store clerks, sports giants, and more. But though its people are diverse in race and interests, the city's ethos is remarkably unified. It is—and don't laugh—a reasonably happy place. Not a mindlessly smiley-face kind of place, but a place where people try to be pleasant and get on with it. Sure, it's had its serious, even tragic, moments—the riots during the '68 Democratic convention; the day in the mid-'70s when the *Daily News,* one of the most intelligent newspapers Americans have ever read, closed down; the week in July 1995 when hundreds of people died because of a brutal heat wave—but overall, Chicago is a seat-of-the-pants kind of town. If you have troubles, they're your troubles, not Chicago's.

Being pleasant doesn't mean that Chicagoans don't have an attitude, though. A few years ago, a boutique called Fiorucci—full of metallic leather bustiers and feathered mules—closed here after a short run, despite successes in New York and Los Angeles. As a local wag said, "Chicago's too real a place for a store like that." One of Chicago's many great literary offspring, Nelson Algren, wrote about his home, "Like loving a woman with a broken nose, you may well find lovelier lovelies. But never a lovely so real."

Chicago's residents genuinely take advantage of the city, broken nose or not, from the crazy ferris wheel on Navy Pier to the sailboat harbors along the lake to the bleachers of Wrigley Field, watching the Cubbies lose another one. The art museums are jammed with locals; so is Orchestra Hall and the Lyric Opera. Everybody schmys on Michigan Avenue, not just the swells who can actually afford to buy things at Nieman-Marcus. Civic festivals, from the over-hyped "Taste of Chicago" to the huge jazz, gospel, and blues fests, draw millions of Chicagoans from every possible race and status, all sitting affably together on their blankets, under the stars.

Still, residents don't often take lazy boat tours of the Chicago River, or gawk at the top of the Sears Tower, one of the world's tallest buildings. We tell ourselves that those obvious pleasures are just for tourists—that is, until Uncle Jerry and Aunt Elaine come in from out of town and we have to show them "American Gothic" at the Art Institute and stand in line forever at Christmastime for a table in the Walnut Room at Marshall Field's on State Street, just so we can sit under the huge tree. We grumble and groan about looking like tourists, and we love it. We love the excuse to schmy in our own city.

Schmying here means, of course, dealing with Chicago's climate. One of the great myths about Chicago is that the weather stinks. Yes, winter lasts a long time—it's freezing or below that about a third of the year—and the skies can be gray for weeks. But the annual low temperatures usually aren't as bad as those in Denver, Minneapolis, Spokane, and Omaha—they're more on the level of Kansas City and Albuquerque. Don't get scared by the fact that it was 27 degrees below zero (without the wind chill factored in) on New Year's Day 1985, or that Chicagoans are 177 percent more likely to own a snowblower than the rest of the country. Be like a Chicagoan and dress for the season. It's winter—it's supposed to be cold. People here take a perverse pride in their ability to handle the elements, though they don't revel in the cold like Montrealers or Minnesotans, throwing carnivals, for god's sake, amid heaps of snow. No, the pleasure here comes in facing down the annual invasion of ice and cold and slush and still doing business as usual. It takes a lot to shut this city down, so pile on the fur, goose down, wool, electric socks, and bun-warmers, no matter how stupid you end up looking. Summers can be, and generally are, hot and humid—the average high in July is over 85 degrees—but those lucky enough to live near the lake (or play near it) don't suffer so much. The phrase "cooler by the lake" really means what it says—in fact, it can be up to 10 degrees cooler along the shore. (And the opposite is true as well—in winter it can be up to 10 degrees warmer.)

Summer allows you to hang at Oak Street Beach, schmying with tanned and toned natives who can look surprisingly like the real-life cast of *Baywatch*. In winter you can cross-country ski through Lincoln Park and then sip a hot chocolate overlooking a lagoon so picturesque that it would make even Fragonard's teeth hurt. In spring you can inhale the scent of the formal gardens in Grant Park beginning to bloom. And in autumn... well, September, October, and November all are consistently gorgeous. Acres of trees lining the shores of Lake Michigan become a living, breathing Impressionist painting, their muted colors blending in with one another in a way that would have awed Monet. The air is crisp as an apple and a cool, pristine breeze settles over the city.

So enjoy being a tourist here. Prepare to be tired, because you will be—if you schmy like you're supposed to.

Central Chicago Neighborhoods

you probably didn't know

Why do they call Chicago the Second City?... If you're speaking in terms of population, these days Los Angeles beats Chicago. (New York still wins, though.) Legend has it, though, that the term "Second City" refers to more than just population. After the Great Fire in 1871, much of the city was rebuilt, and locals starting referring to the new, glistening sections of town as the "second city." The phrase eventually caught on to describe the city as a whole, maybe because it fits a certain state of mind— Chicagoans' decades-long low self-esteem binge— implying that our town lacks the beauty, excitement, grandeur, and power of New York. The truth of that, of course, you'll have to decide for yourself.

Why do they call it the Windy City?... No doubt, Chicago is windy—it sits on a big body of water, and winds whip across it throughout the year. But other cities are just as windy, if not windier (Oklahoma City and Atlanta, for example, annually average faster winds than Chicago). Although a record 69mph wind blew through the city on April 14, 1984, the average is a measly 10.2 miles an hour. There are various legends as to why Chicago became known as the "Windy City," but the most popular blames it on the fact that over the decades it has hosted so many presidential nominating conventions, with all those politicians generating so much hot air that they were referred to as "windy-mouthed." That certainly hasn't changed.

What is "The Loop"?... Once upon a time, the el tracks made a loop around a compact and dense area of downtown. Well, they still do—the el tracks haven't been moved—but the encircled area long ago burst at its seams. Nowadays when Chicagoans speak of the Loop, they're referring to anywhere east and south of the Y-shaped Chicago River, north of Roosevelt Street, and west of Lake Michigan. The Loop means downtown, the financial heart of things, a cultural and commercial nerve center packed with landmarks and theaters and smart hotels (all of which exist in other parts of town as well, but not in such concentration). This is where Chicago's big-city pulse throbs most insistently.

So why does the Loop seem so empty?... Chicagoans may claim that they like the great outdoors, but every day thousands of Loop office workers and shoppers never see a speck of sunlight. That's because they're underground squirreling through the **Pedway**, a subterranean maze of covered walkways that connect numerous train stops, much of the Loop, and its environs on weekdays, from 6am to 6:30pm. "You are Here" signs are marked throughout, though getting lost is half the fun, or at least half the adventure.

What's so great about State Street?... Lots, actually. When the glitz and glam of North Michigan Avenue becomes too much to take, State Street's old-time urban aura can be a pleasant antidote. Its strength lies not so much in the reflection of its past as the Loop's main artery, but in its current reincarnation as a middle-class, bargain-hunters' paradise, upscale **Marshall Field's** notwithstanding. In the last few years a gargantuan three-story **Toys 'R' Us** opened (10 S. State St.), which caused a brouhaha among purists who saw this as the final step in the suburbanization of the street. A few architectural gems have avoided the wrecker's ball, lo, these many years, and are worth a look up: **Carson Pirie Scott & Co.** (1 S. State St.), designed by Louis Sullivan and completed in 1904, and Daniel Burnham's 1890, 15-story **Reliance Building** (32 N. State St.), both of which presaged much of today's modern architecture. Architectural insignificance, however, is the key to one of the street's other highlights—called **Block 37**, just across the street from Field's. Starting out as an urban nightmare—it was razed to make room for a huge shopping-and-office development that never got off the ground, literally—the square block has evolved into one of the most pleasant oases in the area, with an outdoor art gallery during the summer months and an ice skating rink in winter.

What's so magnificent about the Magnificent Mile?... The Magnificent Mile isn't, in fact, a mile at all—this stretch of Michigan Avenue starting at Oak Street and running south to the Chicago River measures slightly less than a mile in length. Magnificent it is, though, without a question. Once lined with some of the city's most renowned architecture, the street has evolved over the years from a sleepy yet chic thoroughfare of five-story limestone buildings, to a bustling, traffic-choked canyon of cash-cow retailers and gleaming office buildings. Yet, it's still elegant, wide, and surprisingly light-filled, with water on both ends (the lake at the north end, the river at the south). The Mag Mile is the true retail center of the city, as well as a business center and an upscale residential neighborhood. And at Christmas time, when the trees are strung with tiny white lights that make the street glitter like a diamond necklace, it's an especially gorgeous sight.

> **Chicago in the movies, part 1—downtown**
> *The 1938 period piece* In Old Chicago *starred Tyrone Power and Don Ameche as two sons of Mrs. O'Leary, the lady who accidentally started the Chicago Fire. Brian DePalma's mob pic* The Untouchables *(1987), starring Kevin Costner, Sean Connery, and Robert De Niro, had one great shootout scene with a baby carriage bouncing down the steps at Union Station. Chicago almost saw its destruction during 1980's* The Blues Brothers, *when John Belushi and Dan Aykroyd drove their Blues-mobile through Daley Plaza. And who could forget* The Beginning of the End, *a horrible 1957 sci-fi flick with Peter Graves in which giant grasshoppers invade Chicago?*

Does size really matter?... To most of us, no, but that doesn't stop us from boasting about the John Hancock Center and Sears Tower, two of the world's tallest buildings (both of which were recently, and sorely, overtaken by twin towers in, of all places, Kuala Lumpur—who wants to go to Kuala Lumpur anyhow?). We've also got the biggest urban zoo (the Lincoln Park zoo), the longest uninterrupted public coastline in any major U.S. metropolitan area, and the biggest Banana Republic, Pottery Barn, and Ralph Lauren Polo stores in the country.

Does Chicago really have more Polish people than anywhere save Warsaw?... Well, there are about two million people in Warsaw—presumably almost all Poles, right?—and, according to the librarian at the Polish Museum of America (tel 773/384–3352, 984 N. Milwaukee Ave.), about 1,000,000 Poles and Polish-Americans living in Chicago. Nowhere else comes close.

How can I sound like a real Chicagoan?... Pronounce the city's name Chicawgo, not Chicahgo.

What's "coffee and"?... A Chicago idiom, the phrase means coffee and a piece of cake, coffee and a pastrami sandwich, coffee and a slice of pie—whatever you might have after a movie or play. "Come on," you might say, "let's get some coffee and." I know, it sounds like a word is missing, but trust me, it's not.

Is there anyone in town who who doesn't idolize Michael Jordan?... No.

What will happen when Michael Jordan retires—again?... The city will basically curl up and die.

Who's going to take the place of Harry Caray in the hearts and minds of Cubs fans?... No one. Longtime Cubs announcer Caray's death brought a definite pall over the '98 baseball season. His widow, Duchie, did sing "Take Me Out to the Ball Game" during the seventh-inning stretch on opening day, which was a touching aftermath to a gray winter made grayer still by Harry's death in Palm Springs. All season long Cubs management invited guest singers—Jay Leno even sang it when he was here for a week taping "The Tonight Show." Still, Chicagoans are a loyal bunch and as far as most of us are concerned, they could get Barbra Streisand and Luciano Pavarotti to sing and it still wouldn't be as sweet to our ears as the warbling of grumpy old Harry.

Well, I brought my car—now where am I going to park it?... Parking on the street in most neighborhoods is a huge pain in the kiester—meters are enforced by an army of persnickety meter readers, and a parking space on side streets, where it's free, is a rare commodity. In addition, the city of Chicago loves, loves, loves to have cars towed, and the companies that do the actual towing are not known for service with a smile. (It'll cost you at least

$100 to ransom your car.) Most decent restaurants have valet parking for $5 or $6, which is a good deal considering the cost to your psyche of driving around the block for a half-hour looking for a space. There are privately owned parking garages all over the city, which are generally well-lit, safe, and convenient, if pricey. Municipal lots, where the prices are lower than the private garages' (how does $5.50 for 24 hours sound to you?), are mostly downtown.

Where can I hear music for free?... While there are clubs all over town that feature live music (see Entertainment), the city itself sponsors some of the best sounds every summer—and it's free. Chicago's line-up of three-day music festivals, which takes place at the **Petrillo Music Shell in Grant Park**, rivals the music you'll hear anywhere else in town. The best events are the **Chicago Blues Festival** and the **Chicago Gospel Festival**, both in June; the **Chicago Country Music Festival** in July; the **Chicago Jazz Festival** in August; and **Viva! Chicago**, the Latin music festival, in September. In addition, the **Grant Park Music Festival** (also at the Petrillo Music Shell) includes nighttime outdoor concerts ranging from classical to show tunes, performed by the **Grant Park Symphony and Chorus**; they're on Wednesday, Friday, Saturday, and Sunday evenings throughout the summer.

Can I go to the opera and the symphony when I'm in town?... It depends on when you come. Just like the weather, Chicago's cultural resources have seasons, too. The **Lyric Opera of Chicago** (tel 312/332–2244), for instance, performs September through February, the **Chicago Opera Theater's** (tel 312/292–7521) season is June through July, so neither of them will be around if you're here in the spring. The **Chicago Symphony Orchestra** (tel 312/435–6666 or 800/223–7114) plays September through June; in the summer they retire to Ravinia, while downtown the **Grant Park Symphony and Chorus** (tel 312/742–7638) concerts begin in June and run through August.

What if I gotta go?... Chicago's a pretty user-friendly place when it comes to finding decent, clean public bathrooms. Hotels, of course, are the best bets. **The Drake**, the **Park Hyatt**, the **Ritz-Carlton**, and **Four Seasons** are all reliable way stations. There are little-known and very private bathrooms at **Crate & Barrel** on Michigan Avenue, and at the **Starbucks** coffee shop on Rush Street. And, of course, there are bathrooms within all the department stores and malls, such as **Water Tower Place**.

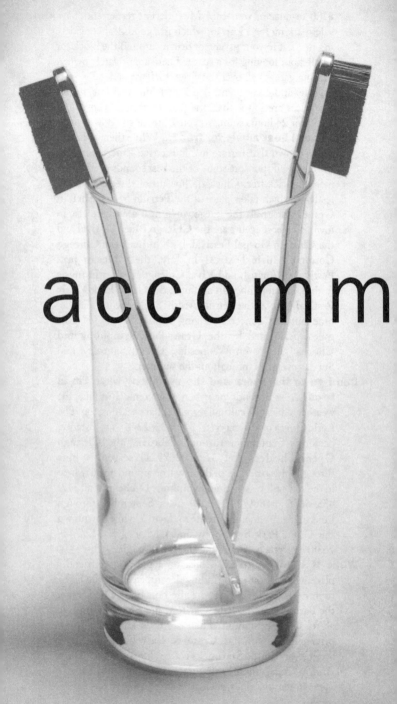

accomm

1

odations

Chicago is a big
convention
town—a *really* big
convention town.
That situation has
both its pluses
and its minuses.

On the upside it means that there are many, many hotels catering to people and corporations with various budgets, from deluxe to demure to depressing (though none of the latter are listed here). The sheer number of hotels also has meant that there is a wide breadth of styles available, from small and intimate European-style inns to you-know-what-you're-gonna-get chain hotels to showy chintz-furnished palaces. The downside, of course, is that some hotels—especially the you-know-what-you're-gonna-getniks—can be about as personal as a K-Mart. They're used to dealing in volume, so don't expect a French-accented concierge who'll remember your name, or rooms with much dash. Because of the number of conventions the city hosts, there are times of year that it is almost impossible to book a room if you haven't done so way in advance. Blocks of hundreds of rooms in many of the bigger hotels are reserved annually for conventioneers. If you visit the city when one of the big conventions is in town, you may be sharing your temporary home with hordes of midlevel vice-presidents traipsing the halls in starchy white shirts, rep ties, and plastic name-tags.

Overall, the selection of hotels in Chicago outshines that of most other cities. In the past decade or so, there has been a hotel building boom, and thousands of newly available (mostly upscale) rooms in such hotels as the **Four Seasons**, **The Fairmont**, and **Swissotel** have forced the old stalwarts—like **The Palmer House Hilton**, which had fallen on musty times—to invest millions of dollars in renovations just to remain viable. And, perhaps because of the competition, even in the biggest of the big convention sleep warehouses, service is more often with a smile than a sneer. After all, the city's hotel employees are aware that the conventioneers only return to Chicago year after year because the service is so consistently good.

Winning the Reservations Game

There's only one real rule when making a hotel reservation in Chicago: don't be a chump. In other words, don't agree to pay what are referred to in the hotel business as "rack prices," meaning the highest nightly fee at which rooms are rented—which is the one you'll be quoted. It's not that you can exactly haggle with the reservations clerk—though you've got nothing to lose by trying—but there are many ways to get a better price. Most hotels have special corporate rates, which may be 10 percent lower than the rack rate. In most cases, you'll have to prove you're really there on business, but some hotels will simply take you at your word. There are often deals for frequent fliers, the elderly, auto-club members, people in the military, or teachers and others who work in education. It pays, literally, to ask about any of these.

Because most conventions occur during the week, Chicago hotels are relatively uninhabited on weekends, even during peak season. Most offer weekend hotel packages year-round, so if you're in town for an entire week you could stay the weekdays at a bland-but-not-too-expensive chain hotel and then move to a fancier place for about the same price or less for the weekend. Some hotels in Chicago also offer special tie-ins with various events and exhibitions. The **Stouffer Renaissance**, for example, works closely with the Art Institute to create weekends geared toward art lovers who may be visiting Chicago just to see the museum's latest blockbuster show. Theater tie-ins are another popular way hotels lure guests.

Hotels well known for the views offered from one side of their building may discount the rooms on the other side, so it's always smart to ask if you can get a cheaper room if you face the city instead of the lake. (After all, there are other ways to see the lake.) Making reservations early is imperative, especially if you are traveling during peak season—January, April, May, and June, when the weather is the most pleasant and/or when the biggest conventions take over the town. During non-peak months, however, rooms may be discounted up to 50 percent off the rack price. You can also get a 50-percent-or-more discount if you go through **Hot Rooms** (tel 800/468–3500), a Chicago-based service that works with about 15 downtown and Gold Coast hotels such as the Drake, the Blackstone, and the Knickerbocker. You can call Hot Rooms 24 hours a day, seven days a week, and there's no fee (though if you make a confirmed reservation and then cancel there is a $25 fee). Hot Rooms operators are familiar with other local hotels as well, and can direct you to similar sites should your first choice be unavailable, though of course they'll try to get you into another Hot Rooms hotel if possible.

Is There a Right Address?

Most of the city's best (and most expensive) hotels are along, or at least nearby, the **Magnificent Mile**, from **The Drake** at Michigan Avenue's northern tip to the **Chicago Hilton and Towers** farther south. Recent additions to the city's hotel scene, including the **Four Seasons**, are in the North

Michigan Avenue area, the retailing center of the city, which has many of the best restaurants within walking distance as well. In addition, it's one of the city's safest neighborhoods. But busting out of the Mag Mile area and staying in other neighborhoods can make for a different perspective, especially if you've visited the city before. If you want to be near the action, but not in the center of the storm, you might try staying in the **Gold Coast** neighborhood just north of Michigan Avenue. Its quiet, tree-lined streets are some of the city's poshest. It's peaceful and understated, yet near enough to the beach and shopping that you won't need a cab every time you walk out the door of your hotel. If you're a glutton for punishment, and your plans include a three-day stint attending Cubs games, you're better off staying in **Lake View**, which has a few small, inexpensive places within walking distance of Wrigley Field. Ditto Lake View if your shopping tastes lean more towards the funky than the fancy. Nightclubs, bars, and jazz and blues clubs all proliferate here. For business trips or museum-hopping, **The Loop** is a good bet, given its proximity to the financial district, convention center, and the Art Institute, et al, but keep in mind that there aren't too many restaurants in the area, and nightlife will most likely require a cab ride. The Loop is so dead after-hours and on weekends, it can seem eerie. Some of the city's newest high-rise

Chicago in the movies, part 2—the neighborhoods

About Last Night (1986), one of the more stupid-but-famous movies made here, takes place in and around Lincoln Park, with brat packers Demi Moore, Rob Lowe, real Chicagoan James Belushi, and Elizabeth Perkins. The movie's set designer went loco and decorated an el stop—usually grungy and in need of paint—with Christmas lights and bunting during a holiday scene (a good use of our tax dollars, right?). While You Were Sleeping propelled Sandra Bullock to stardom, but the 1995 movie, filmed in Lake View, is totally implausible—believe me, real el token clerks are never as cute as the one she played. The first 10 minutes of 1989's When Harry Met Sally take place in Hyde Park at the University of Chicago (though Billy Crystal and Meg Ryan behave so stupidly, it's hard to believe they even got into the U of C to begin with). And for a taste of the South Side, try the 1975 comedy Cooley High (set in 1964), or the riveting 1994 documentary Hoop Dreams, which chronicles the lives of two ghetto b-ball stars.

hotels—including the **Sheraton**, **The Fairmont**, and **Swissotel**—are way east of Michigan Avenue in quasi-neighborhoods such as **Illinois Center** and **Cityfront Center**. They have great views all around, but it's a trek (usually involving a cab) to get anywhere; there's nothing to do in the immediate area, so it can assume a surreal, where-is-everybody feel. The hotels near **O'Hare Airport** are, well, near the airport. They cater to a business crowd (though they attempt to be attractive to others as well by offering weekend packages), and basically are convenient, safe, clean, and about as dull as a dishrag.

The Lowdown

Big bucks de luxe... Guests schlep Marshall Field's and Lord & Taylor bags right upstairs from Water Tower Place to the twelfth floor, where they enter the enormous greenhouse lobby of **The Ritz-Carlton**. The tone is set by plush furnishings, an oddly loud but fanciful fountain, English tea carts piled high with pastries and dainty sandwiches, and other guests surrounded by mountains of Louis Vuitton luggage and hovering uniformed bellhops. The hotel spends more than a quarter-million dollars a year just on flowers, and it shows. You'll probably feel every cent was well spent, though it does seem pretty chintzy that guests paying upwards of a couple hundred dollars a night have to fork over another $8 for each visit to the hotel's health club—especially considering that the **Four Seasons** across the street, which is owned by the same company, doesn't charge guests to use its facility. The Four Seasons—which sits atop Bloomingdale's, if that's your shopping preference—in many ways seems like a huge English country manor in the sky. The beds at both the Ritz and Four Seasons are so comfortable that a few years ago guests began to ask where they could buy one; now they can, believe it or not, through the hotels' gift shop. Unlike the rest of the city's expensive hotels, **The Drake** has an old-timey, aristocratic feel that some might find dowdy. But if you like the kind of environment where old ladies in white gloves and Republicans wearing wingtips feel comfortable, then this is the place. The barber shop, or as they call it, gentleman's grooming service, shouldn't be missed.

Chicago classics... The huge pink neon sign on the roof of **The Drake** has become as much a part of the city skyline as the nearby Hancock Center, which is about five times as tall. Built in 1920 by Ben Marshall, the famous architect to Chicago's rich and famous, and modelled after Renaissance palaces, the Drake hasn't lost its elegance. Its guest rooms, decorated in reproduction English furniture, aren't as plush as some other luxe sleeperies, but few can match it in inherent grace. Similarly, **The Palmer House Hilton**, the city's oldest hotel and the longest continually operated hotel on the continent, still offers a pretty fabulous welcome to the jillions of businesspeople passing through its portal, especially after a $120 million top-to-toe renovation. Located smack in the middle of the Loop, this Chicago institution has a spectacular gilded lobby with a soaring, mural-covered ceiling, sweeping staircases, and furniture covered in thick velvet brocades and moire taffetas. The sprawling **Chicago Hilton and Towers** is the sort of place where waiters have been known to work for 50 years, where one doorman started the day the hotel opened in 1927 and retired decades later when he was 95 years old. Though the ornate lobby is rife with square conventioneers and tour groups dressed for a big day on the bus, the hotel has plenty of big-city glamour. Unlike the other Chicago classics, the quietly refined **Omni Ambassador East** is small enough that the concierge will remember your name. When you mention to a local that you're staying here, they nod a knowing nod and just say, "Ahhhh." Yet, in true Chicago spirit, it doesn't take itself too seriously; the minibars are stocked with frozen Snickers bars. At the **Regal Knickerbocker**, another venerable smaller hotel, gangsters and socialites once partied, and later, Hugh Hefner ruled his Playboy empire; nowadays it's trying to make a comeback with a multi-million-dollar renovation, this time molding its image as a business hotel. If you have a good imagination, you might be able to conjure the grandeur that once was the **Ramada Congress Hotel**, open since the 1893 World Columbian Exposition, and not focus on its current shabby state.

Dowdy but lovable... Originally built in 1924 as a private men's club, the enormous **Allerton** is, while clean, on the shabby—but not shabby-chic—side. It's been rehabbed in chunks, at different times over the decades, giving it a dotty, old-fashioned charm. (Its room rates are the best bargains on Michigan Avenue, which doesn't hurt.) The **Blackstone**, by no means a first-class hotel, is campy in its nod to the past, with loads of red velvet and polished wood and giant brass wall sconces; it's so old and over-the-top it's hip. All sorts of movies have been shot here, including scenes from *The Untouchables* and *The Hudsucker Proxy*. **The Raphael** also has a dowdy charm, with a slighty goofy staff—well-meaning but just a bit odd—and the lobby's gloomy tapestries and Gothic-style decorative features; guest room interiors range all over the place, from contemporary to ornate. **The Talbott Hotel**'s fox hunt decorating theme is a tad on the twee side, but the hotel—converted in 1989 from a 1920s-vintage apartment building—has the casual comfort of a well-worn blazer, an unpretentiousness that is especially refreshing on the fringe of the Gold Coast. For post-modern dowdiness, there's the **Sutton Place Hotel**, which opened in 1988 and quickly became the city's trendiest hotel; it has managed to hold onto that cachet despite a less than stellar atmosphere. Where once it had slim muscle guys in Armani-inspired uniforms scurrying about, now there are garishly red-coated bell-men with big boufs and tacky little name-tags. Some of the furniture is nicked up and really could use an upgrade—which, supposedly, it's getting. Even so, with the great location (a block from Oak Street Beach and around the corner from the city's best shopping) and a restaurant that's ground-zero for fabulous people-watching, the Sutton Place continues to attract a fast-talking, deal-cutting clientele.

Best views... There are only three things you really want to see out your windows in Chicago: the lake, the skyline, or the Chicago River. At the **Stouffer Renaissance** you can get all of the above, and sometimes from the same room (ask to face north), at least if you stay on one of the top floors. It helps that all the rooms have bay windows, which add a 3-D drama to the panorama. Across the river, the **Westin River North** has panoramic views of the Loop from all its south-facing rooms. At the modern but luxurious **Fairmont**, suites are lined up on the east side of the

ACCOMMODATIONS | THE LOWDOWN

hotel to monopolize the best vistas of the lake and the city's downtown nine-hole golf course, **Metrogolf Chicago** (See Getting Outside). Also in Illinois Center, there are unobstructed views from every angle of the triangularly shaped **Swissotel**, even from the forty-second-floor health club and pool, though otherwise the Swissotel is bland as vanilla, and the Wacker Drive location feels isolated. There are great lake views from the **Chicago Hilton and Towers**, too, but its perspective of Grant Park and its gorgeous formal and wildflower gardens is the real knock-out. Though more expensive, the north-facing rooms at **The Drake** are the only ones in the city to overlook the lake, the Gold Coast, and Lincoln Park. At the postmodern **Sheraton Chicago**, the views are pretty terrific from both sides—it's how far up or down you are that makes all the difference. If you're facing north, try to get a room on a high floor for best views of North Michigan Avenue and the lake, but if you're on the south side, book a lower floor for spectacular views of the Chicago River. Since sleeping rooms at the **Radisson Hotel and Suites** don't even start until the fourteenth floor, plenty of them enjoy truly beautiful vistas of lake and city. Expensive hotels don't have a monopoly on spectacular views, either; you can go as cheap as the vintage **Ramada Congress Hotel** and get a clear, wide-open view of Grant Park and Lake Michigan, while the reasonably priced **Days Inn** gives you an eyeful of the lake and of Navy Pier from east-facing rooms; face west and your city panorama is one of the finest.

Gold Coasters... Spiffy, uniformed doormen greet you beneath a dramatic, old-fashioned gold-and-creamy-white canopy at the Georgian-style **Omni Ambassador East**, located on a quiet residential street only a block from the lake in the affluent Gold Coast. The neighborhood location gives this Chicago classic an air of seclusion that helps endear it to celebrities: Everyone from Judy Garland to Rob Lowe has eaten at its famous Pump Room restaurant. Nearby, **The Claridge** offers the same neighborhood feel, convenience, and personal attention, all at lower prices, though its plainer furnishings, all in beiges and maroons, move it a couple of notches down on the glamour scale. (A few suites do have fireplaces). Both hotels are far enough away from the hustle and hassle of Michigan Avenue, yet close enough to walk there.

If everyone else stays on Michigan Avenue, I don't want to... The **Hyatt on Printers Row** is too hip for Michigan Avenue and extremely un-Hyatt-y—a small hotel in a national historic landmark, built in a South Loop neighborhood constructed right after the Great Fire, and recently gentrified with condos, a few trendy boutiques, and bookstores. Don't worry about being far from restaurants—downstairs is one of the city's best, Prairie. Also south of the river, though on the north bank of the Loop, the contemporary-style **Clarion Executive Plaza** offers great city- and riverscapes; the boxlike gray **Stouffer Renaissance**, dripping with glitzy pretension, is on the same street, but two blocks farther in from the lake; and the sleek **Westin River North** sits across the river from them, well inland from Michigan Avenue. In trendy River North, there's the **Best Western River North** and the **Ohio House Motel**—good for those who'll spend most of their time out enjoying the neighborhood, rather than basking in the standard motel-issue rooms. A trio of quaint, quiet, quirky hotels run by the same management, the **Park Brompton**, **The Surf Hotel**, and the **City Suites Hotel Chicago** are smart choices for budget-minded travelers willing to stay far from the downtown crowd. Each is within walking distance of many of the city's gay bars and dance clubs, Wrigley Field, the Lincoln Park Zoo, and only a few blocks from the lake, tennis courts, and the Waveland Golf Course (and only a 15-minute bus ride from the Mag Mile). It's even folksier at **Arlington House**, which isn't so much a hotel as a hostel in residential Lincoln Park. Way off in Hyde Park, near the University of Chicago and the Museum of Science and Industry, there's not much lodging choice except for the **Ramada Inn Lakeshore**. Though it's isolated from the rest of the city (you shouldn't walk to other neighborhoods from here, though trains and buses are an option), you get a great view of the whole downtown skyline in the distance.

Lobbies to die for... You may feel breathless when you enter the gigantic lobby of the the **Chicago Hilton and**

Towers, all gilded and full of green and pink marble. The octogonal sunken lobby of **The Fairmont** is conspicuously filled with cushy velvet divans, glass-top tables, and flowers that fill the high-ceilinged space with a faintly sweet aroma. Step off the seventh-floor elevator at the **Four Seasons**, and room after room, salon after salon, unfolds before you as if you're in some Merchant-Ivory film—tufted sofas and chairs, inlaid marble floors, highly polished English-y furniture, Chinese porcelain bowls, and a legion of uniformed men and women dashing about, presumably carrying out every whim of every guest. The lobby at the **Hampton Inn & Suites** has a collection of artifacts from Chicago buildings that have since gone bye-bye, including artifacts from Adler & Sullivan's Garrick Theater, the former Chicago Stock Exchange, and others from buildings born of the hands of Frank Lloyd Wright, John Wellborn Root, Ben Marshall, and others.

Family values... Suite hotels are generally a great solution when you've got kids in tow, giving you what amounts to two rooms for the price of one, usually with cooking facilities to boot. For families on a budget, the **Lenox Suites**, located just a block off Michigan Avenue, has one- and two-room suites with kitchenettes (stocked with free coffee and juice) and separate sitting- and dining areas. Somewhat pricier but still handy are the **Doubletree Guest Suites** and the **Embassy Suites**, which have indoor pools as a bonus. (The Embassy also has in-room Nintendo). If cooking for yourself is about the furthest thing from your mind, and you've got the money, the family suite at the **Four Seasons** is definitely the way to go. There's a king-size bedroom for Mom and Dad and a smaller kids' bedroom with twin beds. Each suite has Nintendo, two bathrooms, kid-sized bathrobes, and a minibar filled with jelly beans, chocolate chip cookies, and M&Ms; milk and cookies for the kids (and the adults, if requested) is served at bedtime. In addition, the hotel provides guests in all rooms with a crib, diapers, strollers, formula, and baby food on request, and arranges for babysitting. The **Holiday Inn Chicago City Centre**'s spacious and bright—if standard—rooms are kid-friendly (and free for children under 18), and the location near the beach will save you on transportation. The hotel is big enough that if the kids run around and get out of hand for a while, no one will notice.

For lovers and those who want to be... When you and your companion need to get away from it all (the office, the wife, the husband, the kids, the other lover), discretion is the key ingredient. At the **Sutton Place Hotel** you'll find everything you need in your room—including a VCR (rent a steamy movie) and, in the chic black-and-white tiled bathrooms, a deep-soaking tub big enough for two. Take a left out the front door and you'll be in the center of a lot of neon-lit nightlife, but if you opt to take a right and walk down the otherwise quiet street, there's little chance of running into whomever it is you're trying to avoid. Just steps away from Michigan Avenue, it's surprisingly cozy and intimate at **The Tremont**, whose traditionally furnished rooms are done up with abandon in Laura Ashley–like chintz, all matching frilly bedskirts and flowered draperies and valences. Etched-glass double doors divide the bedroom from the living room in the suites at the **Four Seasons**, adding just the right tone of romance to the sumptuously furnished rooms; the room-service food here is so good you never have to leave your room at all, and the beds are reportedly the most comfortable in town. But the ultimate key to romance may be at the **Chicago Hilton** and the **Regal Knickerbocker**, where many guest rooms have two bathrooms—a set-up that not-so-scientifically has been proven to reduce the number of lovers' quarrels.

Suite deals... If you're travelling with the kids or insist on fixing your own eggs in the morning, try an all-suite hotel. Chicago has a number of them, where every guest room has at least a separate sitting area and some kind of kitchenette. Tops in this category are the **Hampton Inn & Suites**, (boring decor but great River North location), the sleek **Embassy Suites** with its echoing atrium, the crisply modern **Omni Chicago** hovering above Michigan Avenue shops, and the traditionally furnished **Doubletree Guest Suites** hotel, a high-rise right off Michigan Avenue that has some of the best views in town. All four also have pools and some kind of gym or health club, as does the somewhat smaller and more personal **Summerfield Suites**, where a book-lined lounge downstairs sets the homey tone. The roomy and reasonably priced quarters at the **Lenox Suites** are downright homey, with sofabeds, kitchenettes, and microwaves (but no gym, nor pool). If you're talking suites—as in "I'm taking a suite of rooms for my entourage,"—that's a different and more luxurious story. The opulent Conrad Hilton Suite, named after the former owner of the **Chicago Hilton and Towers**, sits like a birthday cake on the top of the hotel. With its Jacuzzi overlooking Lake Michigan, grand salon, enormous crystal chandeliers, two bedrooms, library, and 17th-century Flemish tapestries on the walls, it's an exaggerated version of all the regular rooms and suites, which are top-of-the-line themselves, with Chippendale-style furniture and great soothing views of the parks and harbors. Best feature of the Anniversary Suites at **The Ritz-Carlton**: awe-inspiring, all-marble oversized bathtubs facing floor-to-ceiling windows overlooking the city.

Mega-hotels for conventioneers... If you're here at a convention, you're probably staying at whatever place your company put you. At least you've been saved from having to decide among the massive, charm-free convention hotels. If you've been given that unfortunate duty, though, here are the ones to keep in mind. For sheer size, the standouts are the **Chicago Marriott**, a bland white marble box on Michigan Avenue with more than 1,000 rooms and 55,000 square feet of exhibition space, and the **Hyatt Regency**, a mega-hotel with more than 2,000 cookie-cutter guest rooms (each of which includes an ironing board and iron so you can get spiffed up for that 7:30am seminar) and 188,000 square feet of meeting space. Both have about as much charm as a freeway, and you may feel stupid if you aren't wearing a "Hello, my name is..." tag pinned to your gray pinstripe. The Hyatt's attached to the Illinois Center business complex by an underground maze of hallways, which also links it to the **Swissotel**, with more than 600 rooms, creating one big convention megalopolis. An enormous line of yellow cabs snaking around the **Chicago Hilton and Towers** is a sure sign a convention has just hit town, since that hotel is the closest of the bunch to McCormick Place, the city's main exhibition and convention hall. Unlike the others, the

Hilton's rooms are outfitted in residential-like furniture that won't make you feel you're so far from home. Ditto **The Palmer House Hilton**, well located in the Loop, whose more than 1,600 guest rooms fill up during peak convention season. Rooms at the **Sheraton Chicago** are more comfortable than you'd expect from this 1,200-room riverside hulk, and separate check-in areas help to keep conventioneers and other guests out of each other's way. The shiny gold **Hyatt Regency O'Hare** has only two things going for it: size (1,100 rooms and 81,000 square feet of exhibition space) and direct access to the O'Hare Expocenter.

Taking care of business... It seems as though every Chicago hotel is trying to be a "business hotel." Whereas the convention hotels succeed by having hanger-like amounts of space to handle the crowds, business hotels make an effort to see business travelers as individuals. The O'Hare-area **Rosemont Suites**, for example, has computer modem hook-ups in the rooms, voice mail, and halogen lamps so you can actually see your work. All the suites in the **Omni Chicago Hotel** have fax machines and voice mail, not to mention proximity to Michigan Avenue shopping if your meeting's extended and you need another dress shirt. For an extra $15 a night, the **Hyatt on Printers Row** provides a room with a computer modem jack, a coffeemaker, newspaper delivery, and an express Continental breakfast. Business travelers at the **Westin River North** may appreciate the in-room printer/fax/copier, free local calls and long distance access, a speakerphone with dataport, and no in-room fax surcharges, but no doubt the two best business features are the ergonomic desk chair and the stack of Post-it notes in the desk drawer. You'll find in-room fax machines/copiers, modem hookups, and shoe buffers at **The Fairmont**, as well as a slew of homier touches, such as real art on the walls, lots of plants in the rooms, and windows that actually open to catch the breeze. (Not to mention soul-satisfying amenities such as thick terry robes, premium bedsheets, and superbly outfitted bathrooms.) As tony and almost as well-equipped is the **Stouffer Renaissance**, where about a fifth of the rooms have multiple phone lines, data ports for modems, and fax machines; to help harried business travelers stay on schedule, they guarantee room-service delivery within 25 minutes or it's on the house (now if they could get that down to 10 minutes...). The Stouffer offers another rare freebie, too: it waives telephone surcharges on 800-, credit card-, and collect calls, which can save a bundle. The dining table in the two-room suites at the **Doubletree Guest Suites** easily doubles as a large work space, and the second phone line recently installed in every suite is a nice touch. The hotel offers what it calls "female traveler suites," complete with hairdryers, irons, ironing boards, and upgraded bathroom amenities. (So what are men with flyaway hair and wrinkled shirts supposed to do?)

Gym dandies... Well-equipped gym facilities (with Lifecycles, rowers, a Gravitron, treadmills, Nautilus weight stations, Stairmasters, and free weights) and swimming pools—or at least lap pools—are almost *de rigueur* nowadays, so it's no surprise that many of the city's most popular hotels, including the **Westin River North, Stouffer Renaissance**, **Chicago Hilton and Towers, Embassy Suites, Omni Chicago**, and **Summerfield Suites**, have such high-end perks. Most will even lend you workout clothes. A few other hotels, though, have even more going for them. The **Swissotel**'s forty-second-floor health club has dynamite views, the **Doubletree Guest Suites** has a great rooftop gym and pool, and the **Radisson Hotel and Suites'** rooftop pool is actually outdoors. The **Four Seasons** has a quarter-mile outdoor running track and sundeck, as well as a glass-domed, eighth-floor 50-foot swimming pool, surrounded by columns and windows overlooking the city. But even it can't compete with the utter fabulousness of the thirteenth-floor swimming pool at the **Hotel Inter-Continental Chicago**. Surrounded by stained-glass windows, mosaics, wicker chaise longues, huge potted palms, and wrought-metal sconces, the Italianate junior Olympic-size pool (75 feet) was the training ground for the original Tarzan, Johnny Weissmuller. Even if you're not staying here, you should make a special trip to see it. It's that cool. You can have your body fat analyzed in the **Palmer House** fitness center, but the real highlight here is its state-of-the-proverbial-art golf simulator, as well as

Astroturfed, silk-plant-dotted driving and chipping ranges. It's all completely fake (it's on the eighth floor, after all) but if you're into golf, probably pretty amusing. And of course, it's a good excuse for a mid-afternoon gin & tonic.

Cheap sleeps... You don't get much in the way of luxurious perks by staying at the **Park Brompton**, **The Surf Hotel**, and the **City Suites Hotel Chicago**, three small, eccentric Lake View hotels, but you do get to go to bed each evening knowing that you're not spending much. Each of these quirky hotels has its own theme—The Park Brompton apes a countryside English inn, with four-poster beds and tapestry-upholstered chairs; the Surf greets guests with an imposing bust of Louis XIV (or some other wig-wearing poufed-up French guy); and the City Suites boasts its former incarnation as the home to gangsters and their molls—an image carried out by heavy carpeting and drapes, both of which also help to combat the rumble of the nearby el. Convenient to the galleries and eateries of River North are two more decent bargains: the **Best Western River North**, which has a rooftop pool, and **Ohio House Motel**, an incongruous sort of urban motor inn where room doors open directly onto the parking lot and the coffeeshop offers a $2.95 breakfast of two eggs, two strips of bacon, two sausages, and two pancakes (attention, hearty eaters). If a central location is important to you, by far the cheapest place to stay along Michigan Avenue is the **Allerton**—what the hotel obviously saves in decorating costs it apparently passes on to guests. Within spitting distance of Michigan Avenue, the **Motel 6** is a bargain, if you're willing to go for generic furnishings and minimal service. At least the neighborhood's safe, and its restaurant, Coco Pazzo Cafe, is surprisingly chic. Or if you'd like to be south of the river, near the Loop and the museums, there's the **Essex Inn** and the **Best Western Grant Park** (the latter has an outdoor pool and some great views from east-facing rooms). But the hands-down cheapest place to stay in town is **Arlington House**, a hostel with both private rooms and dormitory sleeping arrangements, where the clientele is mainly backpacking students and foreigners. Bring your own linen, or rent theirs—it's that kind of place (though the coffee is free).

May I get that for you, sir?... At the **Four Seasons** they really service you, so to speak. Forget your entire wardrobe? No problem. The hotel has a deal with Bloomingdale's, which is in the same Mag Mile building, through which you can get a new wardrobe delivered to your room (though you'll pay through the proverbial nose). Got a hankering to work out at a great gym with a personal trainer? No problem. They've got those, too. Each room even has a private safe for those traveling with jewels à la the Duchess of Windsor. **The Tremont** will lend its guests a cellular phone for the day. At the **Sutton Place Hotel**, a BMW is available on a first-come, first-served basis for guests to use during their stay.

Oh so near O'Hare... Staying near the airport is usually a matter of convenience—you need to make an early morning flight, or you're forced to stay an extra day because your flight's been delayed or the wing fell off the plane. A courtesy van shuttles people and luggage between the airport and the nearby hotels, which are many but undistinguished. You can while away the hours in your room at the **Sheraton Gateway Suites** by playing Nintendo, which is included in each room; the two-room suites at the **Rosemont Suites** include a microwave, for those too travel-weary to face another restaurant. The Rosemont also scores points for its Frank-Lloyd-Wright-inspired decor, using mahogany trim, barrel chairs, and stained-glass windows. The **Hyatt Regency O'Hare** offers an automated check-in and check-out machine (like an ATM) that takes about 90 seconds; you just stick in your credit card, punch a few buttons, and you're on your way. Give the relatively small and civilized (for an airport hotel, anyhow) **Hotel Sofitel** a round of applause for trying to create a little excitement for its guests: you get a rose on your bed each night at turn-down, and a loaf of French bread when you check out. If nothing else, that could help you skip the airline's mystery-meal-on-a-tray on your flight home.

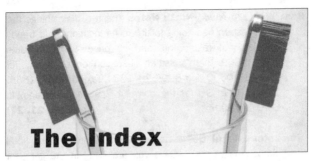

The Index

$$$$$	over $250
$$$$	$200–$250
$$$	$140–$200
$$	$100–$140
$	under $100

Price applies to a standard double room for one night.

Allerton. Though the decor's pretty tired-looking, this big hotel does have a spectacular location right on Michigan Avenue and room rates about as cheap as they come.... *Tel 312/440–1500 and 800/621–8311. 701 N. Michigan Ave., Chicago, IL 60611. 450 rms. $$* **(see pp. 18, 27)**

Arlington House. This friendly and cheap little hostel is on a leafy Lincoln Park Street, about a 15-minute bus ride from downtown and within walking distance of many of the city's best blues, jazz, and dance clubs. There are both private rooms and dormitory sleeping arrangements. What this place lacks in amenities (which is just about everything), it makes up for in low rates, which are even lower if you're a member of the American Youth Hostel Federation.... *Tel 773/929–5380 and 800/538–0074. 616 W. Arlington Place, Chicago, IL 60614. 200 beds, 40 private rms. $* **(see pp. 21, 27)**

Best Western Grant Park. Once a dive called the Ascot, the Best Western Grant Park got a facelift and is now respectable, albeit with standard-issue motel furnishings. Convenient to the Field Museum, the Shedd Aquarium, and the Adler Planetarium. Outdoor pool and workout facilities.... *Tel 312/922–2900 and 800/472–6875. 1100 S. Michigan Ave., Chicago, IL 60605. 172 rms. $$* **(see p. 27)**

Best Western River North Hotel. The two main things the Best Western has going for it are its location amid trendy galleries and restaurants and its price—weekend rates begin at $69. There's also an all-season rooftop pool.... *Tel 312/467–0800 and 800/528–1234, fax 312/467–1665. 125 W. Ohio St. (at the corner of LaSalle), Chicago, IL 60610. 150 rms. $* **(see pp. 21, 27)**

Blackstone Hotel. Designated a National Landmark, this hotel almost makes you believe you are living in the gangster days of Prohibition. Rooms are large and comfortable and generally have good views.... *Tel 312/427–4300 and 800/622–6330, fax 312/427–4736. 636 S. Michigan Ave., Chicago, IL 60605. 305 rms. $$* **(see p. 19)**

Chicago Hilton and Towers. Grand in every way, from the ornate lobby with its 60-foot ceiling to the gilded ballrooms, it has very well-appointed rooms—cherrywood cabinets and quilted bedspreads—and a terrific health club.... *Tel 312/922–4400 and 800-HILTONS, fax 312/922–5240. 730 S. Michigan Ave., Chicago, IL 60605. 1,543 rms. $$$* **(see pp. 15, 18, 20, 21, 23, 24, 26)**

Chicago Marriott. Quite possibly the ugliest hotel in the city, this mega-sleepery has one thing going for it: location, location, location. It's also one of the more reasonably priced hotels on the Magnificent Mile.... *Tel 312/836–0100 and 800/831–4004, fax 312/836–6139. 540 N. Michigan Ave., Chicago, IL 60611. 1,172 rms. $$$$* **(see p. 24)**

City Suites Hotel Chicago. There aren't too many hotels that would boast about their former incarnation as the home to gangsters and their molls, but this small, funky place does. And why not, considering its location right on busy Belmont Avenue amidst restaurants, coffeehouses, night clubs, and stores selling everything from Doc Martens to sun-dried tomato bagels. With the floors heavily carpeted and the windows equally draped, the fact that the el rumbles by 24 hours a day only a few hundred yards away doesn't seem to bug anyone. Simply decorated rooms, suave black-and-white tile bathrooms.... *Tel 773/404–3400. 933 W. Belmont Ave., Chicago, IL 60657. 45 rms. $* **(see pp. 21, 27)**

The Claridge. Basically, this small Gold Coast hotel is a very pleasant, no-thrill, no-frill place. Continental breakfast in lobby and newspaper delivered to your room daily.... *Tel 312/787–4980 and 800/245–1258, fax 312/266–0978. 1244 N. Dearborn Pkwy., Chicago, IL 60610. 167 rms. $$$* **(see p. 20)**

Clarion Executive Plaza. This contemporary hotel gets away with higher tariffs largely because it's situated on the Loop's southern bank of the Chicago River. Rooms are tasteful if not spiffy, but if you stay here, you won't be looking at the furniture—you'll be looking out the window at those awe-inspiring city and river views.... *Tel 312/346–7100, fax 800/346–1721. 71 E. Wacker Dr., Chicago, IL 60601. 417 rms. $$$* **(see p. 21)**

Days Inn. Nothing really going for it but incredible views (at least if you're facing east) and very reasonable room rates. Rooms are clean and functional, but noise from Lake Shore Drive may keep you up at night. There's an outdoor swimming pool, and you're only two blocks north of the small but graceful beach at Olive Park.... *Tel 312/943–9200 and 800/325–2525. 644 N. Lake Shore Dr., Chicago, IL 60611. 578 rms. $$* **(see p. 20)**

Doubletree Guest Suites. What this all-suite hotel lacks in drama, compared to many of its neighbors such as The Drake, Four Seasons, and Ritz-Carlton, it makes up for with two-room suites, lots of service, panoramic views, and an excellent rooftop gym facility and pool. Plus, the hotel houses the Park Avenue Café, one of the city's best and trendiest restaurants. White-gloved bellhops hanging around the lobby are a nice touch, though the Muzak ruins the effect.... *Tel 312/664–1100 and 800/424–2900, fax 312/664–9881. 198 E. Delaware Place, Chicago, IL 60611. 345 suites. $$$$* **(see pp. 22, 23, 26)**

The Drake. Quite possibly the city's most famous hotel, this limestone edifice is so gracious you feel like you have to whisper. The oak-paneled, crimson-carpeted lobby is as ornate as a palace (perhaps that's why Queen Elizabeth once stayed here); the rooms, none of which are decorated exactly the same, are quietly elegant, with fancy draperies and furniture that's expensive but not showy. The hotel's bar, Le Coq D'Or, is one of—if not the—best hotel

ACCOMMODATIONS | THE INDEX

bars in the city. Dig those martinis.... *Tel 312/787–2200 and 800/445–8667. 140 E. Walton Place, Chicago, IL 60611. 535 rms. $$$$* **(see pp. 15, 17, 18, 20)**

Embassy Suites. Rimming the huge central atrium, all suites have a living room with a sleeper sofa and a bedroom with either a king-size or two double beds, as well as mini-kitchens. A complimentary breakfast buffet, indoor pool and workout room, and a very good restaurant, Papagus Greek Taverna.... *Tel 312/943–3800, fax 312/943–7629. 600 N. State St., Chicago, IL 60610. 358 suites. $$$* **(see pp. 22, 23, 26)**

Essex Inn. Far from fancy, but not exactly seedy, the Essex is a good medium-priced choice. Rooms are clean if spare (the closet has no door, just a space in the wall).... *Tel 312/939–2800 and 800/621–6909. 800 S. Michigan Ave. (at 8th St.), Chicago, IL 60605. 255 rms. $$* **(see p. 27)**

The Fairmont Hotel. Overlooking Grant Park, this pink granite high-rise hotel has bigger-than-usual rooms flooded with sunlight. God is in the details here—feather and foam pillows, bedsheets of premium 200-count cotton, standing butlers, tie racks, and the best thick terry robes in town, one edged in light blue, the other in pink (an odd sexist touch, that). Superbly outfitted bathrooms come complete with Neutrogena beauty products, a heat lamp, and (rare for most Chicago hotels) a television. There's a wide choice of restaurants, including one that's very fancy and one where the waitstaff occasionally bursts into song.... *Tel 312/565–8000 and 800/527–4727, fax 312/856–1032. 200 N. Columbus Dr., Chicago, IL 60601. 692 rms. $$$$* **(see pp. 14, 17, 19, 22, 25)**

Four Seasons Hotel. Located in the same postmodern go-go eighties building that houses Bloomingdale's, Henri Bendel, and Gucci, this hotel is one of the few that Chicagoans themselves frequent—the restaurants are top-notch and the bar and lounge are nightlife destinations for folks dressed in anything from jeans to tuxes. Guest rooms are done up in muted peaches, foam greens, and pinks, with shiny English furniture, heavily draped windows, and botanical prints; the mini-bar supplies not only the requisite booze and nuts but a disposable camera.... *Tel 312/280–8800 and 800/332–*

3442, fax 312/280—9184. 120 E. Delaware Place, Chicago, IL 60611–0142. 343 rms. $$$$$
(see pp. 14, 15, 17, 22, 23, 26, 28)

Hampton Inn & Suites. The city's latest newcomer, this River North hotel features one- and two-room suites, some with full kitchens, and on-site laundry facilities. There's a small workout area and an indoor pool but otherwise it's all pretty standard stuff. Plusses: Walk-to-everything location, free local calls and no charge for long-distance access (both a rarity nowadays), and kids under 18 stay free.... Tel 312/832–0330 and 800/426–7866. 33 W. Illinois St., Chicago, IL 60610. 230 rms. $$ **(see pp. 22, 23)**

Holiday Inn Chicago City Centre. A huge high-rise a few blocks from Michigan Avenue, this glass-clad, 26-story monolith hosts lots of tour groups and business travelers. The attached McClung Court apartment complex has a top-drawer sports complex, tennis and raquetball courts, and an outdoor pool, free for guests to use. Room decor is nicer than your average Holiday Inn, but still innocuous.... Tel 312/787–6100 and 800/HOLIDAY. 300 E. Ohio St., Chicago, IL 60611. 500 rms. $$ **(see p. 22)**

Hotel Inter-Continental Chicago. This dual personality palace is actually two side-by-side hotels—one modern, one originally built in 1929 as an athletic club—joined together in 1994. Though the lobby is blandly contemporary, rooms in the older section (recently refurbished) are laden with Biedermeier furniture, heavy draperies, and brass lamps.... Tel 312/944–4100 and 800/327–0200, fax 312/944–3050. 505 N. Michigan Ave., Chicago, IL 60611. 844 rms. $$$ **(see p. 26)**

Hotel Sofitel. A little bit of French-fried hospitality near O'Hare Airport. The marble-floored lobby with its babbling fountain creates a calm, surprisingly un-airport-like atmosphere. Despite the blond wood armoires and floral-print padded headboards, the rooms are pretty ugly.... Tel 847/678–4488 and 800/233–5959, fax 847/678–5710. 5550 N. River Rd., Rosemont, IL 60018. 304 rms. $$$ **(see p. 28)**

Hyatt on Printers Row. Located in a National Historic Landmark—two industrial red-brick buildings, built right after the Chicago Fire, now joined together—this small Hyatt has good-sized rooms with modern monochromatic decor, and equipped with two TVs and a VCR.... *Tel 312/986–1234 and 800/233–1234, fax 312/939–2468. 500 S. Dearborn St., Chicago, IL 60605. 161 rms. $$$* **(see pp. 21, 25)**

Hyatt Regency Chicago. The lobby lounge covers half an acre; its greenhouse look, fountains, pools, and restaurants seem cool at first, but this entire hotel complex is so big, and signage is so bad, that you can't help but get lost at least once during your stay.... *Tel 312/565–1234 and 800/228–9000, fax 312/565–2966. 151 E. Wacker Dr., Chicago, IL 60601. 2,019 rms. $$$$* **(see p. 24)**

Hyatt Regency O'Hare. Except for its huge 11-story skylit atrium lobby with four glass elevators, this gargantuan convention hotel (there are 89 meeting rooms) is pretty standard stuff: contemporary pinkish and brownish rooms, sprawling restaurants serving adequate food, and lots of people wearing name tags.... *Tel 847/696–1234 and 800/233–1234, fax 847/380–4890. 9300 W. Bryn Mawr Ave., Rosemont, IL 60018. 1,100 rms. $$$* **(see pp. 25, 28)**

Lenox Suites. Well-located (just off Michigan Avenue), this all-suite venue has clean but profoundly dull-looking rooms done up in dreary shades of blue and purple. One nice touch: the couches in the living rooms are all sofabeds. There's a small fitness center and valet parking.... *Tel 312/337–1000 and 800/445–6669. 616 N. Rush St., Chicago, IL 60611. 325 suites. $$$* **(see pp. 22, 24)**

Motel 6. You're not going to get any cheaper than this unless you're willing to stay in a place that rents by the hour—and even then, you won't find one so near Michigan Avenue. Rooms are clean, with no frills.... *Tel 312/787–3580, fax 312/787–1299. 162 E. Ontario St., Chicago, IL 60611. 191 rms. $* **(see p. 27)**

Ohio House Motel. Attention budget travelers: this little courtyard motel is hard to beat. Rooms start at $78; the most expensive (a four-person occupancy) is $95. Mini suites are $120. Only a few blocks from the Loop and the Magnificent Mile.... *Tel 312/943–6000. 600 N. LaSalle St., Chicago, IL 60610. 50 rms. $* **(see pp. 21, 27)**

Omni Ambassador East. Home to the world-famous Pump

Room, where everyone from Judy Garland to Rob Lowe has eaten, this quiet hotel ranks high on glitz as well as refinement. Guest rooms, though all outfitted with classic furnishings, are not cookie-cutter similar. It doesn't take itself too seriously: the management has the temerity to claim that every guest who really pays attention will see a celebrity, and the minibars are stocked with frozen Snickers Bars. The Muzak in the lobby is the only false note.... *Tel 312/787–7200 and 800/843–6664, fax 312/787–4760. 1301 N. State Pkwy., Chicago, IL 60610. 275 rms. $$$*
(see pp. 18, 20)

Omni Chicago Hotel. Considering the location and the fact that every room is a suite, this is something of a bargain. The Italian restaurant, Cielo, has superb Mag Mile views. Full health club (including lap pool).... *Tel 312/944–6664, fax 312/266–3015. 676 N. Michigan Ave., Chicago, IL 60611. 347 suites. $$$* **(see pp. 23, 25, 26)**

The Palmer House Hilton. Once one of the city's grandest hotels, the huge Palmer House has spacious standard-issue guest rooms, with traditional, upscale walnut furniture. A bar and a couple of good-looking but so-so restaurants help feed the hordes.... *Tel 312/726–7500 and 800/445–8667, fax 312/263–2556. 17 E. Monroe St., Chicago, IL 60603. 1,639 rms. $$$* **(see pp. 14, 18, 25, 26)**

Park Brompton Hotel. This small out-of-the-way hotel in Lake View is more inspiring for its low prices than its faux-English manor decor. No restaurant or room service here.... *Tel 773/404–3499. 528 W. Brompton St., Chicago, IL 60657. 30 rms. $* **(see pp. 21, 27)**

Radisson Hotel and Suites. Renovated in 1995, the hotel boasts upscale, spacious, well-lit rooms all on high floors. An extra $25 will get you an upgrade to a suite. Fitness center and outdoor rooftop pool.... *Tel 312/787–2900, fax 312/787–5758. 160 E. Huron St., Chicago, IL 60611. 341 rms. $$$* **(see pp. 20, 26)**

Ramada Congress Hotel. Faded hotel, prime location— across from Grant Park, on the edge of the Loop, an easy walk from numerous museums.... *Tel 312/427–3800 and 800/635–1666, fax 312/427–7264. 520 S. Michigan Ave., Chicago, IL 60605. 825 rms. $$* **(see pp. 18, 20)**

ACCOMMODATIONS | THE INDEX

Ramada Inn Lakeshore. Your best bet in Hyde Park—near the University of Chicago, the DuSable Museum, and the Museum of Science and Industry—this high-rise hotel has unexceptional cookie-cutter rooms. Outdoor pool, and many rooms have views of the city skyline and the lake.... *Tel 773/288–5800 and 800/228–2828, fax 773/288–5745. 4900 S. Lake Shore Dr., Chicago, IL 60615. 184 rms. $* **(see p. 21)**

The Raphael. Tucked away in the residential neighborhood east of Michigan Avenue, the Raphael has friendly service and an oddball charm. The lobby features an enormous wood chandelier and tapestries; guest room interiors range from contemporary to ornate. Business people predominate during the week, but there are plenty of leisure travelers on weekends.... *Tel 312/943–5000 and 800/821–5343, fax 312/943–9483. 201 E. Delaware Place, Chicago, IL 60611. 172 rms. $$$* **(see p. 19)**

Regal Knickerbocker Hotel. After a $10.5 million renovation, this ex-grande dame off Michigan Avenue has a beautiful new lobby, a cozy martini bar, and tastefully redecorated and retrofitted guest rooms. The renovation increased the number of rooms—don't expect spaciousness, just graciousness.... *Tel 312/751–8100 and 800/222–8888, fax 312/751–9205. 163 E. Walton St., Chicago, IL 60611. 305 rooms. $$$* **(see pp. 18, 23)**

The Ritz-Carlton. Located above the windowless, marble-clad behemoth known as Water Tower Place shopping mall, this ultra-deluxe hotel offers handsomely outfitted traditional rooms. Well-equipped gym facility and small pool, though they charge a daily fee to use them.... *Tel 312/266–1000 and 800/621–6906, fax 312/266–1194. 160 E. Pearson St., Chicago, IL 60611–0124. 435 rms. $$$$$* **(see pp. 17, 24)**

Rosemont Suites. Spiffy forest-green, beige, and burgundy two-room suites are clean-lined and bright, and have sofabeds, a microwave and refrigerator, and two TVs. You get a free full breakfast every morning delivered to your suite.... *Tel 847/678–4000 and 800/542–0912, fax 847/928–7659. 5500 N. River Rd., Rosemont, IL 60018. 296 suites. $$$* **(see pp. 25, 28)**

Sheraton Chicago. Along the flower- and shrub-lined Chicago River promenade, this postmodern hotel is a blight, but it succeeds where it really counts, with its interiors and service. The main lobby is all pretty wood trim and huge expanses of glass taking in the gorgeous riverscapes outside; there are separate check-in areas for conventioneers and regular guests. The rooms are pretty standard, in muted peaches, browns, and creams, but they're more comfortable than many rooms in competing hotels. Good service despite its size.... *Tel 312/464–1000 and 800/325–3535, fax 312/464–9140. 301 E. North Water St., Chicago, IL 60611. 1,200 rms. $$$* **(see pp. 17, 20, 25)**

Sheraton Gateway Suites. About as generic as possible, this all-suite hotel has one thing going for it: proximity to O'Hare. Otherwise, you get a grim concrete atrium surrounded by drab beige-and-greenish rooms with sofabeds, refrigerator, coffeemaker, and two TVs. Free shuttle to and from O'Hare.... *Tel 847/699–6300 and 800/325–3535, fax 847/699–0391. 6501 N. Mannheim Rd., Rosemont, IL 60018. 297 suites. $$$* **(see p. 28)**

Stouffer Renaissance Hotel. Gray and dreary-looking, this relatively new hotel sits prominently on the Chicago River; inside it's high glitz, with faux French-provincial furniture, oversize crystal chandeliers, a wishing fountain, uniformed bellhops, and ashtray sand branded with a curlicue "R." Guest rooms have marvelous views but are nothing special in the decor department.... *Tel 312/372–7200, fax 312/372–0834. One W. Wacker Dr., Chicago, IL 60601. 550 rms. $$$$* **(see pp. 15, 19, 21, 25, 26)**

Summerfield Suites Hotel. A nice combination of a small, European-style hotel with room-to-stretch-out suites, the Summerfield (formerly the Barclay) is cozy and charming. VCRs in every room, kitchens in most, and a health club and rooftop pool; complimentary Continental breakfasts and hors d'oeuvres.... *Tel 312/787–6000 and 800/621–8004, fax 312/787–4331. 166 E. Superior St., Chicago, IL 60611. 120 suites. $$$* **(see pp. 24, 26)**

The Surf Hotel. Instead of a doorman, this out-of-the-way hotel greets guests with an imposing bust of Louis XIV, or XV, or some other wig-wearing poufed-up French guy. He adds just

ACCOMMODATIONS | THE INDEX

the right loony touch to this small, quirky (and inexpensive) hotel on a sleepy residential Lake View side street. The rooms and suites, though simple, have all the requisite amenities; there's nearby parking for less than $10 a day (and staying out here, you'll probably want a car).... *Tel 773/528–8400. 555 W. Surf St., Chicago, IL 60657. 36 rms. $* **(see pp. 21, 27)**

Sutton Place Hotel. Opened in 1988, it still looks postmodern, but nowadays the framed Robert Mapplethorpe photographs seem a bit passé, and the fake plants in the lobby are definitely tacky. The rooms still have some chic amenities, though, like Sony CD players and VCRs.... *Tel 312/266–2100 and 800/606–8188, fax 312/266–2103. 21 E. Bellevue Place, Chicago, IL 60611. 246 rms. $$$$* **(see pp. 19, 23, 28)**

Swissotel. This wedge-shaped, glass-clad tower takes advantage of the views at the far eastern tip of Wacker Drive, a few blocks off Michigan Avenue, but though it's attached underground to Illinois Center and the Hyatt Regency, it's otherwise rather isolated. Exactly what you'd expect from the Swiss: well-ordered, clean, and with all the usual luxury amenities (king-size beds, remote-controlled TVs, marble baths). One nice twist: each room has its own doorbell. Don't miss the authentic *konditorei* in the lobby, which serves fabulous home-baked goods. The rest of the restaurants here are forgettable.... *Tel 312/565–0565 and 800/654–7263, fax 312/565–0540. 323 E. Wacker Dr., Chicago, IL 60601. 630 rms. $$$* **(see pp. 14, 17, 20, 24, 26)**

The Talbott Hotel. Built as an apartment building in 1927 and converted to a hotel in 1989, the family-run Talbott offers large rooms with a variety of layouts that include either kitchenettes or full kitchens. Complimentary Continental breakfast and evening brownies and coffee.... *Tel 312/943–0161 and 800/621-8506, fax 312/944–7241. 20 E. Delaware Place, Chicago, IL 60611. 98 rms, 50 suites. $$$* **(see p. 19)**

The Tremont. The efficient staff at this small, understated hotel right off Michigan Avenue treats everyone well. The Tudor-style lobby is decked out with burnished brass chandeliers, wingback chairs, and a Chinese porcelain bowl of potpourri; guest rooms are equally posh and Britishy, with VCRs and CD players.... *Tel 312/751–1900 and 800/621–8133. 100 E. Chestnut St., Chicago, IL 60611. 129 rms.* $$$$ **(see pp. 23, 28)**

Westin River North. Westin's takeout of the genteel Hotel Nikko made it just another behemoth; peddling clean nothing–special rooms, mostly to business people. The Hana Lounge lobby bar still exists, but it's lost its Zen-like serenity. Same good views, though.... *Tel 312/744–1900 and 800/645–5687, fax 312/527–2664. 320 N. Dearborn St., Chicago, IL 60610. 422 rms.* $$$$ **(see pp. 19, 21, 25, 26)**

ACCOMMODATIONS | THE INDEX

Chicago Accommodations

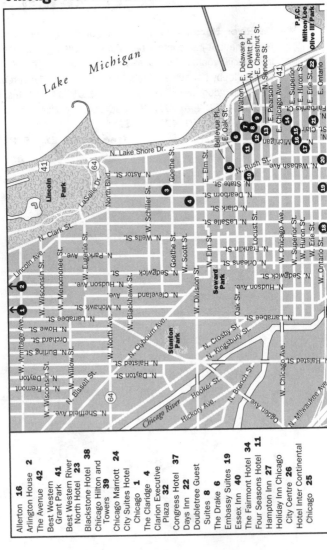

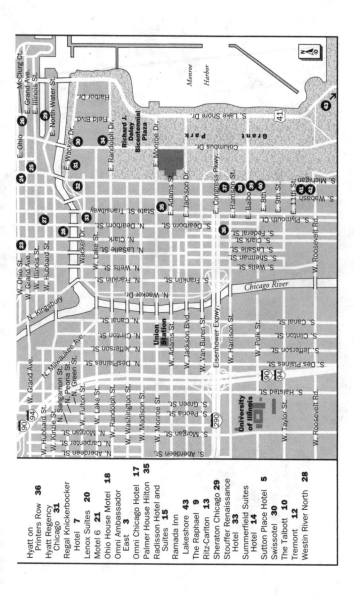

Hyatt on
Printers Row **36**
Hyatt Regency
Chicago **31**
Regal Knickerbocker
Hotel **7**
Lenox Suites **20**
Motel 6 **21**
Ohio House Motel **18**
Omni Ambassador
East **3**
Omni Chicago Hotel **17**
Palmer House Hilton **35**
Radisson Hotel and
Suites **15**
Ramada Inn
Lakeshore **43**
The Raphael **9**
Ritz-Carlton **13**
Sheraton Chicago **29**
Stouffer Renaissance
Hotel **33**
Summerfield Suites
Hotel **14**
Sutton Place Hotel **5**
Swissotel **30**
The Talbott **10**
Tremont **12**
Westin River North **28**

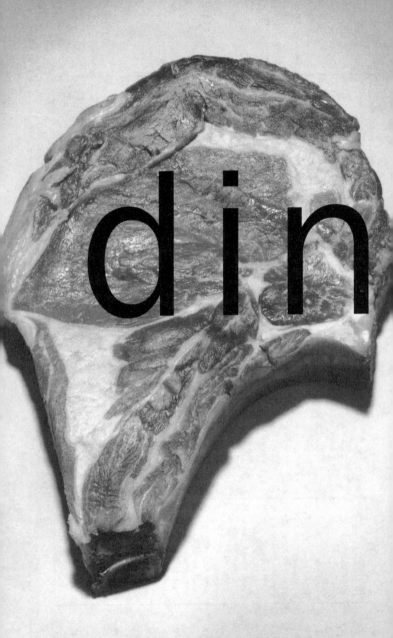

ing 2

The old Chicago stalwarts—deep-dish pizza at pizzerias **Uno** and **Due**, steaks and chops "dis thick" at **Gene &**

Georgetti, and stick-to-your-ribs pierogis at the **Busy Bee**—still exist, but Chicago chefs (and bartenders, for that matter) have moved way beyond the days when that was all that people wanted. Authentic Mexican is hot now, led by the success of **Frontera Grill**, as are tapas as served at **Cafe Iberico**. Thai food made an appearance a decade or so ago and has become one of the city's most reliably consistent cuisines. (For some reason, though, the Chinese food here isn't all that good, with a few exceptions.) **Jane's** serves corn pasta, and **Wishbone**'s specialty is hoppin' John (black-eyed peas over rice with cheddar, scallions, and tomatoes).

How to Dress

Rule of thumb for Chicago restaurants: Wear a jacket to **The Pump Room** and to **Charlie Trotter**, or they won't seat you. (Actually, The Pump Room might lend you an ill-fitting, scratchy blazer.) Though most other places let you wear what you want, scope things out ahead of time, especially at the more expensive restaurants. The listings below warn you whether any dress-code restrictions apply. Chicago isn't a stuffy town, but it's no resort, either; wearing shorts and sunglasses is frowned upon at stylishly chic places like **Ambria**. If in doubt, dress up—you can get away with your Armani tux anywhere if you're dining late after a formal event.

Getting the Right Table

You don't need to worry about greasing the palm of Chicago maître d's—it's not the custom here. And as far as the "right" table goes, the only one to avoid is that near the bathroom or the kitchen (unless, that is, you've reserved the one *in* the kitchen, as you can at **Charlie Trotter**). Of course, certain restaurants have truly prime tables—at **Spiaggia**, they're along the windows overlooking Oak Street Beach; at **Gene & Georgetti**, the first-floor tables seem earmarked for special pals of the host; at **Okno**, sit anywhere but the balcony if you want to see and be seen by the cognoscenti. You can request seating when you call for reservations, though there's no guarantee you'll get it. At most restaurants that accept reservations you should try to make them at least three days in advance. However, at the city's toniest establishments (such as Charlie Trotter, Ambria, and Spiaggia) you should make reservations as soon as you plan your trip, no matter how far in advance, and confirm not once, but twice—say a week before and then the day of your planned meal. If you can, leave a phone number where you can be called to confirm (if they can't reach you, they may drop your reservation).

The Lowdown

Institutions... The really great thing about **Michael Jordan's Restaurant** is just how quickly it became an institution. Of course, it didn't hurt that even the most jaded Chicagoans love Michael Jordan. What's not to love? He's the world's best b-ball player and he actually seems like a pretty nice guy. His sleekly designed restaurant is nice enough, too, even if it's filled mainly with tourists trying to soak up a little Michaelosity before heading to the first-floor gift shop. **The Pump Room** no longer attracts the stars—though black-and-white glossies of former patrons line its walls, from Della Reese to Fred MacMurray—but this historic celebrity haunt still retains something of its old-time glamour. The menu features things like escargot, shrimp bisque, and Caesar salad, just as back in 1938 when it opened. Celebrities—even faux celebrities—don't ever show up at **Ann Sather**, but this north side Swedish restaurant has become an institution anyhow, at least for breakfast. Its gooey cinnamon rolls are famous the world round (okay, maybe just in Chicago's 44th Ward, but that's close enough). Speaking of goo, deep-dish pizza was invented in Chicago more than 50 years ago at **Pizzeria Uno**, a dark, almost seedy, but not-to-be-missed pizza joint (with much more character than the myriad branches of the national chain it spawned). The pizza here is a culinary marvel—delicious, overflowing with toppings and cheese, and deservedly famous. Rub elbows with the city's bureaucrats, from judges to parole officers, at **The Berghoff**, which holds city liquor license No. 1; established in the 1890s, it's been in the same Loop location since 1905. Bratwurst, sauerbraten, and corned beef are consumed here by a couple-thousand or so hungry businesspeople (and tourists) every day. Last but not least, the **Billy Goat Tavern**, a dive-y newspaper reporters' hangout, achieved immortality by inspiring the famous "cheezeburger, cheezeburger—no Coke, Pepsi" sketches on "Saturday Night Live."

See-and-be-scenes... Of course, it depends on who you want to see and by whom you want to be seen. For instance, though some say it's yesterday's restaurant, head to **Bice** at lunchtime if you want to see swank PR and advertising execs cutting deals, elegant thin-as-a-rail women splitting a salad, and lots of European tourists. (At dinner, Bice feeds Chicago's Euro-trash, possibly because the mother ship Bice is a trend-setter in oh-so-trendy Milan.) Besides swarms of folks from its Lake View neighborhood, **Mia Francesca** attracts a modelly crowd. But it's not only the crowd that's hot; so is the food—designer pizzas and pastas that never miss. It takes a bit of effort to get to and into the French-inspired bistro **Marché**, which is always crowded yet doesn't take reservations for prime dining hours; but the payoff is a crowd so eye-blindingly fab that it's almost as good as a night at the theater. In Lincoln Park, a bistro called **Un Grand Café** hosts crowds of your basic table-hopping, Powerbook-using lawyers, moguls, and artists, all of whom, it sometimes seem, know one another. There is also a lot of neck-craning at **Gibson's**, a swinging steak house *on* Rush Street but not typical *of* Rush Street; it's filled with middle-aged divorcées, cigar-chomping guys wearing huge pinkie rings, sleek trophy-wife wannabees, visiting celebs, and neighborhood rich people in search of strong drinks from the heavy-handed bartender and steaks the size of Rhode Island. **Spago** hit town like a comet, immediately attracting Chicago's social and political elite hungry for a taste of Wolfgang Puck's justly famous California cuisine. And the pace hasn't lessened any with time, especially late at night when **Spago Grill** heats up with a chic late-night crowd. It's loud music and a downtown crowd at **Okno**, an artsy Bucktown newcomer with devoted fans that are as much a part of the dining experience as the inventive Asian-influenced food. For a more uptown gallery crowd—artists, collectors, dealers, and hangers-on—try Bucktown's **Con Fusion**, where eclecticism reigns (not to mention that addle-brained name). The it's-hip-to-be-spare decor features peculiar translucent seats that are sturdier than they appear. At **Gordon**, things are a bit more refined, but no less frenetic. Filled with everyone from rich young traders to folks celebrating their 50th wedding anniversaries, this upscale spot offers some of the best food in town, including perfectly done fish, artichoke fritters to die for, and a denseless flourless chocolate cake. At the **Park Avenue Cafe**, the food is good, if a bit highly wrought, yet from almost the first day it opened in 1995 this suave spot off Michigan Avenue has attracted a power crowd.

Deals on meals (under $25)... The most gorgeous people in town continue to eat at **Mia Francesca**, not only because gorgeous people like to stick together (though there's that, too), but because of moderate prices and consistently good trattoria food. If the line here is too long—a nightly problem, since Mia Francesca does not take reservations—and you're set on Italian, try **Scoozi!**, a warehouse-sized River North restaurant with storefront prices. It, too, attracts a great-looking crowd, albeit a bit on the suburban side. Okay, so the gang at **Dick's Last Resort** hasn't just stepped out of *GQ* or *Vogue*, but they know a good thing when they eat it, even if the surroundings at this lowbrow North Pier restaurant are loud, obnoxious, messy, crass, crude, and piggy. The seafood and BBQ is really good, and the price is right. Stay away from the killer margaritas at the **Frontera Grill** and you won't end up spending too much, either—though what you will get is not only the best authentic Mexican food in Chicago, but, according to all the national press attention this place gets, some of the best in these here United States. One of the best-kept dining secrets in town is simple little **Daniel J**, where the husband-and-wife team that owns the place put a high premium on serving terrific, eclectic food—and just wait until you see how they fold their napkins. The word is out, however, about the way-hip **Club Lucky**, where the wait can go on forever. It looks a little like a Forties diner, with plenty of Naugahyde banquettes and an uninspired Italian menu, but the atmosphere and the Wicker Park location are definitely "now." The sprawling space has good sight lines that make it possible to see who's cutting deals with whom, who's sending drinks to whom, and who's basically doing whom. There's no wait, really, at **foodlife**, an upscale mall food court in Water Tower Place, with a healthy, New Age bent. You walk in, get a "credit card," and then hand it to each server as you build your meal, wandering from food booth to food booth. At the end they add it up and, boom, you're spending twice as much as you thought you would (though not as much as in a restaurant with waiters). You really can't spend too much at **Wishbone**, a sprawling Southern-style place in an out-of-the-way location west of the Loop; half the joint is a regular restaurant with waiter service, the other half a cafeteria (at lunch, at least; there's table service at dinner), but both sell hearty country food at country prices. **Jane's** is a casual, moderately priced Bucktown cafe serving inventive food, with many dishes based on health-food ingredients that start out hippie and end up hip. The **Deluxe Diner** serves mostly gourmet versions of traditional diner fare, and while the prices are hardly blue-plate specials, you can get a good lunch or dinner here for half the price of other restaurants serving similar food. The Bucktown address and a funky crowd make this a happening scene.

Steak your life on it... Steaks (as well as chops) at **Gibson's** are good—and enormous and expensive. Near the Oak Street boutiques, this wood-panelled place is subdued. Its prosperous swingy singles crowd isn't. It's a far less chic crowd herding into old-fashioned **Gene & Georgetti** in River North, but judging by the line of big limos with politicos' official license plates, not to mention the chauffeurs loitering out front, it's a no less affluent crowd. The steaks are no less thick and tender, too. And who says size doesn't matter? Not the folks at **The Capital Grille**, where the dry-aged steaks will give you that thrill that you just can't get from London broil, if you catch my drift. One memorable thing about this downtown newcomer is the bartender's jolly, heavy pouring hand—a rare trait indeed these days.

Decor to die for... Though there are easier restaurants to get to than **Marché**, this très chic, grandly decorated grand bistro, located in the up-and-coming River West neighborhood, is well worth the cab fare. Wrought metal and lush swathes of velvet fabric make the room look special; it doesn't hurt, either, that it's filled with the city's beautiful crowd. In the art nouveau dining room of **Ambria**, across from Lincoln Park, the aesthetics are just right—exquisite flowers, dark paneling, stiff white tablecloths, sparkling china and silver, and fine French food presented as if it were art. It's not the black-and-white glossies of Hollywood's stars of yore that make **The Pump Room** such a lovely space, though their old-fashioned glamour certainly doesn't hurt. Its true glitz comes in the form of gigantic chandeliers, lots of big, round tables sparkling with crystal, cutlery, and flowers, and a celebratory feeling. With its huge Mao portrait (à la

Warhol), severe red-black-and-white accents, and bamboo walls, the **WonTon Club**, a few blocks from Michigan Avenue, is one of the city's most cleverly-designed spots. One tip: to enjoy your designer sushi and sake smoke-free, ask to sit away from the smoking section in the center of the restaurant. Whirling dervishes of design, undulating walls, and a glittery panoply of Technicolor sights mark the **Cheesecake Factory** as one of the most inventive places on Michigan Avenue, right up there with the Viacom Store and Niketown. The menu features every imaginable type of food known to man, but the name tells you what really matters: to-die-for cheesecake for dessert. At hotter-than-hot **Okno**, the chartreuse boomerang-shaped tabletops and too-narrow banquettes are a striking counterpoint to the black sky seen through two-story-high windows.

The sporting life... Eating burgers at **Michael Jordan's** isn't exactly the same as being courtside at a game, but at least you're in like-minded, sports-crazy company. Jordan's sleek River North restaurant is filled mainly with tourists staring at the huge video screen in the first-floor bar, waiting for a table in the dining room upstairs. "They" say Michael eats here, too, in a specially-designed-for-him dining room, but don't count on seeing him. The bar at **Harry Caray's** is 60.5 feet long—the same as the distance between home plate and the pitcher's mound. It isn't unusual for the waiters, as well as the patrons, to break into "Take Me Out to the Ball Game" at midnight. The Italian food is pretty good, but the collection of memorabilia is what's really impressive.

Ethnic eating... **Penny's Noodle Shop**, a popular little place up in Lake View, is a wonderful pan-Asian (i.e., Japanese, Chinese, Vietnamese, Thai) noodle shop. Though the **Hi Ricky** chain may have better noodles overall, Penny's *pad see-uw* (traditional noodle dish) is still unsurpassed. There's no strife at **Moti Mahal Indian Restaurant**, either, except occasionally between the surly waitstaff and the patrons. But keep your karma cool and this storefront restaurant in Lake View will reward you with the best cheap Indian food in a city filled with cheap Indian food. It's Cantonese style at **Hong Min**. Dishes with names like "Oceans of Health" (seaweed noodles and veggies) and "Buddha Bop" (brown rice, chestnuts, dates, red beans, and various roots) are the oddly delicious highlights of the vegetarian Korean cuisine at **Amitabul**, up in Lake View. Try any of the seven types of vegetable pancakes. How often do you see a menu offering a side of goat meat for a dollar? At **Suya African Bar & Grill** there's that, as well as many other Nigerian dishes worth your adventurous while. If it's too crowded to get a table immediately, just go next door to its Lake View neighbor **Tibet Cafe** (and vice versa), where the Chinese-like cuisine will bowl you over with its subtlety and grace. There's no subtlety (or grace, for that matter) at **Heaven on Seven**, where the Cajun specialties are fire-breathing hot. But then, in a cuisine with jalapenos and Tabasco in almost everything, what did you expect? Forget virtually everything else that's called "Mexican"—River North's **Frontera Grill** is the real thing, with dishes such as *verdras motuleñas* (tostada of grilled portobello mushroom, zucchini, black beans, oranges, and plantains), *caldo de siete mares* (scallop, shrimp, mussel, and snapper soup), and tacos filled with duck, steak, and even catfish. Cheap is the operative word, garlicky the operative flavor at **Cafe Iberico**, an authentic, smoky, raucous River North tapas bar. Actual Spanish people eat here, which is a good sign. It's mostly tourists and people on dates at Lincoln Park's **Cafe Ba-Ba-Reeba!**, which also serves tapas, though at considerably higher prices. At the **Busy Bee**, probably the city's best-known Polish restaurant, tourists mix 'n' mingle with local Poles and artists from its funky Bucktown neighborhood, all chowing down on the fat pierogis. Wild game, such as elk, duck, and venison are the specialties at **The Berghoff**, a hearty wood-panelled German restaurant that's been around for more than a century. Their own beer, called (naturally) Berghoff, is surprisingly good.

Caffeine scenes... The arty regulars at the **Third Coast Cafe**, just off Michigan Avenue, mix well with the place's other habitués: guys wearing chinos and loafers with no socks, women in Jackie O. wraparound sunglasses who only speak Italian. The best coffee in town, though—called Elaine's Brew—is at **Elaine and Ina's**, a downtown breakfast place beloved by yuppies. The pastries are the thing at **Lutz Continental Cafe and Pastry Shop**, an old-fashioned German coffeeshop with starched table-cloths, on the north side, far from the madding crowd.

The **Medici**, near the University of Chicago in Hyde Park, serves all sorts of coffee concoctions in a really cozy woodsy setting.

If al fresco's your style... Stylish **Bistro 110** has an outdoor cafe where you won't be overcome by the French food's garlicky aroma; you'll have a postcard-perfect view of the Water Tower and Michigan Avenue, not to mention a parade of crazed shoppers schlepping from one store to the next. **Un Grand Café**'s outdoor space overlooks the Lincoln Park Conservatory, lending this boisterous bistro one of the more contemplative outdoor views in town. At the **Heartland Cafe**, a mellow health-foody place stuck in a 1960s timewarp, the front patio tables overlook a sleepy tree-shaded side street in Rogers Park. Competition for seats outdoors at the **Third Coast Cafe** is totally cutthroat, given that most people who do get a streetside seat linger a long time. It's no wonder, though, considering this inexpensive cafe's hot location a block off Michigan Avenue. A lively parade of moviegoers, dog-walkers, window-shoppers, and stroller-pushing yuppies make the outdoor cafe at **Bistrot Zinc**, overlooking a recently gentrified Lake View streetscape, one of the most entertaining in town. They even let you sit out there with your dog at your feet. Avoid the car exhaust and crush of shoppers at the outdoor sidewalk cafe at **Le Colonial** and head for this upscale Vietnamese restaurant's shaded second-floor balcony, where a lucky few get to dine overlooking the sidewalk scene. If manicured lawns and a view of the cobalt-blue lake in the distance is more to your liking, stop in for lunch at the **M-Cafe**, the Museum of Contemporary Art's restaurant, and sit outside on the broad terrace. But watch out for bees.

We never close—well, almost never... When the host at **Cafe Iberico** says the wait for a table is "20 minutes," it can translate into five or 50, depending. Still, it's open late, it's in trendy River North, it's cheap, and it's just the kind of food—tapas—you want at the end of the evening. River North's all-the-rage **Spago Grill** can still be crowded at midnight, so don't be surprised if there's a short wait (head to the cigar bar upstairs). Still, it's worth it just to chow down on the satisfying salads and pizzas anointed by California master Wolfgang Puck. It's even more crowded as night turns into the early morning hours at **Okno**, where the *au courant* linger for their own after-hours party. The food's as stunning and artful as the crowd—well worth a late night in Bucktown. The hepcats who jam into Wicker Park's **Club Lucky** till the wee hours every night (except Sunday) know that the Italian food takes the proverbial back seat to the stylish scene, complete with a great front bar specializing in the best martinis in town. Chinese food has a way of satisfying those late-night hunger pangs as well, and though most of Chinatown goes pretty dead late at night, dingy-looking little **Hong Min** serves top-notch Cantonese food until the wee hours. But sometimes there is no better late-night bite than good greasy hand-cut fries and a burger, both of which are served at the **Wiener Circle** in Lincoln Park, where the short-order cooks behind the counter may scream at you, but it's generally well-meaning: "WHAT DO YOU WANT? FRIES WITH THAT? COME ON, COME ON, FRIES?" The answer should always be yes, no matter what they ask. Everything on that? Yes. Extra salt? Yes, Yes, Yes. These guys are hot dog and hamburger professionals, and if they can't satisfy your late-night hunger, nobody can.

Pizza classics... Chicago is known for its deep-dish pizzas—artery-clogging globs of cheese, rich and chunky tomato sauce, thick crust, and traditional toppings from sausage to olives to onions, etc. Order extra tomatoes and cheese—it's amazingly good. The wait at most of the best pizzerias is long, but you can generally order way before you're seated, so the food will be delivered not long after you hit the table. (That way they can get you in and out as fast as possible.) Try **Pizzeria Uno** or **Pizzeria Due**, around the corner from each other in River North. You can't go wrong at either venue. Another favorite, if only because of its location just off Michigan Avenue, is **Gino's East**—perhaps the only restaurant in town where people will be lined up outside in the dead of winter. Decades of patrons have carved their initials, witticisms, and a few unprintable *bon mots* into the wood tables here.

Designer pizza... At River North's **Scoozi!** the thin, oven-roasted pizzas are deliciously huge oblong things that the waiters present at the table as if they were diamonds from Cartier. They come in two sizes and usually there are six from which to choose, such as the simple margherita (tomato, pesto, and mozzarella), sofisticata (arugula, bacon, and red onion), and forestiera (wild mushrooms, roasted garlic, and fontina cheese). The char-crusted pizzas at **Mia Francesca** are really good, too, though the wait to get into this hot, hot, hot Lake View restaurant can be so long you might as well fly to Roma and back for the real thing. If you do stick around, though, the pizza with mussels and calamari is worth it. And since the whole designer pizza thing really started with Wolfgang Puck anyway, breeze into his **Spago Grill** in River North for pizzas topped with anything from duck sausage to a simple Margarita (tomato and cheese). They'll blow you away with their thin but crispy crusts and fresh takes on the usual ingredients.

The Italian battalion... There was a period a few years ago when every other restaurant that opened in Chicago was a trattoria. Bowls of gnocchi, chicken Vesuvio, and Caesar salads were becoming as common as a burger and fries. A few places, though, stood out from the crowd, and still do, and they're not necessarily all located along Taylor Street in Chicago's tiny Little Italy (the operative word is "little"). In fact, **Spiaggia**, in its coolly upscale space overlooking Michigan Avenue and the lake, is considered by some folks the best Italian restaurant in town. Indulge in mounds of delicious pastas and creamy cannoli at **Maggiano's Little Italy**, a River North red-sauce classic right down to the checked tablecloths; another River North standout on the tonier end of the trend-o-meter is **Centro**. Down in the Loop, there's Tuscan-flavored **Trattoria No. 10**, a favorite of the business lunch crowd. If you insist upon going to Little Italy, you won't be disappointed at **Rosebud**, which is usually jammed (expect a wait, even with a reservation). You'll probably leave with a very full doggie-bag in hand.

French toast... **Ambria** is arguably the city's premier French restaurant—rich, classic dishes, game, truffles, the whole haute thing. It's in the Belden Hotel, just across the street from the Lincoln Park Conservatory; across the lobby is **Un Grand Café**, a boisterous and far more casual (and inexpensive) counterpart serving updated bistro fare. Expect a chic crowd, waitrons scurrying about in starched aprons and black bow ties, and enough Chanel No. 5 in

the air that you'll think you're in Gay Paree. Far less boisterous but no less authentic is **Le Bouchon**, a tiny
Bucktown hole-in-the-wall with simple framed pictures
of France on the walls and a tin ceiling above. The maître
d' has never quite gotten the fact that here in America
reservations actually have meaning, but the inevitable
wait is worth it—you'll get authentic bistro food at reasonable prices. In December, you'll be subjected to really
bad holiday music, but otherwise it's Edith Piaf on the
Muzak and great French fare on your plate at **Bistro 110**,
a handsome, busy Mag Miler. Meals start with a hot 'n'
crusty baguette, ramekin of butter, and head of roasted
elephant garlic—heaven on earth. The wraparound
mural at **Voila!** picks up on the theatrical atmosphere of
the Schubert across the street; pre- and après-theater
crowds lend a bit of buzz to this *commeci, commeça* bistro
in the Loop. Add a "t" and you get **Bistrot Zinc**, an
authentic-looking Lake View restaurant (zinc-topped
bar and marble-topped tables) which cleverly put eye-
level mirrors behind the booths so everyone in the whole
place can see everyone else coming and going. At
Brasserie Jo, in River North, piped-in French lessons
add an eerie note to one's bathroom excursions, but that's
about the only scary thing you'll find here. The food is as
familiar and comforting as a worn afghan on a chilly winter's afternoon: coq au vin, bouillabaise, and anything
served with white beans are standouts. It's fun eating
charcuterie straight from its bright orange pot brimming
with sausages and other meats. One suggestion: order the
floating island for dessert.

Isn't it romantic?... **Bistrot Zinc**'s casually chic atmosphere makes it the perfect spot to drape yourself lan-
guidly in a booth, sipping a cosmopolitan while staring
lovingly into the eyes of your beloved. For an even more
relaxed atmosphere (but still in a booth) try the **Deluxe
Diner**, where spotlights over the crazy booths make you
feel totally alone together. Up on North Halsted, **Oo-
La-La!** is invitingly dark—the individual votives on each
table cast a romantic glow on everyone's face—and the
satisfying pastas leave you with a well-fed glow.

Eating solo... The long counter or a cozy table in the back
room at **Ann Sather** is a great place to settle in with a
book or to just watch the passing crowd of locals, which

ranges from funky old guys to leather-clad lesbians. You don't have to like Swedish food—most folks come for the breakfasts, anyway. Everything at River North's smart little **Big Bowl Cafe** is served in a big bowl—get the gimmick?—soups, Asian-style noodles, and other quick and casual solo meals. (The tables are small and close together, so eavesdropping on your neighbors is really easy, too.) The loquacious bartenders at stylish French **Bistro 110** are great company when dining alone at the copper-topped bar, ideal for a stop-off during a Mag Mile shopping spree. Mag Mile people-watching both inside and out the windows make the **Third Coast Cafe** a great, inexpensive eating-alone place, along with piles of newspapers and magazines if you want to read. The booths at the **Deluxe Diner**, in Bucktown, are big cushy affairs and—bless the management's heart—they'll actually seat one person at them, so you can spread out the paper, scan the personals, whatever. The arty atmosphere and crowd at **Wishbone** makes eating alone easy too: you can read, just look around, appear depressed and brooding and in need of Prozac—no one cares. What the place does care about, though, is serving as-authentic-as-possible-in-Chicago Southern home cookin'.

Noshing between galleries... River North's gallery scene can be exhausting. Fortunately there are a bunch of nearby places to rest those weary bones. If you've been searching for that perfect Old Master drawing, a plate of homemade pasta at **Scoozi!** may be called for (and at lunch, there's generally no wait at this huge, pretty restaurant). Two other Italian places are nearby: the northern Italian **Centro**, with large portions and sophisticated patrons, and the more plebian **Maggiano's Little Italy**, a charming spot that helped spark the family-style serving trend in the city. The vaguely pan-Asian **Big Bowl Cafe** is a great lunch stop, too: cheap, stylish, flavorful. There's always the chic Mexican favorite, the **Frontera Grill**; or sprawling **Papagus Greek Taverna**, where the best deal is to sample the long list of hot and cold appetizers. **Earth** may use natural ingredients and everything in the place may be recycled, but the art-dealing and -hopping crowd it attracts is far more Manolo Blahnik than Birkenstock. A light lunch of a seaweed roll and sushi at the **Won Ton Club** is just the sort of artfully presented food that goes well with a day of gallery going—and it tastes good, too.

Near Mag Mile shopping... When schlepping those Crate & Barrel, Marshall Field's, and Cartier bags gets tiring, stop into **Bistro 110**, where the lively atmosphere—not to mention the incredibly garlicky food—will regenerate you. If you're doing that Water Tower Place thing, you really can't go too wrong at **foodlife**, an upscale mall food court with a health-food-y twist. Want a bit more calm amidst the storm? Park yourself at chic **Le Colonial** for a Bombay gin martini and some simple yet elegant Vietnamese food. Think pre-pre-war Viet Nam: Frenchified food, strong drinks, encroaching palm fronds, ceiling fans turning lazily far above your head. Or head to the **M-Cafe**, on the first floor of the Museum of Contemporary Art, where you order at the counter but they bring the food to your table. Sophisticated soups, sandwiches, salads, and pizzas are on the menu; culture is in the air. Try the salmon "pastrami" or salad Niçoise (with beautifully seared fresh tuna) at **Mrs. Park's Tavern**, a relatively folksy adjunct of the tony **Park Avenue Cafe**, tucked discreetly off Michigan Avenue. Beware of expensive wines by the glass, though. It's not easy to find an inexpensive place to eat around here, so no wonder **Johnny Rockets**—a pastiche of a 1950s diner transplanted from L.A.'s Melrose Boulevard—is usually crowded. It's a good choice if you've got kids in tow, as is **Gino's East**, for pizza that'll keep them happy for a few more hours.

Morning glories... With a fire roaring all winter and beautiful murals covering the walls—not to mention snappy waitresses who barely let you swallow a sip of coffee before they're there topping it off—it's no wonder that **Ann Sather** has a line for weekend breakfasts snaking down Belmont Avenue. Just off Michigan Avenue, **Elaine and Ina's** is a more expensive place for breakfast, but the long lines of Cherokee-driving, cellular-phone-using, Banana Republic-outfitted patrons that come here every weekend for pancakes and designer scrapple don't seem to mind. Concerned that your cholesterol is too low? Are your arteries too free-flowing? Could you use a little meat on them there bones? If you answered yes to even one of the above, head on over to **Lou Mitchell's**, which has been around since 1935, for over-the-top hearty breakfasts—omelettes, French toast, all the classics. For a quick bite before Saturday gallery-hopping or shopping, plop down at a table sporting a red-and-white-checked tablecloth at River North's **The Corner Bakery** for some of the best baked goods in the city. The smell alone will thrill you. The menu also features some of the best tuna salad in town served on dense olive bread, a garlicky Ceasar salad, and just-gooey-enough macaroni and cheese. If you're sick and tired of plain ole eggs, try the *machacado con huevo* (scrambled eggs with shredded jerky, serrano chile, and salsa verde and black beans), *huevos motuleños* (fried eggs on a tostada with tomatoes, ham, fried plantains, and black beans), or *huevos ahogados* (poached eggs with tomatillo-chile sauce and Swiss chard) at River North's **Frontera Grill**, all served in this casual Mexican restaurant's comfy, colorful dining room. At River West's **Wishbone**, folks happily chow down the Southern-style breakfasts (have some grits with them eggs). The gay-as-a-goose freebie magazine *Babble* calls **Oo-La-La!**'s weekend breakfast the "diva brunch," and are they ever right. The guys look awfully good for this early in the day, sating themselves with the strong bloody Marys, great eggs Benedict, or banana-stuffed French toast.

Absolutely fabulous... Don't let the understated decor of this chic townhouse restaurant fool you—suave **Charlie Trotter** pampers its guests in grand style. There's nothing to distract you from the task at hand: being wowed by the food and the service. The international menu's always changing, always fabulous. **Spiaggia**'s floor-to-ceiling windows overlooking Lake Michigan add the perfect sparkle to the city's best Italian restaurant. With its elegant art nouveau decor, **Ambria** (across from Lincoln Park) is where you want to go for classic French, especially if someone else is paying. If fancy to you means being forced to wear a coat (and a tie, please), then eat at **The Pump Room**, under the huge glittering chandeliers, where celebrities have ordered their steaks medium-rare for years. Quietly elegant **Everest**, with its panoramic view of the city and its intriguing French-plus cuisine, makes for a luxurious night out.

Off the eaten track... **Daniel J** isn't really anywhere to speak of other than on a drab street in a drab part of town west of Lake View, but oh, the food! Family-run—he's the chef, she's the hostess—it places its priorities on inventive but not outlandish recipes, perfectly executed. Try the oven-baked crab cakes. Don't ask why **Reza's**, a terrific Persian restaurant, is in Andersonville, the Swedish part of town, but it is. The mostly vegetarian **Heartland Cafe** is in a far-north section of the city, but if you're in the mood for a relaxing time (hippie-style, that is), it's the place to go. Do whatever it takes to get to **Lutz Continental Cafe and Pastry Shop**, on the north side, if for no other reason than to bury your face in a huge linzer torte while sipping an espresso. Cheaper neighborhood rents translate into lower meal checks than you'd expect at **Le Bouchon**, for French bistro fare in Bucktown, and **Club Lucky**, for hip Italian in Wicker Park. Inexpensive Southern home-cooking, served in a casual cavernous space with big paintings of chickens lining the walls, is all that's needed to attract the hipoisie to **Wishbone's** seriously out-of-the-way location (out-of-the-way unless you work for the "Oprah Winfrey Show," since her studios are across the street). It's worth a schlepp to Bucktown to the renowned Polish diner the **Busy Bee**, just for the pierogis.

The children's hour... **Ann Sather** is casual enough for the kids, but homey-chic enough for the adults. It's located in a former funeral home, which kids find hilarious. It takes a certain tastelessness to really like **Dick's Last Resort**, a loud, obnoxious, messy eatery at the North Pier. But loud can be a plus when you're out with kids. Let your hair down and you and the kids just might have a little quality time, snarfing down great BBQ while listening to live music, usually Dixieland jazz or the blues. You can also get barbecue at the faux-ramshackle **Bub City Crabshack & BBQ** in the Lincoln Park area, but order the kids to order crab: they get a mallet, then a bib, then a hot steamin' plate of what the menu calls a "mess o' crabs" (Dungeness crab, snow crab, and crab claws). River North, as you'd expect, is jam-packed with child-pleasers. **Michael Jordan's Restaurant** is so kid-friendly it has a separate menu for the little ones. And it's soooo cute it'll make you want to throw up, but the kids won't know. Serving "Fastbreak Fingers" (chicken fingers), "Center Court Cheese" (grilled cheese sandwich), "Bankshot Cole Slaw," and "Courtside Cookies," it's fun for the very short and young. Older kids probably will be more than happy at **Maggiano's Little Italy**, a festive place where favorites like spaghetti-and-meatballs are served family-style, or

Ed Debevic's, a 1950s-themed eatery that's like one long "Happy Days" rerun. With its swirling, whirling, eye-popping interior, not to mention its huge menu, the **Cheesecake Factory** will provide endless fun for the family, even if you all roly-poly out the doors 10 pounds heavier from downing those huge slabs of cheesecake. Hot 'n' spicy, messy, and colorful, the Cajun food at **Heaven on Seven** is about as kid-friendly as a cuisine can get. The location's handy, too, in a movie multiplex right off the Mag Mile.

Healthful eating... Things that should, but hardly ever do, enter your body, like roots, seaweed, ginseng, and soybean sprouts, are just some of the healthy things you'll find at **Amitabul**, a self-styled "vegetarian Korean Zen" restaurant in Lake View that actually makes all this dreadful-sounding stuff taste really good. The organic food at River North's **Earth** includes vegetable strudel, herbed chicken, vegetable tofu with brown rice—followed by an incredibly rich and creamy rice pudding that immediately undoes all the nutritional good you've done yourself (at least they use antibiotic-free cream!). The **Heartland Cafe** is a touch of Santa Cruz in Rogers Park—lots of tofu on the menu, most of it so delicious it could convert you. Peace, love, and live music abound, though the waitstaff could go a little lighter on the patchouli oil. While the **Big Bowl Cafe**, a stylish restaurant in River North, isn't strictly vegetarian, there are enough interesting veggie choices to satisfy any non-meat-eater, including delicious no-fat (baked) spring rolls. Mellow **Jane's** in Bucktown isn't strictly vegetarian either, but its motto—"vegetarian & clean cuisine"—pretty much sums it up: whole-food ingredients, put together with flair.

Retromania... In the mood for the type of swank 1940s supperclub that Bogey himself might have frequented? Try **Club Lucky**, where the hepcat crowd hangs, sipping the best martinis in town (and giving the forgettable Italian food a miss). If Frankie Valli and the Big Bopper are more your style, go for burgers and shakes to **Ed Debevic's**, a snappy Fifties-memorabilia-jammed diner in River North; or **Johnny Rockets**, a cartoonish diner where *American Graffiti* meets the Magnificent Mile. Far out, literally and figuratively, is the **Heartland Cafe** in

Rogers Park—so 1960s, so mellow, so much tofu. Chicago restaurateurs have mercifully skipped the urge to create a 1970s-style dining experience, but the go-go Eighties are alive at brassy **Bice**, an offshoot of the high-glam Milanese original, which attracts the sort of people who make sure that the next table hears them order "two bottles of Dom."

Near the theaters... With more than one concentration of theaters in the city, devoted theatergoers have to scout out good choices nearby each. Near the Music Box and Mercury theaters, try **Bistrot Zinc** for French comfort food, **Amitabul** for Korean stir-fries, or **Hi Ricky** for scrumptious Asian noodles, especially the chow fun. Another French cafe, **Voila!** draws a post-theater crowd with its late-night kitchen, across from the Schubert and only a short walk from the Goodman; nearby **Rhapsody**, in the Symphony Center complex, tunes up with a refined eclectic menu. The vaguely Italian **Tomboy** and very, very Persian **Reza's** are in Andersonville, home to many small, off-off-off-*off* Broadway theaters. **Mia Francesca**, a chic trattoria, and the Swedish standby **Ann Sather** are just a stroll away from the Theater Building and the Bailiwick theater complex in Lake View.

Near the United Center we stand... Finding a place to eat before or after a Bulls game is easy—even though the immediate neighborhood looks pretty bleak, within a short car ride are some good bets. You can't miss pan-Asian **Red Light**, with its huge crimson beacon sitting atop the restaurant like a turban. Loud, busy, crowded, and flashy, it's better than you'd expect, once you get past the waitron attitude. Chicago's nearby Little Italy is just that: little. But there's nothing little about the portions at two of its most well-known (and fun) restaurants: **Mia Francesca's** on Taylor and **Rosebud**, where the pastas are some of the best in town. For some down-home cooking, try the hoppin' John or blackened catfish at the funky **Wishbone**.

You gotta get a gimmick... When you order one of the two dozen "flights" of wine (four half-glasses of vino related by region) at the retro-chic **Hudson Club**, the presentation ceremony is half the fun. The other half is cleansing your palate between tastes, discussing each wine's relative bouquet, sounding pretentious as you do it, and getting the sort of buzz only drinking four wines at once can give you. At unpretentious **Cucina Bella** up in Lake View, they actually give you aprons when you eat in their frenetic, garlic-pungent, too-much-fun kitchen. It's fun eating in the kitchen at Charlie Trotter, too, but here it's a bit more buttoned-up: no aprons for the patrons, thank you, at this four-star restaurant. The culinary feast, however, is completely sensual—you can taste the food, hear the chefs, watch the glory of preparation, smell the aroma, and almost reach out and touch the excitement. It's worth every penny (and it takes a lot of pennies to eat here). Reserve this table way ahead. The **WonTon Club** bills itself as a sake lounge (and noodle shop and sushi bar—go figure) but it's really the sake in which it specializes. Who knew there were so many brands? The waitstaff can help you decide which to order. Try a few, but watch out—it hits you like a lead balloon.

The Index

$$$$$	over $50
$$$$	$40–$50
$$$	$30–$40
$$	$20–$30
$	under $20

Price categories reflect the cost of a three-course meal, not including drinks, taxes, and tip.

Ambria. The city's premier French restaurant, with an ever-changing menu that may include melt-in-your-mouth sweetbreads with portobello and endive; Beluga caviar; or pomegranate-glazed squab. Impeccable service and prices to match.... *Tel 773/472–5959. 2300 N. Lincoln Park West. Reservations advised. $$$$* **(see pp. 44, 48, 53, 57)**

Amitabul. This spare but cheery Lake View storefront offers delicious Korean food, with a frank menu that tells you, for instance, not to order the sizzling yin & yan if you can't handle heat and spices.... *Tel 773/472–4060. 3418 N. Southport Ave., Southport el stop.* $**(see pp. 50, 59, 60)**

Ann Sather. Homey, yes; cozy, not, unless you're in the front room which, unfortunately, is the smoking section. This is a Swedish restaurant, with Swedish potato sausage, Swedish meatballs, and sandwiches on limpa bread on the menu to prove it.... *Tel 773/348–2378. 929 W. Belmont Ave., Belmont el stop (also at 5207 N. Clark St., tel 773/271–6677). AE not accepted.* $
(see pp. 45, 54, 56, 58, 60)

The Berghoff. This old-timey oak-panelled German restaurant decorated with murals and stained glass attracts hordes at lunchtime, chowing down on hand-carved roast beef, turkey, and corned beef sandwiches in the stand-up bar. Classic wiener schnitzel, sauerbraten, and apple strudel in the vast dining room are your best bets.... *Tel 312/427–3170. 17 W. Adams St., Adams el stop.* $$
(see pp. 45, 50)

Bice. Despite the pretension, this restaurant has all the regular Italian dishes you'd expect and some you wouldn't, like pasta in pesto with green beans and potatoes.... *Tel 312/664–1474. 158 E. Ontario St., Chicago Ave. el stop. Reservations advised.* $$$$ **(see pp. 46, 60)**

Big Bowl Cafe. You'll be (excuse the pun) bowled over by the terrific dishes here, from the grilled-vegetable soup with angel hair noodles to the ginger chicken, vegetable, and shrimp with roasted garlic.... *Tel 312/787–8279. 159 1/2 W. Erie St., Chicago Ave. el stop (also at 6 E. Cedar, tel 312/640–8888).* $ **(see pp. 55, 59)**

Billy Goat Tavern. Within a block of both the *Sun-Times* and the *Chicago Tribune*, this dive—and that's a charitable description—is a media hangout, its walls covered with scores of sepia-tinted newspaper clippings. Greasy but delicious burgers are about the only thing worth eating.... *Tel 312/222–1525. 430 N. Michigan Ave., Michigan Ave. buses. No reservations. No credit cards.* $ **(see p. 45)**

Bistro 110. A stylish bistro with a wicker-chaired garden room, great bar, and energetic dining room, just off the Mag Mile. Try the great roasted red snapper, if they have it, or one of the wonderful garlicky pastas or the half-chicken.... *Tel 312/266–3110. 110 E. Pearson St., Michigan Ave. buses. Reservations advised. $$$* **(see pp. 51, 54, 55, 56)**

Bistrot Zinc. So French, so chic, this oo-la-la bistro boasts Gallic soul food: onion soup, leek tarts, steak frites, braised rabbit, tarte Tatin, and caramel-oozing apple crepes. A casual (and cheaper) salads-and-sandwich menu is served in the bar area, which opens to the street.... *Tel 773/281–3443. 3443 N. Southport Ave., Southport el stop. Reservations advised. $$$* **(see pp. 51, 54, 60)**

Le Bouchon. Zis is really one of ze best (cheap-ish) Frunch bistros in town. Delicious steak frites, cassoulet, great onion tart, *d'accord*, and chicken dishes.... *Tel 773/862–6600. 1958 N. Damen Ave., take a cab. Reservations advised. $$* **(see pp. 54, 58)**

Brasserie Jo. A perfect recreation of a Parisian hotspot, right down to the piped-in accordion music, this restaurant serves authentic brasserie dishes like Alsatian onion tarts and onion soup.... *Tel 312/595–0800. 59 W. Hubbard St., Michigan Ave. buses. Reservations advised. $$$* **(see p. 54)**

Bub City Crabshack & BBQ. A big messy ol' restaurant serving the obvious: crab, as well as great big ol' sloppy dishes of BBQ brisket, chicken, pork, and terrific gumbo. The friendly buzz, loud country music, and good-time feeling are infectious, even if they're fake.... *Tel 312/266–1200. 901 W. Weed St., Clark/Clybourn el stop. $$$* **(see p. 58)**

Busy Bee. *The* Polish diner. All the dishes you'd expect—delish pierogis made with meat, potato, and cheese, stick-to-your-ribs Polish sausage, potato pancakes, and boiled beef (always a crowd pleaser)—at seriously low prices.... *Tel 773/772–4433. 1546 N. Damen Ave., Milwaukee Ave. el. AE not accepted. $* **(see pp. 44, 50, 58)**

Cafe Ba-Ba-Reeba! The boisterous, jammed-with-yuppies

DINING | THE INDEX

atmosphere is a lot of fun, and the food on the ever-evolving menu—from the tortilla española to the marinated octopus to the full meals (such as paella)—is nearly as good as a trip to the Costa del Sol.... *Tel 773/935–5000. 2024 N. Halsted St., take a cab. Reservations advised. $$* **(see p. 50)**

Cafe Iberico. A real tapas bar—sprawling, raucous, loud, crowded, smoky. Great shrimp dishes, tortilla española, baked goat cheese, and terrific pitchers of sangria add to the party atmosphere.... *Tel 312/573–1510. 739 N. LaSalle St., State St. el stop. AE not accepted. Reservations advised. $$* **(see pp. 44, 50, 51)**

The Capital Grille. Its downtown location and swank surroundings lend this recently opened steak house a power feel, even if the guy at the next table is really just a wholesaler from Peoria. Gigantic dry aged steaks, chops, and fresh seafood prevail.... *Tel 312/337–9400. 633 N. St. Clair St., Michigan Ave. buses. Reservations advised. $$$* **(see p. 48)**

Centro. The patrons all reach for their pockets when a cell phone rings, but at least they know good northern Italian food. Try the garlic-bathed chicken Vesuvio.... *Tel 312/988–7775. 710 N. Wells St., Chicago Ave. el stop. Reservations advised. $$$* **(see pp. 53, 55)**

Charlie Trotter. If not the best restaurant in Chicago, this one certainly gets called the best most often. The $85-a-person prix-fixe might include Maine lobster with preserved papaya, scallops, and foie gras, California pigeon breast with spring vegetables, and on and on.... *Tel 773/248–6228. 816 W. Armitage Ave., take a cab. Reservations required. $$$$$* **(see pp. 44, 57)**

Cheesecake Factory. In this John Hancock Center restaurant, huge crowds of people come and go, and a wild interior design looks like an LSD trip. But it all leads to an unforgettable ending: More than a dozen types of cheesecake.... *Tel 312/337–1101. 875 N. Michigan Ave., Michigan Ave. buses. $$* **(see pp. 49, 59)**

Club Lucky. The Italian food here—all the basics from fettucine alfredo to chicken Vesuvio to cannoli—takes the proverbial back seat to the oh-so-swank scene. Low prices lure an artsy crowd.... *Tel 773/227–2300. 1824 W. Wabansia Ave., take a cab. $$* **(see pp. 47, 52, 58, 59)**

Le Colonial. This upscale (i.e., pricey) restaurant serves the best Vietnamese in town. The attitude-free staff explains how to eat some of the more exotic dishes, like shrimp paste wrapped around sugar cane.... *Tel 312/255–0088. 937 N. Rush St., take a cab. Reservations advised. $$$* **(see pp. 51, 56)**

Con Fusion. Living up to its name, this stark Bucktown spot serves Asian-y, California-ish, global-esque cuisine—yet somehow it all works perfectly. The menu changes at the chef's whim, but may include gravlax marinated in gin, tuna tartare, pears in a star-anise sauce, and rack of lamb with Japanese eggplant, etc..... *Tel 773/772–7100. 1616 N. Damen Ave., Milwaukee Ave. el stop. Reservations advised. $$$* **(see p. 46)**

The Corner Bakery. Originally known for terrific muffins and pastries (unbelievably good individual bundt cakes), over the last year or so this River North spot has expanded its menu to include sandwiches, pastas, pizzas, and salads.... *Tel 312/344–7700. 516 N. Clark St., take a cab (also at 1121 N. State St., tel 312/787–1969, and 676 St. Claire Place., tel 312/266–2570). $* **(see p. 57)**

Cucina Bella. Simply decorated with knick-knacks and bottles of wine, this homey Lake View storefront serves food that the owners themselves refer to as "authentic Italian comfort food," and that just about says it all.... *Tel 773/ 868–1119. 543 W. Diversey Pkwy., Diversey el stop. $* **(see p. 61)**

Daniel J. This simply decorated, family-run storefront wows diners with every dish on the menu—from the oven-baked crab cakes, to the mahi mahi with toasted coconut, pineapple, and macadamia nuts, to the stone-baked thin-crust pizzas.... *Tel 773/404–7772. 3811 N. Ashland Ave., take a cab. Reservations advised. $$$* **(see pp. 47, 57)**

Deluxe Diner. Like the name says, it's a diner, but the chicken pot pie is more chicken than pie, the meat loaf more meat than loaf, the tuna melt gooey and good, and the fries even

better.... *Tel 773/342–6667. 1575 N. Milwaukee Ave., Milwaukee el stop. No reservations.* $$
(see pp. 48, 54, 55)

Dick's Last Resort. Loud, raucous, everything chugged down with beer. Slobber over slabs o' ribs, messy chicken, and what they themselves call "squirty" crab's legs; live music, usually Dixieland jazz or the blues, is usually on tap too.... *Tel 312/836–7870. 435 E. Illinois St., Michigan Ave. buses.* $$ **(see pp. 47, 58)**

Earth. At this earthy-looking brick-walled place, with huge fiddle-leaf fig trees and lots of flowers, the menu serves equally earthy fare—organic ingredients and very little meat.... *Tel 312/335–5475. 738 N. Wells St., Chicago Ave. el stop. Reservations advised.* $$ **(see pp. 55, 59)**

Ed Debevic's. This homage to the 1950s must've taken a dozen high-priced creative directors to dream up. The food is all delish, cheapish, and fattening. But hey, who knew from diets in the Fifties, anyhow?.... *Tel 312/664–1707. 640 N. Wells St., take a cab.* $ **(see p. 59)**

Elaine and Ina's. Long lines of prototypical yuppie families line the block every weekend morning for corn–black-bean–cheese scrapple and sour cream pancakes that are so good you'll forget how fattening everything is.... *Tel 312/337–6700. 448 E. Ontario St. No credit cards.* $
(see pp. 50, 56)

Everest. Take the elevator 40 stories up from the Chicago Stock Exchange and treat yourself to an exceptional French meal accented with North American ingredients such as Maine lobster and Texas venison. Pre-theater meal is $39; fixed-price meals start at $69 a head.... *Tel 312/663–8920. 440 S. LaSalle St., Adams St. el stop. Reservations required.* $$$$$ **(see p. 57)**

foodlife. The grand pasha of mall "food courts," this 13-station food-o-rama at Water Tower Place offers a spread that includes rotisserie chicken, stir fries, pastas, tofu burgers, tacos and burritos, and great desserts, and you pay just once. Beer and wine, as well.... *Tel 312/335–3663. 835 N. Michigan Ave., Michigan Ave. buses.* $ **(see pp. 47, 56)**

Frontera Grill. This award-winning Mexican restaurant in River North is about as authentic as it gets, with a weekly changing menu of delightfully nongreasy, nontaco dishes. Colorful artwork, wooden tables, and bright Southwest-inspired walls.... *Tel 312/661–1434. 445 N. Clark St., take a cab. Reservations advised. $$* **(see pp. 44, 47, 50, 55, 57)**

Gene & Georgetti. In the shadow of the Ravenswood el, this dark, old-fashioned, two-level steak house specializes in aged prime steak. Many judges and local politicians eat here regularly.... *Tel 312/527–3718. 500 N. Franklin St., Merchandise Mart el stop. Reservations advised. $$$*
(see pp. 43, 44, 48)

Gibson's. Huge booths, dark panelling, big ferns, good lighting. Try the steaks, of course, from porterhouse to T-bone, sirloin to filet mignon, but don't skip well-prepared fish dishes either. Great baked potatoes, slathered in sour cream, naturally.... *Tel 312/266–8999. 1028 N. Rush St., take a cab. Reservations advised. $$$* **(see pp. 46, 48)**

Gino's East. Really good pizza. Really long lines. But don't despair, they'll take your order while you wait for a table or booth in this dark, cave-like subterranean restaurant.... *Tel 312/943–1124. 160 E. Superior St., Michigan Ave. buses. No reservations. $$* **(see pp. 52, 56)**

Gordon. Quirky to the max—chic interior decor with erotic drawings in the bathrooms. If the cold lemon soufflé in a pool of warm caramel is available, order it. A jazz trio appears on weekends.... *Tel 312/467–9780. 500 N. Clark St., take a cab. Reservations advised. $$$$* **(see p. 46)**

Un Grand Café. This boisterous Lincoln Park bistro is the perfect place for a full-fledged dinner or a late-night omelet and a glass of wine. Without reservations you'll wait a long time to sample its steak frites and bouillabaisse.... *Tel 773/348–8886. 2300 N. Lincoln Park West, take a cab. Reservations advised. $$$* **(see pp. 46, 51, 53)**

Harry Caray's. A big, loud restaurant like its namesake, the late Cubs announcer, the dining rooms are sprawling affairs jammed with people eating better-than-average traditional Italian food. Don't miss the deep-fried calamari or the

DINING | THE INDEX

chicken Vesuvio.... *Tel 312/828–0966. 33 W. Kinzie St., Merchandise Mart el stop. $$* **(see p. 49)**

Heartland Cafe. Terrific semi-vegetarian restaurant with omelets and stir-frys, okay pasta. The burgers are made from buffalo meat—not just any buffalo meat, but farm-raised buffalo meat. Live music most nights; there's a health food store attached, too.... *Tel 773/465–8005. 7000 N. Glenwood Ave., take a cab. No credit cards. $*
(see pp. 51, 58, 59)

Heaven on Seven. Transplanted from its seventh-floor Loop location to the second floor of a cinema complex off Michigan Avenue, this raucous joint whips up authentic Cajun food—hoppin' John (blackeyed peas and andouille sausage), fried catfish, fried oysters, and jambalaya. Skip the tacky souvenir shop.... *Tel 312/280–7774. 600 N. Rush St., State St. el stop. (Also at 111 N. Wabash Ave., Adams St. el stop, tel 312/263–6443, lunch only, no reservations.) $$* **(see pp. 50, 59)**

Hi Ricky. Asian noodle and soup dishes, as well as unusual satays (shrimp, tofu). Loud and casual, and you can eat for about $10.... *Tel 773/388–0000, 3730 N. Southport Ave., Southport Ave. el stop. Tel 312/491–9100, 941 W. Randolph St., take a cab. Tel 773/276–8300, 1852 W. North Ave., Milwaukee Ave. el stop. $* **(see pp. 49, 60)**

Hong Min. Located in a bordering-on-seedy storefront in Chinatown, this is one of the best Chinese restaurants in town—Cantonese and Mandarin dishes such as steamed fish or barbecued pork in black bean and garlic sauce. BYOB.... *Tel 312/842–5026. 221 W. Cermak Rd., take a cab. AE not accepted. $$* **(see pp. 49, 52)**

Hudson Club. With its glamorous 1940s-style airplane hangar-like interior, folks would come here even if the food weren't good; thankfully, it is. Eclectic menu includes everything from oven-roasted beets to cornflake-crusted shrimp. 100 wines by the glass.... *Tel 312/467–1947. 504 N. Wells St., Chicago Ave. el stop. Reservations advised. $$$*
(see p. 60)

Jane's. Whadyya know—an artsy Bucktown restaurant that isn't pretentious! Brick walls, a high, high, high exposed-beam

ceiling, good lighting, and pictures on the walls by local artists all create a mellow atmosphere. The inventive menu may include an unbelievably filling tofu-stuffed burrito.... *Tel 773/862–5263. 1655 W. Cortland St., take a cab. $$*
(see pp. 44, 48, 59)

Johnny Rockets. Red and black and white all over, with minijukeboxes at each booth—you get the picture.... *Tel 312/337–3900. 901 N. Rush St., State St. el stop. No credit cards. $* **(see pp. 56, 59)**

Lou Mitchell's. A Chicago breakfast institution, this place serves the definitive "hearty" breakfast, with homemade breads and cakes, omelets oozing butter and cheese, and great stacks of pancakes and French toast. Long lines.... *Tel 312/939–3111. 625 W. Jackson Blvd., take a cab. No credit cards. No dinner; closed Sun. $* **(see p. 56)**

Lutz Continental Cafe and Pastry Shop. Ageless and quaint, this cozy German pastry shop serves lush pastries, cakes, and tortes, as well as espresso, cappuccino, and American coffee. Try the petit fours.... *Tel 773/478–7785. 2458 W. Montrose Ave., take a cab. AE not accepted. $* **(see pp. 50, 58)**

M-Cafe. Located in the Museum of Contemporary Art, this lunch-only spot serves delicious, artfully presented (but too tastefully small) brioche sandwiches, soups, and salads, as well as Vietnamese spring rolls, goat cheese pizzas, and crispy chow fun noodles.... *Tel 312/280–2660. 220 E. Chicago Ave., Michigan Ave. buses. $* **(see pp. 51, 56)**

Maggiano's Little Italy. Red-and-white-checked tablecloths, sepia-tinted pictures of the Old Country, and enormous platters of traditional pastas, like red-sauced mostaccioli, fettucine alfredo, and spaghetti and meatballs. Family-style service keeps the prices down.... *Tel 312/644–7700. 516 N. Clark St., take a cab. $$* **(see pp. 53, 55, 58)**

Marché. Yes, there's paillard of this and grantinée of that on the menu at this grandly decorated bistro, but the chef here uses French cuisine merely as inspiration. Try the aromatic couscous with grilled vegetables, the haricots verts with fennel and tomato, or any of the spectacular desserts.... *Tel 312/226–8399. 833 W. Randolph St., take a cab. Reservations advised. $$$$* **(see pp. 46, 48)**

DINING | THE INDEX

Medici. A short distance from the University of Chicago, this college and neighborhood hangout serves great burgers, natch, as well as salads, pizzas, and beer.... *Tel 773/667–7394. 1327 E. 57th St., take a cab. $* **(see p. 51)**

Mia Francesca. About as sizzling as sizzling restaurants in Chicago get, this sparely adorned trattoria has managed to stay hot thanks to moderate prices and consistently good food. The menu changes daily.... *Tel 773/281–3310. 3311 N. Clark St., Belmont Ave. el stop (also Mia Francesca's on Taylor, 1400 W. Taylor St., tel 773/829–2828. Reservations advised.) AE not accepted. $$*
(see pp. 46, 47, 53, 60)

Michael Jordan's Restaurant. Surprisingly good food at this good-looking celebrity restaurant (warm, woody, lots of video screens) that doesn't try to rip off its patrons with obscenely high prices. Try Juanita's macaroni and cheese.... *Tel 312/644–DUNK. 500 N. LaSalle St., Chicago Ave. el stop. $$$* **(see pp. 45, 49, 58)**

Moti Mahal Indian Restaurant. The crowds crowding into Moti Mahal's storefront space say it all. Tandooris excel; so do vegetarian dishes like aloo gabhi (potato and cauliflower in a gingery sauce) and sag paneer (spinach and homemade cheese). In exchange for low prices, however, you also get service with a sneer. BYOB.... *Tel 773/348–4392. 1031 W. Belmont Ave., Belmont Ave. el stop. $*
(see p. 49)

Mrs. Park's Tavern. A good (cheaper) alternative to the swellegant Park Avenue Cafe upstairs (see below), this red-white-and-blue space dotted with folk art serves salads, sandwiches, pastas and more. Open late.... *Tel 312/280–8882. 198 E. Delaware Pl., Michigan Ave. buses. $$*
(see p. 56)

Oo-La-La!. The food at this great-looking place at times is terrific and at other times merely okay. The pastas are your best bet, from the plain-as-day pasta pomodoro to the *fettucine al sapori forti* (pasta with pine nuts, raisins, and garlic). Fish is sometimes way overcooked.... *Tel 773/935–7708. 3335 N. Halsted St., Belmont Ave. el stop. $$*
(see pp. 54, 57)

Okno. This Bucktown trendster is the most creative restaurant in town, with its coriander-encrusted seared tuna served in a bamboo steamer and vegetarian "Chinese take-out" appetizer served in—what else?—take-out cartons.... *Tel 773/395–1313. 1332 N. Milwaukee Ave., take a cab. $$$*

(see pp. 44, 46, 49, 52)

Papagus Greek Taverna. The Greek decorations may be slightly on the kitschy side, but the food is pretty good—your basic moussaka, spanakopita, and baklava. Busy, noisy, dimly lit, and convenient to River North (in the Embassy Suites hotel).... *Tel 312/642–8450. 620 N. State St., Grand Ave. el stop. Reservations advised. $$*   **(see p. 55)**

Park Avenue Cafe. All the dishes on the frequently changing menu here are presented handsomely. Desserts are especially terrific—mango sorbet with caramelized banana, carrot cheesecake soufflé—oy! The decor is as smoothly sophisticated as the well-heeled patrons.... *Tel 312/944–4414. 199 E. Walton St., Michigan Ave. buses. Reservations advised. $$$$*   **(see pp. 46, 56)**

Penny's Noodle Shop. This 30-odd-seat sliver of a place beneath the Chicago el tracks attracts a neighborhood crowd with delicious Thai dishes like peppery *pad se ue* (traditional noodle dish), to crisp and savory Chinese greens with oyster sauce, to Vietnamese spring rolls, to Japanese *udon* with fish cakes. BYOB.... *Tel 773/281–8222. 3400 N. Sheffield Ave., Belmont Ave. el stop (also at 950 W. Diversey Pkwy., Diversey el stop., tel 773/281–8448). No credit cards. $*   **(see p. 49)**

Pizzeria Due. An old reliable in an old brownstone—thick deep-dish 'zas oozing cheese, sausage, and virtually every vegetable imaginable, just like you like 'em. Long waits.... *Tel 312/943–2400. 610 N. Wabash St., Michigan Ave. buses. $*   **(see pp. 43, 52)**

Pizzeria Uno. Basically the same as above.... *Tel 312/321–1000. 29 E. Ohio St., Michigan Ave. buses. $*

(see pp. 43, 45, 52)

The Pump Room. Glitz galore in a chandeliered dining room with big booths, bigger tables, and biggest portions. Mostly steaks and chops traditionally prepared. Neat little bar, too,

DINING | THE INDEX

and dancing to a trio on weekends.... *Tel 312/266–0360. 1301 N. State St., take a cab. Reservations required, jacket required.* $$$$ **(see pp. 44, 45, 48, 57)**

Red Light. The menu at this more-or-less Chinese restaurant includes all the usuals plus some not-so-expecteds: claypot red curry chicken, five-spice squid, tea-smoked squab, a terrific roasted duck. And forget tired red-bean ice-cream: try the coconut sorbet with hot fudge.... *Tel 312/733–8880. 820 W. Randolph St., take a cab. Reservations advised.* $$ **(see p. 60)**

Reza's. Huge and boisterous, this Persian restaurant offers more than 100 choices on the menu, from lamb kabob to *kashkeh bodemjan* (eggplant, curds, and whey) to quail to grilled duck breast in pomegranate sauce. And nothing costs more than $12.95.... *Tel 773/561–1898. 5225 N. Clark St., take a cab (also at 432 W. Ontario St., tel 312/664–4500). AE not accepted. Reservations advised.* $$ **(see pp. 58, 60)**

Rhapsody. The seasonal menu is divided between—what else?—"preludes" (lobster tempura, grilled foie gras) and "concerto" (garlic chicken, rib-eye steak).... *Tel 312/977–4468. 65 E. Adams St., Adams St. el stop. Reservations advised.* $$$ **(see p. 60)**

Rosebud. Everything served in this rambling, bustling Little Italy restaurant is big: heaping pastas, a garlicky chicken Vesuvio as big as Vesuvius itself.... *Tel 312/942–1117. 1500 W. Taylor St., take a cab.* $$$ **(see pp. 53, 60)**

Scoozi!. A feast for the eyes, with purposely decrepit walls, immense sprays of flowers, mirrors, and golden-glow lighting. Best on the menu: pastas.... *Tel 312/943–5900. 410 W. Huron St., Chicago Ave. el stop. Reservations advised for lunch.* $$ **(see pp. 47, 52, 55)**

Spago/Spago Grill. Malibu-chic hits the Midwest! Bustling loud Spago and the less-expensive and more casual Spago Grill serve the trademark leanish-cuisinish cuisine of chef-owner Wolfgang Puck (who cooks here only occasionally).... *Tel 312/527–3700. 520 N. Dearborn St., take a cab. Reservations advised.* $$$$ **(see pp. 46, 51, 53)**

Spiaggia. Soaring ceilings, pastel colors, views of the lake, and loads of waitstaff scurrying around set the scene at this exquisite Italian restaurant.... *Tel 312/280–2750. 980 N. Michigan Ave., Michigan Ave. buses. Reservations advised.* $$$$$ **(see pp. 44, 53, 57)**

Suya African Bar & Grill. Owned and operated by a Nigerian immigrant, this laid-back African grill in Lake View serves gutsy dishes such as *egusi* (soup with melon seed, spinach, and bitter leaf).... *Tel 773/281–7892. 3911 N. Sheridan Rd., Sheridan Rd. el stop.* $ **(see p. 50)**

Third Coast Cafe. Hot location a block off Michigan Avenue and good inexpensive food (home-baked scones oozing raspberries, fresh-tasting eggs, really good salad niçoise). No wonder it's one of the neighborhood's most popular hangouts.... *Tel 312/664–7225. 888 N. Wabash St., Michigan Ave. buses.* $ **(see pp. 50, 51, 55)**

Tibet Cafe. In this serene storefront cafe in Lake View, the food is all vaguely Chinese, but not Chinese: from *thang*, a clear soup with spinach and egg drop, to the Himalayan *khatsa*, spicy cauliflower and tofu. Nothing quite washes it all down as well as a *boe cha*, Tibetan tea with milk, salt, and butter.... *Tel 773/281–6666. 3913 N. Sheridan Rd., Sheridan Rd. el stop.* $ **(see p. 50)**

Tomboy. In the "new" gay neighborhood—Andersonville—this hangout has a neighborhood crowd to prove it. Nothing-special Italian-inspired dishes served in a large, noisy room: come here for the fun, gabby crowd and boy-and-girl-ogling, not the food. BYOB.... *Tel 773/907–0636. 5402 N. Clark St., take a cab.* $$$ **(see p. 60)**

Trattoria No. 10. If you're searching for a great Italian meal in the Loop, Trattoria No. 10 has a burnt-orange ambience straight out of Tuscany, and food—particularly the ravioli—to match.... *Tel 312/984–1718. 10 N. Dearborn St., Adams St. el stop. Reservations advised.* $$$ **(see p. 53)**

Voila! French! The bistro menu here features all the regulars: onion soup, *croque monsieurs*, and various *plats du jour* such as steak frites, shepherd's pie (if you feel like crossing the English Channel), and an unusual seafood beignet.

Located in the Loop.... *Tel 312/580–9500. 33 W. Monroe St., Adams St. el stop. Reservations advised.* $$$

(see pp. 54, 60)

Wiener Circle. Burgers are better than the dogs here, and the fries are some of the best in town. Customers hunker down at wood picnic tables out front in the wake of carbon monoxide spewed from passing buses.... *Tel 773/477–7444. 2622 N. Clark St., take a cab. No credit cards.* $

(see p. 52)

Wishbone. At this hip, casual restaurant, dig into Southern home-cooking, such as pan-fried chicken or the house specialty—hoppin' John (black-eyed peas over rice with cheddar, scallions, and tomatoes) and great pecan pie.... *Tel 312/850–2663. 1001 W. Washington St., take a cab. Reservations accepted.* $$

(see pp. 44, 47, 55, 57, 58, 60)

WonTon Club. Sophisticated Asian-inspired meals may begin with sushi or seaweed rolls, then segue to duck potstickers or hot-hot-hot tuna tartare, followed by tea-toasted salmon or wasabi-seared tuna.... *Tel 312/943–6868. 661 N. Clark St., take a cab. Reservations advised.* $$$

(see pp. 49, 55, 61)

North Side Dining

Ambria **17**
Amitabul **5**
Ann Sather's **12**
Bistrot Zinc **6**
Charlie Trotter's **18**
Cucina Bella **14**
Daniel J. **3**

Hi Ricky **4**
Lutz Continental Cafe
  and Pastry Shop **1**
Mia Francesca **11**
Moti Mahal Indian
  Restaurant **13**
Oo La La! **10**

Penny's Noodle Shop **9**
Reza's **2**
Suya African Grill **8**
Tibet Cafe **7**
Un Grand Café **16**
Wiener Circle **15**

Chicago Dining

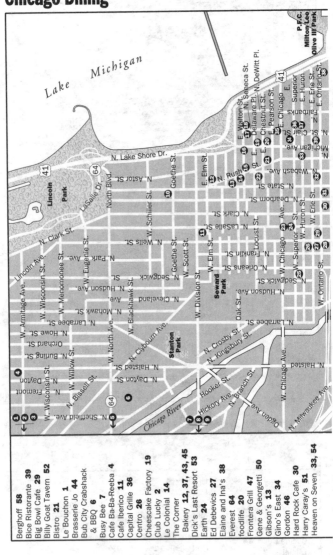

Berghoff **58**
Bice Ristorante **39**
Big Bowl Cafe **29**
Billy Goat Tavern **52**
Bistro **21**
Le Bouchon **1**
Brasserie Jo **44**
Bub City Crabshack
 & BBQ **6**
Busy Bee **7**
Cafe Ba-Ba-Reeba **4**
Cafe Iberico **11**
Capital Grille **36**
Centro **26**
Cheescake Factory **19**
Club Lucky **2**
Le Colonial **14**
The Corner
 Bakery **12, 37, 43, 45**
Dick's Last Resort **53**
Earth **24**
Ed Debevics **27**
Elaine and Ina's **38**
Everest **64**
foodlife **20**
Frontera Grill **47**
Gene & Georgetti **50**
Gibson's **13**
Gino's East **34**
Gordon **46**
Hard Rock Cafe **30**
Harry Caray's **51**
Heaven on Seven **33, 54**

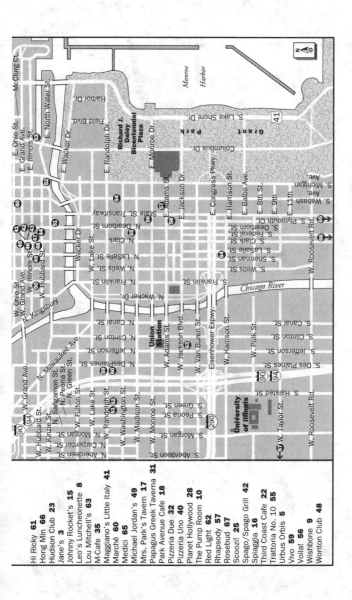

Hi Ricky **61**
Hong Min **66**
Hudson Club **23**
Jane's **3**
Johnny Rocket's **15**
Leo's Luncheonette **8**
Lou Mitchell's **63**
M-Cafe **35**
Maggiano's Little Italy **41**
Marché **60**
Medici **65**
Michael Jordan's **49**
Mrs. Park's Tavern **17**
Papagus Greek Taverna **31**
Park Avenue Cafe **18**
Pizzeria Due **32**
Pizzeria Uno **40**
Planet Hollywood **28**
The Pump Room **10**
Red Light **62**
Rhapsody **57**
Rosebud **67**
Scoozi! **25**
Spago/Spago Grill **42**
Spiaggia **16**
Third Coast Cafe **22**
Trattoria No. 10 **55**
Urbus Orbis **5**
Vivo **59**
Voila! **56**
Wishbone **9**
Wonton Club **48**

3

sions

Chicago has a way
of derailing even
the most sensible
itineraries. Sure,
you may think
you're going to
walk from your

hotel to the Art Institute of Chicago, but you find yourself passing through **Lincoln Park** and instead decide to sit in the shadow of the bronze statue of William Shakespeare and read a detective novel. Or you plan to lounge on **Oak Street Beach** and work on your tan, but wind up renting roller-blades at the concession stand and hotdogging it up and down the boardwalk until the sun sinks beneath the horizon. Day after day your plans don't quite get fulfilled, and yet you've done so much.

It's not merely that Chicago is a big city—after all, Detroit is a big place, too—but it's a big city with an unusually wide array of things to do. It's not a sunny resort area where you either sit on the beach or windsurf, 'nuff said, or a cement canyon where you walk around museums and sample tony restaurants. It's both of those things: windsurfing at **Montrose Beach** in the morning and high tea at the **Ritz-Carlton** in the afternoon one day; the next, brunch at **Spiaggia** and a stroll through the **DuSable Museum of African American History**, with the afternoon spent learning to sail at **Belmont Harbor** and the evening at a first-rate play at the **Steppenwolf Theatre**. The only real challenge is apportioning your time so you don't feel cheated in the end.

Getting Your Bearings

Chicago, bless its heart, is about as easy a big city in which to get around that exists. The city is laid out like a grid, with the intersection of north–south **State Street** and east–west **Madison Street** in **the Loop** being its blessed heart. Addresses get incrementally bigger in all directions as you move away from this point, with about 100 numbers per block, 800 per mile. So, at the same place on each perpendicular street you'll more or less find the same address; 3000 North Sheridan Road, for instance, is as far north as that same address on every other north–south street. There are a few diagonal thoroughfares, such as **Lincoln** and **Ridge** avenues, but their number systems by and large are in keeping with the grid streets—2000 Clark Street, for example, is at Armitage, the same way 2000 Lincoln Park West is. The lake is east—always. The most significant street to know is **Lake Shore Drive**, which hugs the coast north–south. The other main north–south drags include **Broadway, Clark Street, Halsted Street, Dearborn Parkway, LaSalle Street**, and **Michigan Avenue**. Six of the Loop's east–west thoroughfares are named after presidents—**Washington, Mad-**

ison, Monroe, Adams, Jackson, and **Van Buren**. Farther north, **North Avenue, Fullerton, Diversey,** and **Belmont** are zeniths of neighborhood activity. Laid on top of this grid-like scenario are the el and bus routes, which traverse the city in such a way that a car, while helpful, is unnecessary. Getting from the Loop to Wrigley Field for a Cubs game is a one-train deal. You can take a bus from the Lincoln Park Zoo to Marshall Field's and, as you glide down Stockton Drive and then Michigan Avenue, you get a magnificent sightseeing tour thrown in for free. The **Chicago Transit Authority (CTA)** is one of the few remaining subway systems in the United States that operates most days around the clock (though some stations are closed after traditional work hours and on part or all of the weekends, so it's imperative to check). Generally, the entire system is referred to as the "el" because parts of it are elevated, like a roller coaster. At places it curves from side to side like a roller coaster, too. There are six separate subway routes, denoted in different colors on the maps, copies of which are available at every subway token booth. And then there are buses, which follow various routes illustrated on blue-and-white signs posted at the bus stops (generally every two blocks along the route). The fare on trains and buses is currently $1.50

The City Architecture

Chicagoans take their architecture very seriously. They argue about it on the el; they discuss it over breakfast reading the Tribune; they take special trips to the Loop to see the latest controversial building. And they have good reason for such passion, for Chicago's a city of hundreds of architectural gems, a living, breathing hothouse of important buildings, controversial construction, and innovation. Chicago is known as the birthplace of modern American architecture. Why? Well, after the Great 1871 Fire singed four densely built square miles of mostly wooden buildings, the 1869 stone **Water Tower** on Michigan Avenue was one of the few buildings left standing (and it's not much to look at). So the city had to be rebuilt, coincidentally just as new technologies (like the elevator, steel skeletons, and fireproof terra-cotta cladding) were making it possible to build taller, more interesting buildings. The city's building boom attracted the country's greatest architects, from Louis Sullivan to Henry Hobson Richardson to Frank Lloyd Wright. (It's still home to great architects, such as Helmut Jahn, Stanley Tigerman, and Larry Booth.) The boom encouraged them and others to experiment with form and function—and did they ever.

DIVERSIONS | INTRODUCTION

(plus a 30-cent transfer for use between bus lines, which must be used within two hours of its issuance). For a map or free advice on how to get from one place to another, call the CTA (tel 312/836–7000). Just remember, Chicago is flat, streets run for the most part straight north–south, east–west, and the lake is always, always, always east. Now go have fun.

The Lowdown

Must-sees... You should not leave the city limits without going to the **Art Institute of Chicago**, even if it's just to stand slack-jawed with the crowd that is usually massed before what may be the museum's most famous holding, Georges Seurat's *Sunday Afternoon on the Island of La Grande Jatte*. The thing is, it's actually an incredible painting, the only one I know of to have a Broadway musical based on it. And no visit to Chicago would be complete without walking around the 72-foot-long apatosaurus at the **Field Museum of Natural History**, the highlight of the museum's grand "DNA to Dinosaur" exhibit. Odds are, once you get home, some neighborhood wisenheimer will ask if you walked through the giant heart at the **Museum of Science and Industry**—and in this case, the wisenheimer knows whereof he speaks. It may sound kitschy, but it's an oddly impressive experience, as is this whole huge hands-on museum where adults are just as enthralled as kids. Graceful, ornate **Buckingham Fountain**, along Lake Shore Drive in Grant Park, is another don't-miss-it, if for no other reason than because over the years it's become a city icon. The froth of pink marble in the center is surrounded by four bronze seahorses (one for each of the states flanking Lake Michigan—Illinois, Wisconsin, Michigan, and Indiana) cavorting in a pool of water; add a computer-generated light show at night and it is always and forever dazzling.

Special moments... You must, must, must take a long, lazy drive up (or down) **Lake Shore Drive**. The experience is what they call a two-fer: you see the lake on one side, *and* the **Loop skyline**, **Grant Park**, the **Gold Coast**, and **Lincoln Park** on the other. Day or night, it's a stunning vista. Walk around **the Loop**—better yet, take a guided tour given by the **Chicago Architecture Foundation**—to get a feel for the business that makes this powerful city really tick. As crowds of stockbrokers and lawyers scurry around you, stand still on a corner and crane your neck to study America's most perfect assemblage of classic skyscraper architecture. Speaking of walking, take a jaunt up (or down) **North Michigan Avenue**, the city's prime shopping thoroughfare, with huge stores and malls housing the city's most glamorous places to buy stuff. Whether or not you spend a dime, the dazzling retail display can induce a sense of well-being in all but the most hardened consumer. And if you're in town during baseball season, make time to attend a **Cubs** game at **Wrigley Field** (see Entertainment). The ballpark is in the middle of a tight residential neighborhood; parking stinks, so take public transportation if you can.

Only in Chicago... No matter how happy you are to be in Chicago, there's always room for the blues. Whether you visit the **Checkerboard Lounge** on the South Side or **Kingston Mines** on the North Side (see Nightlife), you won't regret it. After all, Chicago is the home of the blues. You shouldn't miss **Robie House**, either, perhaps Frank

---

Get yer free art right here!

*Art should free your mind, not free your wallet of all its money. Some museums in Chicago are always free: the **DuSable Museum of African American History**, the **Oriental Institute**, and the **David and Alfred Smart Museum of Art**, all three in Hyde Park; and the **Mexican Fine Arts Center Museum**. Others at least have a free day, to wit: Monday: **Chicago Historical Society, Chicago Academy of Sciences, International Museum of Surgical Sciences**. Tuesday: **Adler Planetarium, Art Institute of Chicago, Museum of Contemporary Art**. Wednesday: **Field Museum of Natural History**. Thursday: **Chicago Children's Museum** (tel 312/ 527–1000, at Navy Pier), **Museum of Science & Industry**. Friday: **Spertus Museum of Judaica**. See The Index for details. Just be warned: Museums are generally most crowded on their free-admission days, when it's often impossible to get close to any of the exhibits and you'll have to wait your turn for the interactive displays; parking can be a hassle, too.*

Lloyd Wright's most famous residential building within the city limits (it's in Hyde Park); it may inspire you to trek on out to suburban **Oak Park** to see more of Wright's iconoclastic Prairie Style architecture, born and bred here in Chicago. Then go stuff your face with a world-famous deep-dish pizza from either **Pizzeria Uno** or **Due**, the city's premier pizza makers (see Dining). Other cities, from New York to London, may claim that they make authentic Chicago pizzas, but none—and I mean none—make them as good as pizza makers in Chicago. There is no room for argument here.

Prowling the Gold Coast... According to a 1994 study by Roosevelt University, Chicago's Gold Coast is second only to Manhattan when it comes to the highest concentration of moolah in the country. From the lake to roughly about LaSalle Street, Chicago to North avenues, this is Chicago's fancy-shmanciest area, incorporating exclusive shopping and tree-shaded residential streets lined with gorgeous townhouses, pre-war apartment buildings, and more than a few very ugly modern towers. Roaming around is a pleasure. The former **Playboy Mansion** (1340 N. State St., at Lake Shore Dr.) is now condos, but you can still try to imagine what Hef was up to all those years. The **Archbishop's Residence** (1555 N. State Pkwy.) is a Queen Anne-style red-brick mansion, typical at least in size of the many ornate palaces, built after the Chicago Fire, that used to line Lake Shore Drive. Other architectural highlights include McKim, Mead & White's 1892 **Patterson-McCormick Mansion** (20 E. Burton Place), originally built for Joseph Medill, who was mayor of Chicago and part owner of the *Chicago Tribune*; the 1914 **Three Arts Club** (1300 N. Dearborn St.), by the architectural firm of Holabird & Roche; the **Louis Sullivan Townhouses** (1826–1834 N. Lincoln Park West), designed by Sullivan himself; and **Charnley House** (1365 N. Astor St.), designed by Adler & Sullivan. In fact, all of **Astor Street**, from Division Street to North Avenue, is a designated national landmark. Check out the **Chicago Historical Society**, at Clark Street and North Avenue. It's a really wonderful museum—not boring or staid like a lot of historical society digs. Alongside memorabilia from the Civil War (including Lincoln's deathbed) and from the Chicago Fire, there's neat stuff like a poster advertising John Wilkes Booth playing Hamlet in a Chicago theater a week before he shot Lincoln, as well as the first copy of *Playboy* magazine. When walking around finally starts to get to you, head over to the **Oak Street Beach**, where sunbathers, Rollerbladers, walkers, runners, and saunterers provide a good dose of live theater. At the south end of **North Avenue Beach** (or, depending on where you are, the north end of Oak Street Beach), you can rest and play chess at the **Chess Pavilion**, where chess challengers from around the city gather to square off. Beneath a concrete sculpture that looks almost airborne, schmoozers and players alike sit around at all hours, some playing the game, some watching, some just contemplating the passing crowd. Bring your own chess pieces and you too can play on the built-in boards. It's almost always a wonderful Chicago scene. Along **Oak Street** itself is a prime shopping area, one block crammed with world-famous designer boutiques, from Armani to Versace, set in exquisite brownstones (see Shopping for details). Once your throat becomes parched, take a load off at the **Third Coast Cafe** (see Dining) for a half-caf skim latté and scone; **P.J. Clarke's** (tel 312/664–1650, 1204 N. State Pkwy.) for a terrific burger and fries and really good Caesar salads; **Albert's Café** (tel 312/751–0666, 52 W. Elm St.) for yet another latté and a frilly French pastry or sandwich; or for some of the best people watching, the **Brasserie Bellevue** (21 E. Bellevue Place, in the Sutton Place Hotel), a glass-enclosed "sidewalk café" where the food is utterly beside the point.

Museumscapes... There's a velvet rope in front of Seurat's pointillist masterpiece, *Sunday Afternoon on the Island of La Grande Jatte*, perhaps the most beloved picture at the **Art Institute of Chicago**. Everyone wants to get close to it, to be near it, to see it, to remember it. "Hey, remember when we studied that?" visitors ask each other, pointing to the picture. In fact, you hear that sort of thing all over the museum—in front of Rembrandt's *Young Girl at the Open Half-Door*, Renoir's *On the Terrace*, Cassatt's *The Bath*, and Balthus's *Patience*. So, if you've only got the stamina to see one museum in the city, this should definitely be it. Though its collection does not have the depth of some other, larger museums, it's many famous holdings make it seem like Art History's Greatest Hits. The museum, which was built in 1892, sits on a majestic site on Michigan Avenue with the Loop's lakeside Grant Park as its backyard. Don't miss what's left of the Trading Room of the original Chicago Stock Exchange, the rest of which was demolished for stupid reasons in 1972 (to make way for a modern skyscraper); luckily, portions of the beautifully stencilled walls, moulded pilaster capitals, and art glass were preserved and incorporated into the re-creation you'll see here. (The Exchange's two-story entry arch was also saved and re-erected in a nearby garden at the museum.) Also, check out the Rubloff paperweight collection. It sounds dumb—paperweights—but their magnificent sparkling colorings and designs make them as gorgeous as fine jewelry. Also, whether you're a Martha Stewart devotee or not, the Miniature Thorne Rooms—68 tiny but scarily intricate re-creations of spectacular period interiors—is worth a visit to the museum alone. In its new, crisply grand space just off Michigan Avenue, the **Museum of Contemporary Art** has really captured the imagination of the city, with glamorous social events and annual 24-hour art extravaganzas. At last there's room to exhibit more of the museum's permanent collection, which includes works by artists such as Bruce Nauman, Richard Serra, Jeff Koons, and Chicago master Ed Pashke; fortunately, the bigger (more expensive) space hasn't stopped the museum from hosting edgy video- and computer-related works and performance art. Nearby is the **Terra Museum of American Art**, which displays pictures from the 18th century through today by all the grand poobahs of American Art, such as Homer, Cassatt, Hopper, and Audubon. Some people find the Terra pretty staid, but it is a perfect place to bone up on American Art 101, being one of the few museums in this country solely devoted to American artists. In Hyde Park, the **David and Alfred Smart Museum of Art** displays the University of Chicago's eclectic art collection—including paintings by Degas and Matisse, sculptures by Rodin and Henry Moore, and an outstanding Greek vase collection. The best thing here is the original dining room set designed by Frank Lloyd Wright for his now-famous **Robie House**, a few blocks away in Hyde Park.

Ethnic museums... Jewish art and artifacts, from ritual objects to paintings and sculpture, are on display at the **Spertus Museum of Judaica**, which is of limited interest except for the moving Zell Holocaust Memorial and the Children's Artifact Center, a clever hands-on exhibit that lets kids learn through archaeology the history of the Middle East. If you're already heading down to the Hyde Park area, there are two other museums to make the trek worthwhile, and they're both fairly small—you can easily do them in the same day as the Smart Museum. On the University of Chicago campus, the **Oriental Institute Museum** showcases the art and artifacts of the Near East—ancient Persia, Iraq, Egypt, Israel, Syria, and Turkey—from about 9000 B.C. to the tenth century A.D., with many pieces of art, archeological finds, and other things pillaged from other cultures during a time when pillaging wasn't so un-p.c. Highlights include Egyptian mummies and, from an Assyrian palace, a 40-ton sculpture of a winged bull. The **DuSable Museum of African American History**, also in Hyde Park, traces the black experience in America; displays honor Martin Luther King Jr., Rosa Parks, Sojourner Truth, and others. For good luck rub the nose of the bronze bust of Haitian-born Jean Baptiste-Pointe DuSable, a trader born of mixed African and European blood; he was the first known non-Native American settler in Chicago. In Pilsen, the **Mexican Fine Arts Center Museum** show-cases contemporary Mexican and Mexican-American art with new exhibits every couple of months, while on the Northwest Side the **Polish Museum of America** high-lights both traditional and modern Polish and Polish-American art, including the Stations of the Cross from the first Polish church in America. It's one of the largest museums in the country devoted to the art and history of one ethnic group, but given that there are more Poles in Chicago than in any other city in the world other than Warsaw, that shouldn't come as too big a surprise.

The wonders of science... As it happens, Chicago has a whole raft of museums devoted to the sciences, strung out along the shore of Lake Michigan. The starting point has to be down in Hyde Park at the truly great **Museum of Science and Industry**. One of its most beloved exhibits is also one of the simplest: Stand in one spot in

DIVERSIONS | THE LOWDOWN

the oval-shaped Whispering Gallery and you can mur-
mur to a person standing all the way on the other side—
they'll hear you loud and clear. It's an ever-amazing
thing to do, and more so because while doing it you real-
ize you've also learned how sound travels. It's like that all
over the museum, where visitors learn almost by osmosis
as they walk through, pull, touch, explore, and wonder at
the more than 2,000 interactive exhibits, including an
actual Boeing 727's fuselage, an authentic U-505 Nazi
submarine, and a reproduction of a Southern Illinois
coal mine. Go north up the lakeshore to Grant Park, and
you'll find another of the big kahunas of Chicago's
museum world, the **Field Museum of Natural History**,
with its mighty dinosaurs, hairy beasts, and permanent
and temporary exhibits devoted to all things natural,
from anthropology to zoology. Enormous exhibits, such
as "Africa," "Oceana," or "Inside Ancient Egypt"—
which includes the *masaba* (tomb) of Pharaoh Unis and
23 actual mummies—feature interactive experiences
that allow visitors to not only see how other cultures
and environments exist, but to feel a visceral connection
to them. Across a road from the Field is the **Shedd
Aquarium**, a splendid facility that's practically as good
as an indoor Sea World. The Shedd got some unwel-
come publicity a few years ago when it opened its
Oceanarium, which tries to re-create the coast of the
Pacific Northwest—lots of people weren't thrilled about
the display of the Beluga whales, whom they felt were
living in unnatural living quarters (as if most of us
aren't). But the Oceanarium is, in fact, a marvel, where
you can walk along a trail that mimics the coastal envi-
ronment as you encounter whales, dolphins, sea otters,
and harbor seals (you can also watch the sea mammals
through underwater windows). Once you've checked
out the water, look up to see the sky at the nearby
Adler Planetarium with its high-tech, special-effects-
laden 68-foot-high Sky Theater. If you can, go on a
Friday night—after the show the Adler uses its incredible 20-inch computerized telescope to instantly project
18-foot by 24-foot live images of outer space to the
audience. For those bored by the usual museum displays,
head to the oddly fascinating **International Museum of
Surgical Sciences**, housed in a couple of great 1917 former residences on Lake Shore Drive, for a tour of med-

ical devices through the ages, as well as a re-creation of a turn-of-the-century drug store (it's not exactly Walgreens).

Talk is cheap... Have you slept with your mother-in-law lately? Or perhaps you are a very confused cross-dressing hermaphrodite. Did your father break up your marriage by running over your spouse with a bulldozer? If you've answered yes to any of these questions, you belong as a guest on one of the three talk shows that tape in Chicago. If you'd just like to be an audience member at one of the tapings, however, call **"The Oprah Winfrey Show"** (tel 312/591–9222), **"The Jerry Springer Show"** (tel 312/321–5365), or the infamous **"Jenny Jones Show"** (tel 312/836–9400) at least a month in advance for tickets. Most shows tape twice a day, three days a week, August through May. Sorry, but none will tell you that day's topic until you get there for the taping.

Kid-pleasers... Be warned, the museums that are particularly kid-friendly, such as the **Field Museum of Natural History**, the **Shedd Aquarium**, and the **Museum of Science and Industry** (see "The wonders of science" above), are absolute mob scenes on free days, especially in the summer or over holidays when school is out. Still, if that's the only time you're here, brave the crowds—these are not to be missed, even if your kids are only toddlers. The **Spertus Museum of Judaica** has a children's museum and a hands-on archaeology exhibit, which older kids can enjoy. Of the city's two zoos (see "Cruising the zoos," below), the smaller **Lincoln Park Zoo** is better for the under-eights, while older kids will probably prefer the more spread-out **Brookfield Zoo**. A **boat tour** on the lake (see "Tour time," below, or Getting Outside) makes sightseeing pretty palatable for children, and, of course, no thrill-seeking youngster would want to miss the zooming elevator ride to the way-high observatories at the **Sears Tower** or the **John Hancock Center**.

Art al fresco... In front of Chicago's big skyscrapers, there are a lot of big sculptures. Here are my favorites in the Loop, where approximately 65 pieces are within easy walking distance of one another. The most famous, and probably the only one you should go out of your way to see, is the great untitled 1967 Picasso sculpture at the **Daley Plaza** (Dearborn and Randolph streets). It's become a virtual icon of the city, as much so as the Hancock building or Wrigley Field. There's a miniature version there, too, for the visually-impaired and/or touchy–feely. **Flamingo**, Alexander Calder's bright-red, spidery-looking 1974 stabile, soars 53 feet into the air in the shadow of the sullen-looking **Federal Center** (219 S. Dearborn St.). Touted as vandal-proof, it does look like it's still in perfect condition, so the boast must be true. *Les Quatre Saisons* is a fancy way of referring to Marc Chagall's 1967 *Four Seasons* at One First National Plaza (Dearborn and Monroe streets); an extraordinary piece, it's a 70-foot-long, 14-foot-high, four-sided colorful mosaic. Jean Dubuffet's *Monument with Standing Beast* at the State of Illinois Building (100 W. Randolph St.) is an exuberant 10-ton, black-and-white fiberglass gift from the artist himself. At more than 100 feet high, they say it's a bat, but Claes Oldenberg's 1977 *Batcolumn* at the Social Security Administration Building (600 W. Madison St.) just looks like a big phallic symbol to many. Check out Louise Nevelson's 1983 *Dawn Shadow* from the street at Madison Plaza (Madison and Wells streets) if you must, but the view from the nearby el platform is better. The last of the best is Joan Miro's 1981 *Chicago* near the Chicago Temple (69 W. Washington St.), a bronze, concrete, and ceramic structure that mostly resembles a totem pole gone haywire.

Cruising the zoos... Chicago is lucky to have two world-class zoos. Even for those who find zoos slightly depressing—after all, would most of these animals really choose to be in Chicago if they had their druthers?—both the **Lincoln Park Zoo** and the **Brookfield Zoo** can be terrifically fun. The **Brookfield**, spread out over 200 acres 14 miles due west of the Loop, is by far the bigger of the two. Its 2,000 animals (representing 425 species) are housed in more naturalistic settings than most of those in the Lincoln Park Zoo: Tropic World, for instance, is a football-field-sized indoor rain forest, complete with three different ecosystems, one each for South America, Asia, and Africa. While the trees, rocks, lush foliage, phony-but-fun-anyhow thunderstorm, and 50-foot waterfall won't fool you, it apparently does fool the myriad birds, apes, and other critters that live there. There's more, including a five-acre "Habitat Africa," the mandatory synchronized-swimming dolphin show in the Seven Seas Panorama and Dolphinarium (there's a really bad word for you), a reptile house, a pachyderm house, a baboon "island," bear grottos, zebra and camel areas, and a separate children's zoo. The Motor Safari Tram tours the zoo and allows you to get on and off at various points. Now, it's heresy in Chicago to whine about the **Lincoln Park Zoo**, the most visited zoo in the entire country; but, truthfully, it's a bit harder to love than Brookfield. However, it's one of the last zoos in the country that doesn't charge admission, and it's a neighborhood zoo, where kids show up after school and families stroll around on summer evenings or weekends. Set on 35 urban acres smack dab in the middle of Lincoln Park, it's the obvious choice for quick visits—it does manage to be both fun for families and sort of romantic for couples. But some of the animals are still housed in long brick animal houses, reminiscent of 19th-century orphanages, which casts a depressing pall. Zoo officials are trying to make the animals' living conditions better by modernizing and upgrading the spaces and creating naturalistic outdoor habitats. Considering its comparatively petite size, the zoo has a lot to offer, including the Farm-in-a-Zoo and a small children's zoo, inhabited mainly by babies of all manner of species; a trainer is often on hand to let kids pet one thing or another.

Strolling around Old Town... Old Town, the area roughly from Division Street north to Wisconsin Street, and LaSalle Street west to Larrabee Street, used to be funky; now it's rehabbed and refurbished. Its narrow side-streets are jammed with both huge new-money houses and tiny renovated jobs (there's hardly anything rundown anymore). For strolling and strollers (the baby kind), the neighborhood is a perfect place to spend a lazy afternoon, gazing around the not-always-beautiful but definitely always-interesting residential streetscapes. Check out **Crilly Court** (covering about five blocks east of Eugenie Street, bounded by Eugenie, West Street, Paul Street, North Wells Street, and North Park Avenue), built in the 1880s by Daniel Crilly, a local developer, and rehabili-

DIVERSIONS | THE LOWDOWN

tated in the 1940s, which touched off Old Town's renaissance. It's lined with townhouses and apartment buildings that have magnificent gardens behind them, though you can't see them unless you know someone. You can, however, look above some of the apartment buildings' doors to find the names of Crilly's children carved there—Edgar, Oliver, Isabelle, and Erminie. Other beautiful buildings worth a look-see include the Romanesque-style **St. Michael's Church** (458 W. Eugenie St.), part of which actually lived through the 1871 fire. Legend has it that its church bells define the area because, supposedly, you're only really in Old Town if you can hear them. (What that means for the whereabouts of the hearing-impaired is unclear.) On Wells Street, which was to Chicago in the 1960s what Haight-Ashbury was to San Francisco, a few small, funky boutiques remain, but mostly it's upscale Italian restaurants and a couple of nice clothing stores. There's also one terrific bookstore, **Barbara's Bookstore** (1350 N. Wells St.), where you can browse endlessly. It's actually sort of sad to see **Piper's Alley**, which used to be filled with psychedelic stores catering to Chicago hippies and hippie-wannabes and is today an antiseptic hallway with a huge four-screen movie theater attached. **Trattoria Roma** (tel 312/664–7907, 1535 N. Wells St.) and **Topo Gigio** (tel 312/266–9355, 1516 N. Wells St.) are two of the better restaurants along the strip. If you just want a fast, inexpensive bite, try **Old Jerusalem** (tel 312/944–0459, 1411 N. Wells St.), a storefront restaurant serving great falafel, fresh tabbouleh, and other Middle Eastern dishes. And something has to be said here about **Second City** (tel 312/337–3992, 1616 N. Wells St.; see Entertainment), the world-famous improvisational comedy club that has spawned such hilarious luminaries as Elaine May, John Belushi, Shelley Long, John Candy, and Gilda Radner. Mainly tourists go there, and while they usually have a laugh-riot, it's not as funny as it used to be, and it can be expensive. A less expensive alternative is to go after the main show for improv only.

Gallery hopping... Gallery-hopping is a major Chicago pastime, with dozens of galleries from which to choose. Chicago's art scene, mind you, is devoted mostly to contemporary art, and unlike galleries in some, ah-hem, eastern cities, Chicago gallery owners actually welcome browsers. New places open (and close) constantly; pick up a copy of *The Reader*, Chicago's free weekly, or the quarterly *Chicago Gallery News* at almost any gallery, for the latest listing of exhibits. Most galleries are open Tuesday through Saturday, 10–5, with shorter summer hours—call ahead if there's one show you want to make sure you see. The Michigan Avenue area, where the gallery scene began several years ago, is mostly for big-time, big-name collecting. Expect to see works by artists such as Jim Dine, Goya, Picasso, and Cassatt, among others, at leading galleries such as **R.H. Love** (tel 312/640–1300, 40 E. Erie St.), **R.S. Johnson** (tel 312/943–1661, 645 N. Michigan Ave.), and **Richard Gray** (tel 312/642–8877, 875 N. Michigan Ave.) Further west in River North, what were upstart galleries a generation ago are now mainstream, dealing mostly in contemporary American and European art. Literally dozens of galleries within a six-block area sell everything from fine photography at **Catherine Edelman** (tel 312/266–2350, 300 W. Superior St.), hot Latin American art at **Aldo Castillo** (tel 312/337–2536, 233 W. Huron St.), conceptual art at **Roy Boyd** (tel 312/642–1606, 739 N. Wells St.), self-taught artists at **Carl Hammer** (tel 312/266–8512, 200 W. Superior St.), and most everything in between (even art from the Arctic) at **Orca Art Gallery** (tel 312/280–4975, 812 N. Franklin St.). As rents rose in River North, smaller, edgier galleries began to sprout even further west—in an industrial area now dubbed River West, and in the Bucktown/Wicker Park neighborhoods. Both now teem with galleries, restaurants, and, more recently, residential loft conversions, a sure sign of art-world cachet. **Oh Boy!** (tel 773/772–0101, 2060 N. Damen Ave.) showcases American art primarily from the country's mid-section, Louisiana to Wisconsin, while **Yello Gallery** (tel 773/235–9731, 1630 N. Milwaukee Ave.) represents more than a dozen Irish and Irish-American artists (don't miss the funky antique store behind the gallery). Both **Klein Art Works** (tel 312/243–0400, 400 N. Morgan St.) and **Rhona Hoffman** (tel 312/455–1990, 312 N. May St.) are respected River North transplants selling often-large contemporary American works.

T.G.I.F. in River North... Unlike New York (where art gallery openings are exclusive, invitation-only affairs), galleries in Chicago's gallery districts hold their openings just about every Friday evening and are open to anyone who happens to cruise by. In River North particularly, where dozens of galleries are concentrated in a six-block area, an entire evening can be spent meandering around, sipping free wine from small plastic cups (even getting some chocolate-covered raisins from the Carl Hammer Gallery), and checking out the art and your fellow art-lovers. Recently several galleries have instituted what they call First Fridays, in which they stay open till eight-ish the first Friday of every month, whether there's an official opening or not. In addition, both the **Museum of Contemporary Art** and the **Art Institute of Chicago** hold evenings featuring not only their collections but also live entertainment and cash bars. (The Art Institute's is the third Thursday of the month, while the Museum of Contemporary Art sticks to a first Friday date).

Mayhem on the trading floors... Millions of dollars, tons of pork bellies, and tankers full of oil exchange hands every day in Chicago's money pits, one of the best and cheapest shows in town. You'll be amazed at the feral behavior of the traders as they scream, bellow, make what look to be obscene gestures, and just generally behave like pigs at the **Chicago Board of Trade**, the **Chicago Mercantile Exchange**, and the **Chicago Board Options Exchange**. You'll be relieved that there is a glass partition separating the visitors gallery from the trading floor. The scene is pretty much the same at each of these places— toss a coin to decide which to visit (taking in all three would definitely be overkill). Check out the roof sculpture of Ceres, Roman goddess of grain, at the Board of Trade, where wheat commodities are traded.

One good read deserves another... Sometimes you just vant to be alone, to sit, and to read a good book. So head for the **Harold Washington Library Center**—a wonderful civic monument, opened in 1991 after years of political infighting (the usual Chicago thing). The collection, having long ago outgrown its original Michigan Avenue home, had been dispersed among several buildings, while plans to replace the main library ran the gamut from rehabbing the former Goldblatts department store to erecting a new building altogether. The latter won out, resulting in this 10-story, red granite-and-brick neo-classical edifice holding about a zillion books, all in open-stack shelving. In good weather (always iffy in Chicago), another good place to lounge and read just off the Magnificent Mile is **Washington Square** (Walton St. at Dearborn), a patch of green unofficially known as "Bughouse Square." Chicago's first public park, it earned that nickname in the 1920s, when people would gather to hear radicals scream and yell about the ills of the world, a nutty open-air forum much like London's Speaker's Corner. It's across from the magnificent **Newberry Library**, a private research library specializing in Western civilization and the humanities; though you have to get permission to read here, check to see if any special events, for adults or kids, are on tap that day. Or, with book in hand, head up to **Lincoln Park**—either to the formal gardens in front of the Lincoln Park Conservatory or to lounge in the shadow of the fake totem pole, a replica of the original that stood here until some carvers noted its historical significance to the Kwakiutl Indians of British Columbia and had it shipped off to a Canadian museum. Other good outdoor reading spots are the concrete board-walk and lawn along the lake, just south of Diversey Parkway; almost any bench on the **University of Chicago** campus; or the Gold Coast's **Goudy Square Park** (Astor and Goethe streets), if you don't mind the sound of neighborhood rich kids playing in the background.

Cool views... Most people think the best view is the most extensive panorama, where they can gawk at the most square mileage—"Look, it's Indiana! How scenic!" But the truly breathtaking views, the ones that still make Chicagoans catch their breaths, are actually lower to the ground, if not on it, and sometimes from a moving vantage point. For instance, drive (or take a cab) north along **Lake Shore Drive from Congress Parkway**. On your left you'll see the city skyline at its most gorgeous advantage; on your right, the lake will spread out like an ocean. As you round the bend at **Oak Street Beach**, majestic residential buildings begin to line the drive. Another possibility is to get on **the el** almost anywhere in the Loop—the views from either side as you circle the neighborhood bring you face to

DIVERSIONS | THE LOWDOWN

face with some of the city's best architecture, from the Monadnock Building to the Harold Washington Library Center. Other low-to-the-ground great views include standing on the **Michigan Avenue Bridge**, which crosses the Chicago River and neatly divides the city. It's a picture-postcard-perfect view of downtown, looking towards the south; of the Magnificent Mile to your north; and of the river both east and west. Picnic at the tip of **Belmont Harbor**, where the view of downtown and the lake is one of the best; or stand in front of **Buckingham Fountain**, with your back to the lake—before you, the downtown skyline looms like a Hollywood movie set, so gorgeous it almost looks fake. You can see much more than the stars and skies from the **Adler Planetarium** if you know where to look, such as north across Monroe Harbor from Solidarity Drive. In addition to the harbor itself, which in summer is jammed with sailboats and yachts, in the distance you'll get a spectacularly panoramic view of Navy Pier, Lake Point Towers, and the Michigan Avenue skyline. Another great but little-known view spot is from the fourth-floor balcony at **Crate & Barrel** overlooking Michigan Avenue (see Shopping), where you'll see the Magnificent Mile in all its glory from a unique angle.

Tried-and-true views... If you must see the city from the sky, there's nothing like the view from either the **Sears Tower Skydeck** on the 103rd floor of the 110-story building—at 1,450 feet, one of the world's tallest—or from the 94th-floor **John Hancock Center Observation Deck**. Nonstop, ear-popping express elevators zoom you to both observation decks in less than a minute, and what awaits is a breathtaking 360-degree panorama. On a clear day they say you can see up to 60 miles and four states—it *is* Indiana! From the Sears Tower you'll get a better sense of downtown Chicago; from the Hancock, fondly known to locals as "Big John," you'll see the entire lake and the north side, on up all the way to Wisconsin.

Architectural masterpieces... The American Institute of Architecture publishes the *AIA Guide to Chicago*, a detailed guidebook to the city's scores of important buildings; the following are just the top stars. The **Rookery Building** (209 S. LaSalle St.), designed by the firm of Burnham and Root in 1886, is a monumental office tower of scarlet stone in the south Loop; its lobby, designed by Frank Lloyd Wright in 1905, was restored in 1991 to its 1910 appearance. The north half of the **Monadnock Building** around the corner (53 W. Jackson Blvd.) was designed in 1891 by Burnham and Root as well, while the south half is the work of the firm of Holabird and Roche. It's literally a transitional building: Burnham and Root's half has the distinction of being the tallest masonry building in the city, with six-feet-thick walls at its base (to hold the whole thing up!), while the other half, built two years later, is of steel-frame construction. A few blocks north, large expanses of glass lend Daniel Burnham's 1890 **Reliance Building** (32 N. State St.) an elegant profile, which is today mainly significant as a fine example of just how far early architects were able to go in creating glass walls. The building, unfortunately, has seen better times.

Six buildings that scream "Chicago"... The fact that the yellow stone **Water Tower** (800 N. Michigan Ave.) is still standing at all lends it a modicum of significance—it's just so old and, like Chicago itself, a survivor. It doesn't hurt, either, that it's the focal point of the city's most traveled street, or that Oscar Wilde notoriously labelled it a "monstrosity" during his 1882 visit to Chicago. For all its fame, it's really just a cover for a 38-foot-high standpipe. Ungainly and sinister looking and just a block north, Skidmore, Owings & Merrill's 1970 **John Hancock Center** (875 N. Michigan Ave.) sticks out like a sore thumb on the city's skyline, but it's one of its best-known buildings. You couldn't miss it if you tried. A few blocks south, the white terra-cotta-clad **Wrigley Building** (400 N. Michigan Ave.) is an ode to the chewing-gum empire of the building's namesake. Lit at night like a birthday cake (which many say it resembles), the building sits at the foot of the Magnificent Mile. Known as the "corncob buildings," the 62-story **Marina City** (300 N. State St.), built by Bertrand Goldberg in the early 1960s and just west of the Wrigley Building, is perhaps Chicago's best-known silhouette. That galls some people, since the two round buildings (filled with pie-shaped apartments) aren't very architecturally significant, and worse, they're not in such pristine shape, inside or out. Still, it's their exterior shape, which most people only see from afar, that locals love. Owned today by the Kennedys (yes, those Kennedys) but originally built in 1931 by Marshall Field, the elephantine **Merchandise Mart** (350 N. Wells St.) is still, at 4 million square feet, one of the world's largest wholesale markets, its enormous floors lined with furniture, knick-knack, and fabric showrooms open to the trade only (the first two floors are a bland retail—see Shopping). It sits along the Chicago River west of Marina City, dominating the neighborhood like a Buddha. **Wrigley Field** (Clark and Addison streets) may not be the most up-to-date ball park in the nation—it was built in 1914—but like the Chicago Cubs, it's much beloved. Its grass field and residential neighborhood location are almost unique in professional baseball nowadays.

Architecturally significant *and* they scream "Chicago"...

While **Carson, Pirie, Scott & Co.** (1 S. State St.) may be merely a place in the Loop to buy socks and underwear to some, to others it is Louis Sullivan's masterpiece. Built between 1899 and 1904, the steel-frame building was originally the Schlesinger & Meyer Company Store. But its retailing history takes second place to its architectural importance, which lies in its extraordinary use of ornamentation on the ground floor—especially the world-famous front door—topped by floor after floor of sleek terra-cotta clad walls punctuated by what was known as the "Chicago window," a central window with smaller, movable windows on either side. The 1922 Gothic-style **Tribune Tower** (435 N. Michigan Ave.), across the street from the Wrigley Building at the foot of the Magnificent Mile, was built after a well-publicized contest in which the newspaper's owner, the powerful Colonel Robert McCormick, rejected more modern designs. Look for chunks of great buildings through the ages, such as Westminster Abbey, St. Peter's Basilica, and even the Berlin Wall, embedded into the tower's base. Ludwig Mies van der Rohe, who fled Nazi Germany and settled in Chicago, much to the city's great advantage, designed many important buildings—as well as most of the **Illinois Institute of Technology** on the South Side—but none as important, perhaps, as the two glass-and-steel apartment houses at **860–880 North Lake Shore Drive**, which he designed in 1952. Their distinctive box-like profile became the basis for hundreds of other high-rise buildings around the city and the world.

The Wright stuff... Chicago is a Frank Lloyd Wright-o-phile's dream. Not only did he live and work in suburban Oak Park, which has a superb collection of his homes, but his work survives throughout the city of Chicago as well. He built the **Robie House** (and designed all its interior furnishings), now a National Historic Landmark, in 1909 near the University of Chicago campus. Lined with leaded-glass windows and topped with a low-slung cantilevered roof, the house exemplifies his uncluttered Prairie Style, which rejected Victorian-era ornamentation in favor of a look that was clean-lined, functional, and in harmony with its natural surroundings. Also in **Hyde Park**, other Wright houses include **Blossom House** (4858 S. Kenwood Ave.) and **MacArthur House** (4852 S. Kenwood Ave.), both built in 1892 when Wright was only 25 years old and an employee of Louis Sullivan, and the **Heller House** (5132 S. Woodlawn Ave), which dates to 1897. All are privately owned, but at least you can walk by and gawk. Wright designed more than 30 buildings between 1899 and 1913 in nearby **River Forest** and **Oak Park**, suburbs 10 miles due west of the Loop. **His home and studio** (951 Chicago Ave., Oak Park), where he lived and worked from 1889 to 1911, is open daily for tours. The **Unity Temple** (875 Lake St., Oak Park) was built from 1905 to 1908 and, like many of his buildings scattered throughout the Chicago area, is a National Historic Landmark. Both the **Oak Park Visitors Center** and the **Chicago Architecture Foundation** offer guided tours of Wright's Oak Park work (see "Tour Time," below).

Home sweet historic home... The **Prairie Avenue Historic District** (South Prairie Avenue between 18th and 20th streets) was a once-fashionable neighborhood known as "Millionaire's Row," lined with many fine homes built from the 1870s to the 1890s by the city's wealthiest families, from George Pullman to Marshall Field. Unfortunately, most of them were torn down years ago; the few that remain are being, or have been, restored, along with the street itself, which is cobblestoned and lit by gaslights just as it was in the nineteenth century. There are two star attractions here. **Clarke House** (1800 S.

Prairie Ave.), built in 1836, is Chicago's oldest still-standing building. While the wooden structure is original, the location isn't—in fact, it's been moved twice, once after the 1871 fire, which it miraculously survived. Today it's a museum, still boasting some of its original furniture. The only surviving house by the great Boston architect Henry Hobson Richardson—built in 1886 for John J. Glessner, founder of International Harvester—is today known as **Glessner House** (1801 S. Prairie Ave.). With a large interior courtyard, the 35-room house's exterior seems to turn away from the street, punctuated by small windows. On the unbelievably ugly University of Illinois campus, **Hull House** (800 S. Halsted St.) is where Benny Goodman learned to play the clarinet. It's even better known as the building where social worker Jane Addams performed her good works. If you find yourself in the Bridgeport neighborhood, drive or walk by the bungalow at **3536 S. Lowe Avenue**, former home of the pasha of Chicago politics, the late Richard J. Daley, who also happens to be the father of the city's current mayor.

Blasts from the past... On the streets nearest the lake on the North Side, once lined with beautiful houses and today mostly with apartment houses and condos, **Hutchinson Street** (4200 north, at the lake) stands out as a real prize. Most of the houses there were designed and built from 1894 to 1913 by architect George W. Maher and reflect the changing tastes of the time. Nearby **Hawthorne Street** (3400 north at the lake) is another street well worth strolling down, with most of its mansions originally built between 1880 and the 1930s. A few blocks away, **Alta Vista Terrace** (3800 north at Grace St.), built between 1900 and 1904, is known as the "Street of 40 Doors;" it's lined with 40 tiny but beautiful rowhouses with facades representing various eras— Gothic, Georgian, Palladian, each house facing its twin across the street. It's beautiful and sort of weird.

Lincoln Parking... The residential neighborhood of Lincoln Park is named after—you guessed it—Lincoln Park. The vast park itself remains its heart, with its zoo, conservatory, and loads of sports facilities (see Getting Outside). Just because you've finished hiking the park, though, doesn't mean you've "done" Lincoln Park. Them thar streets are paved with gold, or at least with houses lived in by people who make a lot of it, and almost every house is a delight. There's no dominant architectural style; rowhouses or single-family dwellings, built of brick, clapboard, or stone, they're invariably well-tended, with gardens often in the front and back. Most are old and rehabbed, but the few brand-new houses tend to be showy. Just walk around, point at the ones you like best, and imagine how if you had a million dollars you'd buy this one or that. And then go shopping. There are stores galore along the neighborhood's streets—not just the regulars like The Gap and Banana Republic, but scores of unique shops as well—such as **2nd Hand Tunes** (2604 N. Clark St.), which sells used albums (yes, vinyl LPs) and CDs; **Raymond Hudd** (2545 N. Clark St.), a ladies' (yes, ladies') hat shop; and **Blake** (2448 N. Lincoln Ave.), a drop-dead chic women's boutique that should probably be on Oak Street. (See Shopping.) When it's time for "coffee and…," try **Starbucks** (Webster and N. Halsted St.) or any of the other latté cafes that have sprung up like so many toadstools around town. For great dogs and fries hit **The Wiener Circle** (2622 N. Clark St.); for something more substantial (and French) put on some decent clothes and eat at **Un Grand Cafe** (2300 N. Lincoln Park West); or, if you feel like blowing your wad, **Ambria** (also at 2300 N. Lincoln Park West)—all three are listed in Dining.

It's a small world… Walk around **Andersonville** and you'll see remnants of what is still thought of as the city's Swedish neighborhood, from the **Swedish-American Museum Center** (tel 773/728–8111, 5211 N. Clark St.) to the sweet-smelling **Swedish Bakery**, the **Svi Restaurant**, **Wikstrom's Gourmet Foods**, and a branch of **Ann Sather** (which serves beautifully thin Swedish pancakes with lingonberries), all of which line the 5200 block of North Clark. But try finding an actual Swede. Today the neighborhood's ethnic mix includes Vietnamese, Thais, and Arabs, as well as a growing gay population. **Rogers Park**, the old **Jewish neighborhood** around Devon Avenue (6400 north), while maintaining some of its delis, bakeries, and butchers with window signs in Hebrew, has in the past decade become very international, with immigrants from India, Russia, and elsewhere living in what appears to be relative harmony.

Here you'll find some of the city's best Indian restaurants, sari shops, and video stores renting and selling the best and the worst the Indian film industry has to offer. A few Korean restaurants and Russian groceries dot the street as well. The **Southwest Side** around **Marquette Park** is home to many Lithuanians. Vietnamese immigrants have settled in what has recently been dubbed **Little Saigon** around Argyle Street and Broadway, which houses restaurants, shops, and the **Vietnam War Museum** (954 W. Carmen St., tel 773/728–6111). Though Poles have spread throughout the city, Polish businesses, restaurants, and nightclubs still line the area around **Milwaukee Avenue** from Division Street to Irving Park Road. Highlights include the **Polish Museum of America** and the **Busy Bee Restaurant** (see Dining), which serves cheap and, well, let's just say hearty Polish "cuisine." **Bridgeport**, known the world over as the home of the powerful Daley family (though the current Mayor Daley moved his family to a fancy townhouse development in the South Loop), centers on Thirty-fifth Street and Halsted; just southwest of there is **Canaryville**, also still largely Irish. Around **Lincoln Square**, near Lawrence and Western avenues, you can still hear German spoken, and you can still buy homemade sausage. There's a bustling but small **Chinatown** on the **South Side**, with Cermak and Wentworth avenues as its focal point, filled with restaurants, retail, and Chinese people. A very little **Little Italy** along Taylor Street (around 1500 west) is still populated by many Italians and home to a slew of restaurants. **Greek Town**, on Halsted between Adams and Monroe streets, has several restaurants but is really an invention of clever marketing, not an authentic neighborhood.

Up-and-comers... **Pilsen** has come full circle, from Bohemia to bohemian. Settled from about 1870 to the early 1950s by immigrant Czechs (the name Pilsen comes from what was once Bohemia's second-largest city), it evolved into a Mexican neighborhood, and its main drag, Eighteenth Street, is still lined with Mexican diners and tacquerias, small, family-owned grocery stores, bakeries, and music shops blaring the latest salsa onto the street. The **Mexican Fine Arts Center Museum** is here, as well as many colorful outdoor murals, and side streets around the intersection of Eighteenth and Halsted streets are lined with generally well-kept narrow row houses and tenements, their stoops serving as places for old people, kids, and families to sit and watch, as well as be a part of, the lively passing parade. In recent years, however, lower-case-b bohemians have returned in the form of local artists who have discovered Pilsen's large loft-like spaces and reasonable rents. Now as you stroll the streets, in addition to salsa wafting through the air and families shopping and kibitzing in Spanish, you'll also see a healthy number of pierced-nosed, goatee-ed people who you can bet aren't rolling tortillas in their spare time. **Wicker Park**, **Bucktown**, and **Ukrainian Village**, all of which are northwest of the Loop, were also originally home to various Eastern European immigrant groups. But, like Pilsen, in the past decade these neighborhoods have been "discovered" by artists and others seeking cheaper rents—which of course attracted real-estate developers who rehabbed apartment after apartment, which jacked up the rents, forcing many of the second wave of settlers to move elsewhere. Still, the neighborhoods have a funky, urbane feel; while still home to many artists, they're getting yuppier by the day, creating an odd mix of small clubs featuring loud live music, coffee houses sponsoring poetry readings and performance art, art galleries, antique stores, and upscale restaurants attracting BMW-driving suburbanites.

An offbeat place to get your hair cut... Big Hair (tel 773/348–0440, 2012 W. Roscoe St.) is a decidedly strange place with thrift store decor, music, and stylists dedicated to, well, really big hair, all for only $8.

You bowl me over!... Chicago has two of the neatest bowling alleys around. Tiny, four-lane **Southport Lanes** is housed in an old Schlitz tavern and fortunately still looks it. No newfangled things like automatic pin resets here—there are actual and *live* pin-boys to do the job. There are pool tables, too, and an outdoor cafe. For a more *moderne* experience, try the **Diversey River Bowl**, a more traditional-looking alley that's known to insiders as the "rock 'n' bowl"—its sound system blares everything from Motown to Melissa Etheridge, for a real party atmosphere. Completely fun.

School daze... Chicago has many universities within its borders, but three really deserve a visit. The **Illinois Institute of Technology** may not be the city's most prestigious institution of higher learning, but it's definitely its most architecturally significant one—in fact, in 1976 it was designated one of the 200 most important works of architecture in the United States by the American Institute of Architecture. Designed from 1942 to 1958 primarily by the great Mies van der Rohe, it is a classic example of a then very unclassic modernist style which has since become classic. **Crown Hall** (3360 S. State St.) and the **Robert F. Carr Memorial St. Savior Chapel** (65 E. 32nd St.) are the most distinguished buildings on the 100-acre campus. It's not particularly pretty—frankly, it's a fairly monotonous collection of boxy low-rise buildings laid out one after another like children's building blocks. Talk about "less is more." Still, there is an undeniable look to the place—clean and spare, and oddly satisfying in its rectilinear-ness. For a different take on campus life, stroll around the urbane 175-acre **University of Chicago**, founded in 1892 by John D. Rockefeller, in Hyde Park. A Gothic-style fantasia, with many buildings adorned with intricate gargoyles, fine-pitched arches, and towers, the campus seeks to copy its British rivals, Oxford and Cambridge. Many of the buildings have lushly planted courtyards, as well, and benches throughout make terrific spots for a lazy day spent reading out-of-doors. There are some big, ugly, modern buildings, too, but they're well integrated into the campus. Don't miss the extraordinarily beautiful **Rockefeller Chapel** (1156 E. 59th St.), which houses the world's second-largest carillon. Both the **Oriental Institute**, with its fine collection of archaeological finds, and the **David and Alfred Smart Museum of Art** are worthwhile stops as well. Hyde Park itself is one of the best-integrated middle-class neighborhoods in any urban area, with some Frank Lloyd Wright masterpieces scattered about, but one word of warning: It borders some very nasty places, so meandering around at night is not a very good idea. You can take the el to **Northwestern University** in Evanston, but if you have a car, use it—the ride north along the lakeshore is beautiful. Founded in 1855, the campus is filled with Gothic buildings and looks just as you imagine a college should look: bucolic, impressive, daunting, solid.

Tours are available, whether you're considering sending Junior there or not.

Lake views in Lake View... Just north of Lincoln Park lies Lake View, bordered by the lake, Ashland Avenue, Diversey Parkway, and Irving Park Road, an also-gentrified neighborhood of funky stores, even funkier small theaters, and beautiful tree-lined residential streets. Broadway, Halsted, and Clark streets are the area's main north–south drags; Diversey Parkway and Belmont Avenue are the main east–west streets. Each of these is lined with stores and boutiques specializing in everything from condoms to ultra-chic fashions. And, of course, **Lincoln Park** snakes along Lake View's eastern edge, with the **Waveland Golf Course** (see Getting Outside), tennis courts, baseball diamonds, and other recreational facilities. A lot of people might warn you to stay away from the five square blocks that surround **Wrigley Field** on a game day (that is, when the Cubs are at home, generally losing) unless you're actually attending the game— the traffic is at a standstill, the sidewalks are jammed, there are honky-tonk bands playing on the corners, and souvenir hawkers everywhere. But, for the adventurous, that's exactly when to go, because it's fun, plain and simple. There's electricity in the air, anticipation of a good time, and hope that maybe the Cubs will pull it off. Your best bet is to go to the game, but even if you're just walking around before heading elsewhere, it's a scene worth being a part of. A bit south of the ballpark lies what is considered **"Boys' Town,"** the city's sort of gay ghetto. On any given night the sidewalks along Halsted Street between Belmont Avenue and Irving Park Road are jammed with gay men in search of everything from a good time at the clubs to a quart of milk at the 24-hour 7–11. Here you'll find restaurants (like **Oo-La-La!**), bars (like the grandpappy of Chicago's gay scene, **Little Jim's**), dance clubs (like **Roscoe's**), boutiques (like **We Are Everywhere**, which specializes in T-shirts, sweatshirts, cards, mugs, and other paraphernalia), and even a sex club or two (like the **Unicorn** bath house). The streets nearest the lake, though now mostly lined with apartments, used to be lined with beautiful houses; see "Residential streetscapes," above, for descriptions of **Hutchinson Street** (4200 North, at the lake),

Hawthorne Street (3400 north at the lake), and **Alta Vista Terrace** (3800 north at Grace St.).

Where to dog-watch... You wouldn't expect a city with mile after mile after mile of beaches not to have one devoted exclusively to dogs, would you? **Doggy Beach** is where all the best dogs go—or, at least, where all the best dog-owners go—a fenced-off beach midway between Belmont Avenue and Addison Street, at the lake (obviously). Every summer day literally dozens of dogs from sleek weimaraners to teensy Chihuahuas run wild in the sand and water, much to the delight of passersby, much to the chagrin of the Chihuahuas. It's a terrific sight.

Overhyped experiences... "Taste of Chicago," an annual week-long feast that culminates July Fourth weekend, started out as a way to sample some of the finest food Chicago's restaurants had to offer, but it has evolved over the years into a hyperbolic and not-too-cheap outdoor gorge-fest. Much of the food is fried and fatty and messy, as well as astonishly mundane, considering that some of the city's best restaurants ply their delicacies here. The food festival—the world's largest—is not only a pig-out, it becomes a pigsty, as more than four million people jam into Grant Park on Columbus Drive between Jackson and Randolph streets. Both the **Gold Coast Art Fair** and the **Old Town Art Fair** are losers, too, unless you like sentimental color photographs of the city's skyline, pastels of children and dogs, abstract oil paintings that defy description, landscape watercolors, and lots and lots and lots of pottery. Artlovers are better off going to galleries in River North. Both **Planet Hollywood** (tel 312/266–9850, 633 N. Wells St.) and the **Hard Rock Cafe** (tel 312/943–2252, 63 W. Ontario St.) have better food than you'd expect, but what, ultimately, is the point? And if anyone tells you to go to the Biograph Theater to see anything other than a movie, don't listen. Yes, it's true that gangster supreme John Dillinger was tricked into attending a screening of *Manhattan Melodrama* on July 22, 1934, and instead became the object of his own real-life drama when tricky-fingered government dicks gunned him down in the alley next door. But there aren't any blood stains remaining or a faded chalk outline for you to gawk at—

all that remains is… an alley. Unless you want to take a snapshot of the garbage cans from the Mexican restaurant next door, don't bother. There were such high expectations when the Chicago White Sox (see Entertainment) moved into the new **Comiskey Park** in 1991, it probably would have been impossible for it to live up to them. The park was supposed to be a modern show palace, a place to see baseball with the whole family. Well, yes, it is that, of course, but the whole experience is so false, so phony, and so expensive. You get the feeling that even though baseball is being played, way down yonder (most of the time you're watching the game through your toes), what's really going on is that you're getting your pockets picked. The Baton Show Lounge, Chicago's supposedly glitzy, glamour-filled drag show popular with tourists and suburbanites alike, is, if you'll excuse the expression, a real bust. You get shown to your table; you order overpriced, watered-down drinks (you're required to purchase at least two of these); and you think you're settling in for a fabulous Las Vegas-style evening of drag. Instead, you get a bunch of robotic she-males strutting around lip-synching songs you'd rather not even hear at the gym, let alone a nightclub. These men don't merely dress like women, walk and talk like women, and wear slit-to-here gowns that show off a pair of great gams—some of these guys *are* women, having artificially provided themselves with many of the opposite sex's physical attributes. So where's the illusion? Hell, shoot up Sam Donaldson with hormones and silicone, give him a dress, put "Mame" on the record player, and he, too, could work at the Baton.

Tour time… It's not unusual to see red double-decker tour buses moving slow as snails through bumper-to-bumper traffic on Michigan Avenue, as tourists from who-knows-where get told who-knows-what by who-knows-whom. Here are some of the tours that are worth your time: **Art Encounters** (tel 708/328–9222) offers specific programs throughout the year, from tours of the gallery district to visits to artists' and collectors' homes and studios. Well-planned and thought-out art "walks" are generally held 11am to 12:45pm the second Saturday of every month except May, for about $15. Though there are undoubtedly still gangsters in town, the **Untouchable**

Tour (tel 773/881–1195) brings Chicago's gangland past alive, concentrating on the hoodlum hangouts of such guys as John Dillinger, Al Capone, "Bugs" Moran, and others, as well as the site of the St. Valentine's Day massacre (which is now in the shadow of a retirement home) and the hotel from which Al Capone ruled his evil empire. Richard Crowe, who claims he's the only "full-time professional ghost hunter in the Midwest," runs **Chicago Supernatural Tours** (tel 708/499–0300), which feature legends, lore, and ghost stories of Chicagoland cemeteries, murder sites, gangsters, and haunted pubs, all while cruising the city on a bus or, as he likes to call it, a "luxury highway coach." The five-hour daytime or evening tours cost $30 per person and include a snack stop. In the summer, Crowe offers two-hour supernatural cruises on a boat called the *Mercury Skyline Queen*. The first-rate **Chicago Architecture Foundation** (tel 312/922–3432) organizes regular tours of the Prairie Avenue District, including the Glessner and Clarke houses, as well as river cruises, bus tours, and scores of walking tours of specific buildings, streets, districts, and neighborhoods, from the Loop to Hyde Park to the Gold Coast. The foundation also offers both walking and bus tours of Frank Lloyd Wright's greatest hits, a bike tour of suburban Winnetka, and scores of others, more than 50 tours in all. Tour fees vary from $5 for a walking tour of, say, Alta Vista Terrace, to $17 for river cruises (daily, May–October) to $25 for bus tours covering 30 miles of the Loop, Hyde Park, the Gold Coast, and other historic districts. You may also want to stop by the foundation's shop (224 S. Michigan Ave.), one of the best places to buy souvenirs that actually mean something. The **Oak Park Visitors Center** (tel 708/848–1500) offers daily tours of that suburb's incredible collection of the work of Frank Lloyd Wright, a former resident who designed many homes, as well as his internationally renowned Unity Temple, here.

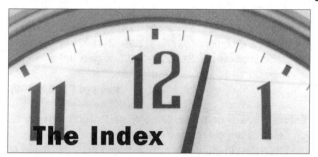

The Index

Adler Planetarium. Besides the great Sky Show in the domed theater, the Adler offers three floors of interactive exhibits about space exploration, the solar system, and the galaxies.... *Tel 312/322–0304; Sky Show information, tel 312/332–0300. 1300 S. Lake Shore Dr. Open 9–5, until 9 on Fri. Planetarium is free; admission charged for Sky Show.*
(see pp. 88, 96)

Art Institute of Chicago. Weary feet are the denouement of a day spent here, checking out every picture you ever studied in art history class, including those by Vermeer, Renoir, Cézanne, and Rothko, to name just a few. The 1892 building is a wonder in itself, not to mention the zillion-square-foot gift shop.... *Tel 312/443–3500. Michigan Ave. at Adams St., Adams St. el stop. Open weekdays 10:30–4:30 (Tue until 8), Sat 10–5, Sun noon–5. Admission charged.*
(see pp. 82, 85, 94)

Brookfield Zoo. Spread out over 200 acres, 14 miles due west of the Loop, Brookfield is home to 2,000 animals (representing 425 species). Take a Burlington Northern train from Union Station to Hollywood and walk to zoo (follow signs). By car, take I-55, I-290, or I-294 to the Brookfield Zoo exits.... *Tel 708/485–0263. 8400 W. 31st St., Brookfield. Open 10–6. Admission charged.*
(see pp. 89, 90)

Buckingham Fountain. Donated to the city in 1927 by Kate Sturges Buckingham, this ornate lakeside fountain presides over the Loop.... *Grant Park, at Congress Parkway, Van Buren el stop.* **(see pp. 82, 96)**

Chicago Architecture Foundation Shop and Tour Center. This first-rate organization devoted to Chicago's architec-

ture and design operates scores of tours (by bus, boat, bike, or on foot) of specific buildings, streets, districts, and neighborhoods.... *Tel 312/922–8687 for recorded tour information, 312/922–3432 to talk to a human being. 224 S. Michigan Ave., Jackson el stop.*
(see pp. 83, 99, 108)

Chicago Board of Trade. Not only stocks and bonds but all sorts of tangible commodities like wheat are traded here.... *Tel 312/435–3590. 141 W. Jackson Blvd., Van Buren el stop. Visitors gallery open weekdays 9–2. Admission free.*
(see p. 94)

Chicago Board Options Exchange. The country's largest stock option exchange.... *Tel 312/786–7492. 400 S. LaSalle St., Van Buren el stop. Open weekdays 9–3. Admission free.* **(see p. 94)**

Chicago Historical Society. This Gold Coast museum has neat Civil War and Lincoln artifacts, dioramas of Illinois history, and some lively, imaginative temporary exhibits.... *Tel 773/642–4600. Clark St. at North Ave. Open Mon–Sat 9:30–4:40, Sun noon–5. Admission charged.*
(see p. 84)

Chicago Mercantile Exchange. Known as "the Merc," this is where futures and options on agricultural commodities (like pork bellies), and financial products (like gold), are traded.... *Tel 312/930–1000. 10 and 30 S. Wacker Dr., Quincy/Wells el stop. Visitors gallery open weekdays 7:30–3:15. Admission free.* **(see p. 94)**

Clarke House. Chicago's oldest surviving building. Tours start at coach house behind Glessner house (see below).... *Tel 773/922–8687. 1801 S. Prairie Ave. Tours Wed–Sun at noon, 1, and 2. Admission charged.* **(see p. 99)**

David and Alfred Smart Museum of Art. The University of Chicago's encyclopedic art collection, which spans from the Renaissance to today.... *Tel 773/702–0200. 5550 S. Greenwood Ave., METRA train to 57th St. and Lake Park Ave. Open Tue–Fri 10–4, weekends noon–6. Admission free.* **(see pp. 86, 104)**

Diversey River Bowl. This bowling alley is know as the "rock 'n' bowl" for its lively piped-in music.... *Tel 773/227–5800. 2211 W. Diversey Ave., Diversey el stop.* **(see p. 103)**

DuSable Museum of African American History. In Hyde Park, the DuSable traces the history of the black experience in America. Fine library and gift shop, too.... *Tel 773/947–0600. 740 E. 56th Pl., METRA train to 57th St. and Lake Park Ave. Open 10–5 (until 6 Thur). Admission charged.* **(see pp. 80, 87)**

Field Museum of Natural History. Lions and tigers and bears, dead and stuffed and on display, along with dinosaurs and enormous interactive exhibits devoted to other cultures and environments.... *Tel 312/922–9410. Roosevelt Rd. and Lake Shore Dr. Open 9–5 daily. Closed Christmas, Thanksgiving, New Year's Day. Admission charged.*
(see pp. 82, 88, 89)

Glessner House. Restored mansion in Prairie Avenue Historic District.... *Tel 773/922–8687. 1801 S. Prairie Ave. Tours start in the coach house, Wed–Sun at 1, 2, and 3pm. Admission charged.* **(see p. 100)**

Harold Washington Library Center. The largest municipal library in the nation.... *Tel 312/747–4400. 400 S. State St., Van Buren el stop. Open Mon 9–7, Tue and Thur 11–7, Wed and Fri–Sat 9–5. Admission free.* **(see p. 94)**

Hull House. Home of social worker Jane Addams and her American settlement-house movement.... *Tel 773/413–5353. 800 S. Halsted St. Open weekdays 10–4, Sun noon–5. Admission free.* **(see p. 100)**

Illinois Institute of Technology. Mies van der Rohe's Chicago masterpiece, this 100-acre campus is a Bauhaus collection unlike any other in the country.... *Tel 312/567–3025. 3300 S. Federal St. Guided tours leave from admissions office (Pearlstein Hall, 10 W. 33rd St.) Mon–Fri at 11am and 1pm.* **(see pp. 98, 104)**

International Museum of Surgical Sciences. Medical implements and devices, as well as a re-created turn-of-the-century drugstore.... *Tel 312/642–6502. 1524 N. Lake*

Shore Dr. Open Tue–Sat 10–4, Sun 11–5. Admission charged. **(see p. 88)**

John Hancock Center Observation Deck. Located on the skyscraper's ninety-fourth floor, the Skydeck provides unparalleled views for miles and miles and miles.... *Tel 312/751–3681. 875 N. Michigan Ave., Michigan Ave. bus. Open 9am–midnight. Admission charged.* **(see pp. 89, 96)**

Lincoln Park Zoo. The most visited zoo in the country, located in the middle of Lincoln Park; highlights include a great 260,000-gallon polar bear tank and the kid-friendly Farm-in-a-Zoo.... *Tel 773/294–4660. 2200 N. Cannon Dr. Open 9–5. Admission free.* **(see pp. 89, 90, 91)**

Merchandise Mart. With more than four million square feet of space, this enormous building houses furniture and fabric showrooms.... *Tel 312/527–7600. 350 N. Wells St., Merchandise Mart el stop. Tours weekdays at noon. Admission charged.* **(see p. 98)**

Mexican Fine Arts Center Museum. In Pilsen, this small but well-respected and popular museum showcases contemporary Mexican and Mexican-American art. Really good gift shop.... *Tel 312/738–1503. 1852 W. 19th St. Open 10–5; closed Mon. Admission charged.*
(see pp. 87, 102)

Museum of Contemporary Art. Founded in 1967, this up-to-the-minute art museum moved in July 1996 into grand new space designed by German architect Josef Paul Kleihus. Terrific cafe, outdoor sculpture garden, and one of the best museum shops in the city.... *Tel 312/280–2660. 220 E. Chicago Ave., Chicago, IL 60611. Open Tue–Fri 11–6 (Wed until 8pm), Sat–Sun 10–6. Admission charged.*
(see pp. 86, 94)

Museum of Science and Industry. With its host of high-tech interactive displays, children love, love, love this museum; adults love it too. The Henry Crown Space Center houses the domed futuristic Omnimax Theater. Great gift shop.... *Tel 312/684–1414 or 800/468–6674. 57th St. and Lake Shore Dr., METRA train to 57th St. and Lake Park Ave. Open 9:30–4 (until 5:30 weekdays, Memorial Day–Labor Day). Admission charged.* **(see pp. 82, 87, 89)**

Northwestern University. Just what you think a university campus should look like: Tudor Revival Mansion, idyllic lawns, and fresh-faced students.... *Tel 708/491–4000. Sheridan Rd. and Clark St., Evanston. Tours run frequently, starting from admissions office.* **(see p. 104)**

Oak Park Visitors Center. Frank Lloyd Wright not only lived in suburban Oak Park, he forever put it on the map by designing many of its finest homes, as well as the Unity Temple. The visitor's center offers daily tours of his home and studio, as well as a walking tour. Take the Lake Street/Dan Ryan el to Marion; walk down North Boulevard to Forest Avenue, turn left another block to the corner of Lake Street.... *Tel 708/848–1500. 158 Forest Ave., Oak Park. Admission free; fee for tours. Call ahead for tour schedule.* **(see pp. 99, 108)**

Oriental Institute Museum. Housed in a Gothic building on the University of Chicago campus, the Oriental Institute exhibits centuries-worth of art from the Near East. Good souk-cum-gift-shop.... *Tel 773/702–9521. 1155 E. 58th St., METRA train to 57th St. and Lake Park Ave. Open 10–4 (until 8:30 on Wed, opens at noon Sun). Closed Mon. Admission free.* **(see pp. 87, 104)**

Polish Museum of America. This museum is devoted to art and artifacts from Poland.... *Tel 312/384–3352. 984 N. Milwaukee Ave. Open noon–5. Admission charged.* **(see pp. 87, 102)**

Prairie Avenue Historic District. The Prairie Avenue Tour Center is located in the coach house behind Glessner House. You can tour it and Clarke House.... *Tel 312/922–3432. S. Prairie Ave. between 18th and 20th streets. Tours Wed–Sun afternoons. Fee for tours.* **(see p. 99)**

Robie House. One of Frank Lloyd Wright's greatest works, the house exemplifies the Prairie Style for which he is famous.... *Tel 773/702–8374. 5755 S. Woodlawn Ave., METRA train to 57th St. and Lake Park Ave. Tours daily at noon. Admission free.* **(see pp. 83, 86, 99)**

Sears Tower Skydeck. The observatory deck here is located on the 103rd floor, eleven floors higher than the one at the

DIVERSIONS | THE INDEX

Hancock Center (see above).... *Tel 312/875–9696. 233 S. Wacker Dr., Quincy/Wells el stop. Open 9am–10pm Oct–Feb, 9am–11pm Mar–Sept. Admission charged.*
(see pp. 89, 96)

Shedd Aquarium. The world's largest aquarium, it features Beluga and Pacific black whales, sharks, turtles, eels, and sea anemones, and a 60,000-gallon penguin habitat.... *Tel 312/939–2438. 1200 S. Lake Shore Dr. Open 9–6. Admission charged.* **(see pp. 88, 89)**

Southport Lanes. There are no newfangled things like automatic pin resets at this four-lane bowling alley; live pin-boys do the job.... *Tel 773/472–1601. 3325 N. Southport Ave., Southport el stop.* **(see p. 103)**

Spertus Museum of Judaica. Jewish art and artifacts, from ritual objects to paintings and sculpture.... *Tel 312/322–1747. 618 S. Michigan Ave., Harrison and State el stop. Open Sun–Thur 10–5, until 3 Fri, closed Sat. Admission charged.* **(see pp. 87, 89)**

Terra Museum of American Art. One of the few museums in the country devoted to U.S. artists.... *Tel 312/664–3939. 666 N. Michigan Ave., Michigan Ave. bus. Open 10–5, until 8 Tue; closed Mon. Admission charged.* **(see p. 86)**

University of Chicago. 175 acres of gorgeous Gothic buildings (with a few modern ones in between) define one of the country's finest universities, associated with more than 60 Nobel Prize winners.... *Tel 773/753–1234. METRA train to 57th St. and Lake Park Ave. Guided tours Mon–Sat at 10am from Ida Noyes Hall, 1212 E. 59th St.*
(see pp. 95, 104)

Hyde Park Diversions

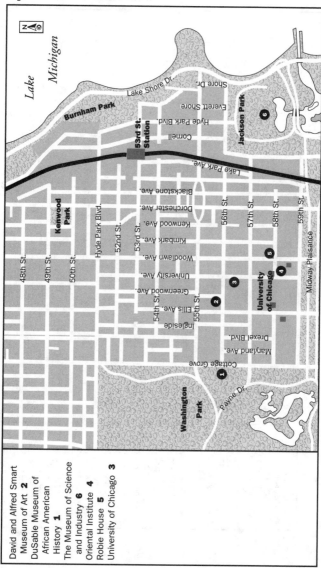

David and Alfred Smart
Museum of Art **2**
DuSable Museum of
African American
History **1**
The Museum of Science
and Industry **6**
Oriental Institute **4**
Robie House **5**
University of Chicago **3**

Chicago Diversions

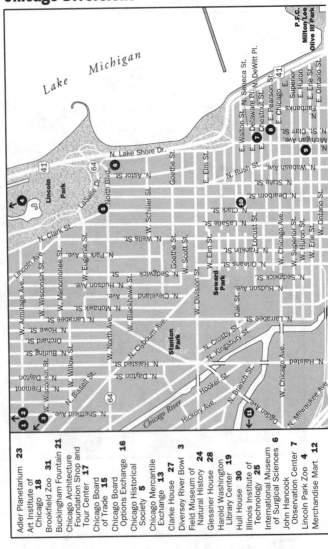

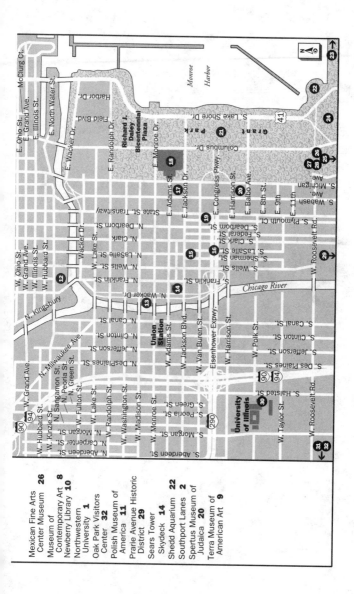

Mexican Fine Arts
Center Museum **26**
Museum of
Contemporary Art **8**
Newberry Library **10**
Northwestern
University **1**
Oak Park Visitors
Center **32**
Polish Museum of
America **11**
Prairie Avenue Historic
District **29**
Sears Tower
Skydeck **14**
Shedd Aquarium **22**
Southport Lanes **2**
Spertus Museum of
Judaica **20**
Terra Museum of
American Art **9**

getting

4

outside

Chicago may be a
big city, but it's a
big city on a
lake—on a big
lake—and what
a difference
that makes.

Chicagoans never get blasé about Lake Michigan sparkling on their doorstep. It is literally the city's living room, where people of all different races and classes meet, mingle, play together, listen to music together, eat together. Chicago uses its lake like no other major city in the world, thanks in large part to forward-thinking urban planning of a century ago. Today, particularly in the summer months, the lakefront takes on the feel of one big urban resort, with boating, swimming, biking, beach volleyball, whatever your pleasure. Forget Club Med. Two huge green parks, named Grant and Lincoln, fan off from the lake, and a string of public beaches within city limits invite one and all to enjoy the water. There's no need to drive to the suburbs or a faraway rural area in search of a golf course or bike path, either. It's all here.

The Lowdown

Parks... At one time, it was possible to walk in a huge arc through the city without touching pavement, via parks and boulevards. Accordingly, the city's motto is *Urbs in Horto*, which means City in a Garden. Nice sentiment— too bad it's no longer true (slums fill much of the city's borders, not flowerbeds and hedgerows). But Chicago does have incredible parks—in fact, it has more than 6,700 acres of parkland. Take 220-acre **Grant Park**, for instance. Spreading out on landfill between Michigan Avenue and the lake (tel 312/747–2200, East Randolph St. to E. McFetridge Dr., at Lake Michigan) it was designed in the 1920s by Daniel Burnham and supposedly inspired by the gardens at Versailles. With the Loop's skyscrapers looming so near, Versailles may not be your first thought when you see Grant Park; it's more like the Luxembourg Gardens in Paris, a highly civilized green space plunked down right in the middle of a big city. Grant Park offers everything a grand city park should—impressive formal gardens, baseball diamonds, tennis courts, ice skating in winter and rollerskating in summer, the Petrillo Music Shell for free summertime concerts and festivals, and vast areas of grass for lounging and loafing, picnicking, or protesting (remember the 1968 Democratic Convention?). Grant Park's most notable feature is the baroque Buckingham Fountain, as seen in the opening credits of the TV show "Married...With Children." It's a well-known make-out spot and the setting for many a marriage proposal.

Even bigger than Grant Park is **Lincoln Park**, running right along the lake north of North Avenue. Here, on 1,200 acres of near-perfect parkland, are meadows, sports facilities, extraordinary formal gardens, extraordinary wildflower gardens, beaches, harbors… the list goes on and on. Since the park borders on several thriving residential neighborhoods, it attracts all sorts of people. For a dizzying burst of humidity, walk into the **Lincoln Park Conservatory** (tel 773/742–7736, 2400 N. Stockton Dr.), three acres of greenhouses erected in 1891, including a palm house, a fern house, a tropical house, and a show house. There's something weirdly Victorian about prowling around here and sniffing out some of the more exotic species in this hothouse. Just outside the conservatory's entrance lies the park's main garden, almost 300,000 dazzling square feet of flowers. By far the biggest attraction in the park is the **Lincoln Park Zoo** (see Diversions). Another park well worth visiting is

A few good men in Lincoln Park

*In Lincoln Park alone you'll find nine famous people further immortalized in sculpture (some, of course, more famous than others). Politicians proliferate, everyone from president **Ulysses S. Grant** (near 1900 N. Lake Shore Dr.) and statesman **Alexander Hamilton** (near Diversey Pkwy.) to **John Peter Altgeld**, a former governor of Illinois, immortalized in bronze near Lake Shore Drive. Then, of course, there's inventor and all-around good American **Benjamin Franklin** at LaSalle Street and Stockton Drive. Our favorite German poet and thinker, **Johann Wolfgang von Goethe**, has been set down at Diversey Parkway, looking proud and very German—and blindingly bright, after a recent regilding. His compatriot, poet and playwright **Friedrich Schiller**, sits near Stockton Drive and Webster Street. The Bard himself, **William Shakespeare**, poses near Belden Avenue, surrounded by flowers. Kid's fave **Hans Christian Andersen** is near Armitage Street, and look for the Italian stallion, **Giuseppe Garibaldi**, between Stockton and Lake Shore drives.*

Jackson Park (E. 63rd St. and Stoney Island Ave., tel 773/643–6363), built on landfill originally used for the 1893 World's Columbian Exposition. Designed by Frederick

CHICAGO | GETTING OUTSIDE

Law Olmsted, who also created Central Park in New York City, this bit of greenery is home to one of the city's greatest attractions, the **Museum of Science and Industry** (see Diversions), which is housed in a stone re-creation of the exhibition's Palace of Fine Arts. Jackson Park also features baseball diamonds, basketball courts, two dozen tennis courts, bicycle and bridle paths, and an 18-hole golf course and driving range (see "Par for the course," below). After visiting the museum, stroll down to the tranquil Japanese garden on the park's southern end. It's a great spot for contemplation, with a soothing waterfall, rocks, water lilies, and a teahouse.

Mittless softball... Chicago is the only place where 16-inch softball has elbowed out the 12-inch version. This variant of the old sandlot game uses no mitts, a slow pitch, and, obviously, a larger ball than the 12-inch variety. Lots of beer and jammed fingers are involved, especially if the ball is new, and for some reason, people with massive beer bellies and really tall, thin guys are the only ones who can drive the ball deep. On the evolutionary scale of softballs, the 16-incher is a coelacanth, a vestige from the days of the game's invention as an indoor winter sport. Leagues play in the parks; to watch a game, try Lincoln Park, or Oz Park in the western sector of the Lincoln Park residential neighborhood.

Playing pick-up... Grant Park (tel 312/747–2200) is known for softball and soccer, on weekends in the playing fields south of the Art Institute and the bandshell. There are more than a dozen fields in the Upper and Lower Hutchinson areas, many of which will be taken by organized office teams or leagues. But come looking prepared—in other words leave your glove at home—and you could get lucky. In addition, there is a three-on-three basketball tournament—sponsored by the Bulls in past years—which features local Be-Like-Mikes and takes place every August on a special temporary court near 900 south, on the lake. You can also find a game of pick-up b-ball on virtually any school playground in the city—after school hours and on weekends. Levels of ability vary; if you're, say, a youngish guy who loves to play but can't jump, you might want to try a playground in the tamer Lincoln Park or Lake View neighborhoods. The courts in **Lincoln Park** (tel 773/742–7726), a short walk south of the zoo, are another good place to look for a pick-up game. Lincoln Park also has great touch football games near Belmont Avenue, usually on Sunday mornings, and organized by league. Two of the latter, **Chicago Sports Monsters** and **Command Performance** (tel 773/327-1348 and 773/975-6624, respectively) can clue you in on schedules and the chance of getting off the bench. According to legend, luminaries such as former Bears back-up QB Mike Tomczak and assorted college linemen have been known to drop in. Every Sunday afternoon in spring and summer, the gay crowd at **Hollywood Beach** (5800 north on the lake) has pick-up volleyball games.

Hitting the beaches... One of Chicago's greatest summertime assets is the beaches that almost continually line Lake Michigan. Some are smooth and sandy, others are craggier and not well-kept, so beware. If there's a sign that says "no swimming," heed its advice. Beaches are open Memorial Day through Labor Day, 9am to 9:30 pm. Various beaches have distinct sensibilities. **North Avenue Beach**, for instance, attracts volleyball players, young families, and lots and lots of singles. **Oak Street Beach** is one of the most popular, due no doubt to its easy-to-get-to location near the Magnificent Mile and lots of hotels; its crowd seems to have arrived there right off the set of "The Bold and The Beautiful"—an alarming number of people with svelte bodies, sleek bathing suits, and slick tans. Farther up in the neighborhoods, **Foster Avenue Beach** (5200 north) attracts families, with convenient parking, a huge grassy area perfect for barbecuing, and a Rollerblading path on the shore just inland from the sandy beach. The most popular gay beach isn't even a beach in the traditional sense—for instance, there is no sand. Located just south of **Belmont Harbor**, though, a large green space has been annexed, more or less, by hordes of gay men (a few lesbians, too, but really, this is a gay male beach) in bathing suits, picnicking, tanning, cruising, and yammering. The last few summers have seen the gay population gradually shift to **Hollywood Beach**, where every Sunday there are pick-up volleyball and frisbee, as well as just a lot of sitting around in the sun. To find it, look for the big rainbow flag that's usually flying from one of the volleyball nets.

Ahoy there... It shouldn't come as a surprise that, between the lake and the river, Chicagoans are gaga for boating—

on sailboats, cigarette speedsters, powerboats, house-boats, rowboats, even kayaks and canoes. At Belmont Harbor, you can take sailing lessons and rent sailboats from the **Chicago Sailing Club** (tel 773/871–7245), which offers a two-week basic course for around $350, or instruction at $40 to 50 an hour for more experienced sailors; **Sailboats, Inc.** (tel 312/861–1757 or 800/826–7010), which has a wider range of boats to rent, also runs two- or three-day clinics for various levels, which may set you back up to $500. If you have your own boat, the **Belmont Yacht Club** (tel 773/477–7575) is for members only, but members of yacht clubs in other cities have reciprocal use of the facilities. Though the club doesn't look all that fancy, to belong here you do have to own a boat, and owning a boat at Belmont Harbor isn't cheap, so you should be in pretty well-heeled company. If that's too rich for your blood, boaters can also dock for about $10 a person at **North Pier** (tel 312/527–2002), alongside sight-seeing cruise boats.

Can you canoe?... For a truly fresh perspective on Chicago's downtown, how about paddling your way between the skyscrapers that line the Chicago River? **Friends of the Chicago River** (tel 773/939–0490) organizes a wide variety of guided canoe trips—some out in the northern and southern suburbs, but some actually on the downtown stretches of the river. There's a least one trip a week in summer; book a week ahead, if possible. All ages and sorts of people sign onto these outings, not just weathered pros. If you're more the seasoned canoer, know that the **Chicagoland Canoe Base** (tel 773/777–1489, 4019 N. Narragansett Ave.) not only sells both antique and new canoes but rents them as well—$35 for one day. Don't expect to negotiate whitewater, but about an hour's drive from the city, the lower Fox River or the Kishwaukee River out near Rockford are good canoeing rivers.

Sightseeing afloat... There's no dearth of boat tours on both the lake and the river. The most popular is the 90-minute **Wendella Sightseeing Boats tour** (400 N. Michigan Ave., tel 312/337–1446; $10 adults, $5 kids under 12), which sets off April through October from the Wrigley Building. The route cruises along the Chicago River as it cuts through the Loop, then along the lake from the Adler Planetarium to Oak Street; take it at night for really stunning views. June through September, **Mercury Skyline Cruises** (Wacker Dr. and Michigan Ave., tel 312/332–1353) and **Shoreline Marine** (departing from both Navy Pier and the Shedd Aquarium, tel 312/222–9328) give Wendella competition. The narration on these boats is pretty much your standard sightseeing spiel, however; for something a bit different, book a seat on one of the weekly sightseeing boat tours run by **Friends of the Chicago River**, whose focus is, predictably, the ecology of the Chicago River system. The **Chicago Architecture Foundation** (tel 312/922–3432) offers insightful narrated boat trips on the river too, focusing not only on the landmark buildings on its shore but also on the history of the river and the city's relation to it. It's best to buy tickets in advance (TicketMaster tel 312/902–1500), as this tour is gaining in popularity. Tickets are under $20.

Pedal pushers... There's no better way to see the city than by biking through it. A blacktop path stretches for about 20 prime lakefront miles, **from 7100 south to 5700 north**, taking in spectacular views of the lake, museums, parks, harbors, and the skyline. Considering the views, it's no surprise that the path is often crowded with walkers, Rollerbladers, joggers, parents with baby carriages, dog-walkers, and others. If possible, avoid this route on Saturdays and Sundays after 8am and weekdays after 3pm. A word of warning: From McCormick Place on north, the path is pretty safe, and riding alone during daylight hours poses no real threat. But much of the path south of McCormick Place runs through areas where few people congregate, and despite city-run bike patrols along the entire length of the path, muggings have been known to happen. One easy way to avoid trouble is the most obvious: Don't ride alone. Another great bike path is the 7-mile **Evanston-Lake Shore trail**, along Sheridan Road in nearby north-suburban Evanston, from about Main Street north to the Evanston-Wilmette border. It's about a half-hour drive from the Loop to the starting point; you can also take the Evanston Express el, or ride your bike up there. The route more or less traces the lakeshore, passing Northwestern University; the northern end of the trail follows on pedestrian sidewalks. For more information on these and other bike trails in the metropolitan area, call the **Chicago Bicycle Federation** (tel 312/427–3325). For a detailed map of the lakefront path, call the **Chicago Park District** at 312/747–2200. Public bike rental is available along the lakefront at Oak Street Beach, Lincoln Park Zoo, at Cannon Drive, and at Buckingham Fountain. In addition, several stores rent bicycles by the hour and day, including **The Bike Stop** (1034 W. Belmont Ave., tel 773/868–6800) in Lake View, and **Wheels & Things** (5210 S. Harper Ave., tel 773/493–4326) in Hyde Park.

Out on a swim... With the lake at your doorstep, or at least steps away from where you're probably staying, there's no real reason to swim in a pool (unless your hotel has a particularly fine one, such as the beautiful pool at the **Four Seasons** or the **Hotel Inter-Continental**'s 13th-floor Italianate junior Olympic-size pool—see Accommodations). But if you must, the Chicago Park District operates dozens of outdoor neighborhood swimming pools, two dozen indoor pools, and a couple of swimming lagoons. Just beware—kids swim in all of these, and you know what that means. The lagoons are at **Douglas Park** (1401 S. Sacramento Ave., tel 312/521–3244) and **Humbolt Park** (1400 N. Sacramento Ave., tel 312/276–0107), both open June through Labor Day, 9am to 11pm. Wednesday nights at 7pm, the gay swim team known as the Smelts practices (all are welcome) at **Gill Park**'s public pool (tel 312/281–4692 for other times and dates, 825 W. Sheridan Rd.).

Par for the course... City duffers got a gift from the golf god in July 1994, when one of the city's ugliest patches of land—a pocket of dirt and sand between the Chicago River and Grant Park, overlooked by some of the most expensive real estate in the city—was converted into **Metrogolf Chicago** (221 N. Columbus Dr., tel 312/616–1234). A *downtown* golf course, no less—perfect for sneaking in a quick nine holes between business meetings. Designed by Perry Dye (son of famous course designer Pete Dye), the nine-hole, par-three course includes hitting stalls, a 65-person driving range, and, of course, locker rooms, a pro shop, and a bar and grill. The center is open year-round (it has heated driving stalls and indoor teaching stalls). A bucket of about 80 balls will run you $9, while green fees are $15 for nine holes. If you're registered at the Swissotel next door, you're guaranteed a tee time (reserve through the concierge). The **Sydney Marovitz Course** (3600 N. Lake Shore Dr.), which many Chicagoans still call Waveland, is a pretty nine-holer right on the lake, convenient for visitors; there's also an 18-hole course in **Jackson Park** (63rd and Stoney Island Ave.), as well as a municipal driving range, and a 35-tee range in **Lincoln Park** (Lake Shore Dr. at Diversey Pkwy.). All city-run courses are open mid-April through November, dawn to dusk; for information on green fees, location, and hours, call the **Chicago Park District office** (tel 312/747–2200; automated phone reservation system at 312/245–0909).

The tennis racket... Right in the dreamy shadows of the city's skyline, there are hundreds of courts to choose from, several of them lighted for night play. City courts are open mid-April through November; some charge fees and take reservations—reserve if you can, since facilities tend to get very crowded on weekends and in the after-work hours. Two convenient locations with lighted courts are **Daley Bicentennial Plaza** in Grant Park (tel 312/742–7648, Randolph St. and Lake Shore Dr., $5 an hour, reservations accepted) and **Waveland** (tel 773/742–7674, Addison St. and Lake Shore Dr., $3 per person daily pass guarantees you one hour on courts, on a first-come-first-served basis).

Rollerblade runner... Stores renting in-line skates have sprung up all over the city, especially along the streets within a block or two or three of the lake, where throngs of Rollerbladers cheerfully mow down runners, strollers, bikers, and dogs. The lakeshore path all the way from Shedd Aquarium north to Hollywood Beach is fantastic for skating; of course, as always along the lake, the farther north you go the less crowded it will be. Try **Londo Mondo Motionwear** (tel 312/751–2794, 1100 N. Dearborn St.,), **Windward Sports** (tel 773/472–6868, 3317 N. Clark St.), and **City Sweats** (tel 773/348–2489, 2467 N. Clark St.), all of which rent in-line skates by the hour and the day. A skate rental booth sprouts up during the summer at **North Avenue Beach** (North Ave. and Lake Shore Dr.) and **Oak Street Beach** (Oak St. and Lake Shore Dr.). If it rains and you've still got the yen to

Rollerblade, head to the **Rainbo Sports Club** (tel 773/271–5668, 4836 N. Clark St.), an indoor Rollerblading and rollerskating rink. It offers nightly open skating, with special times set aside for kids, adults over 25, families, and teens. There's even an adult late night skate that goes until 3am, and Monday night is unofficially for gays. Rent roller skates and in-line skates here for use on site only. Call ahead for current schedule and fees.

What's nice on ice... One good thing about the brutal winters here is that you can ice-skate outdoors—the city maintains more than 100 outdoor ice-skating rinks (call the park district at 312/747–2200 for locations). For a totally cool urban experience, head downtown (or up, depending on where you're coming from) for the Loop's **Skate on State** (tel 312/744–3315, State St. between Randolph and Washington streets.). This wintertime outdoor rink is surrounded on three sides by Loop office towers and Marshall Field's grand State Street store on the fourth. It's free, and if you don't own skates, you can rent them there for $2. There's a warming shelter and a food concession, too, and hokey music wafting through the air. If scenic vistas are more to your liking, the 80-by-135-foot rink at the **Daley Bicentennial Plaza** (tel 312/294–4790, Randolph St. at Lake Shore Dr.) has gorgeous views of the lake and beyond. It's open December through March, assuming the weather is cold and blustery enough. There's skate rental and a warming shelter; a small fee is charged. For year-round skating, damn the weather, try the practical indoor rink at the **McFetridge Sports Center** (tel 773/478–0210, 3843 N. California Ave.). Open hours vary depending on the day and season, so call ahead.

Run for your life... In Chicago, figuring out *where* to run is dead easy. Something about the sight of Chicago's lakeshore paths makes even nonrunners yearn to lace up their Nikes and sprint away. The stretch from Oak Street north to Foster is superb, and therefore very crowded on weekends; go early, late, or on weekdays. Most of the path is blacktop, but there's a separate gravel running path for about a mile from Belmont to Irving Park. If you want to run in a group, call the **Chicago Area Runners Association** (tel 312/666–9836). **Frontrunners/walkers** (tel 312/409–2790), the gay and lesbian running group, meets every Tuesday at 6:30pm and Saturday at 9am at the totem pole at Addison Street and the Lake Shore Drive. Both organizations, predictably, run along the lake. Where else? For serious runners, there's the **Chicago Marathon** every October—(tel 312/527-1105 for registration and information).

The wind's beneath my wings... Windsurfing on Lake Michigan is cool beyond belief, but also dangerous if you don't know what you're doing. And you probably don't. **Windward Sports** (tel 773/472–6868, 3317 N. Clark St.) offers windsurfing classes from late April through August; meet at the store Saturday at 10am or Sunday at 2pm. A two-day course, complete with certification, costs $120; a one-day class is $65.

You sleigh me!... Romantic, fun, jolly, toasty: these are a few words that could describe the winter sleigh rides offered at **Forest View Farm** (1/2-mile west of Cicero Ave. on 167th St., tel 708/560–0306) in suburban Tinley Park. Park your carcass on the velvet seats under a warm blanket, and let the horses pull you and your love slave in an antique carriage into another world; or pile the whole family in the sleigh and raise a rowdy chorus of "Over the River and Through the Woods." (The sleigh drivers must have heard it a gazillion times.) Rides last about 40 wonderful minutes; reservations (and snow) required.

shop

5

ping

In Chicago, shop-
ping is as much a
pastime as voting
twice, walking
through the giant
heart at the
Museum of

Science and Industry, or sitting in the bleachers at Wrigley Field watching the Cubs lose another game. As the hub of the Midwest, it draws millions of people to its shores, many of whom visit to do nothing but spend, spend, spend. Even jaded jet-setters from L.A., Paris, and Rome will find the experience of shopping in Chicago entirely satisfying. Service here is generally peppy, too. The New York assumption that people like to be abused by snotty saleshelp just doesn't exist in Chicago.

Target Zones

Michigan Avenue, from Oak Street on its northern tip, down to the Chicago River, is hands-down the most important shopping street in the city, justly known as the **Magnificent Mile**. Once a sleepy thoroughfare lined with elegant five-story limestone buildings, it has in the past few decades become a marble canyon of sky-high towers, home to the fanciest of the fancy, such as Chanel and Cartier, as well as embarrassing middlebrow fixtures like Victoria's Secret. It is home, as well, to all the best department stores—**Marshall Field's**, **Lord & Taylor**, **Neiman Marcus**, **Saks Fifth Avenue**, and **Bloomingdale's** (a Nordstrom's is in the works, too). In 1995, there was a big brouhaha when a Filene's Basement, known as the mother of all things discounted, opened across from the Water Tower Place shopping mall. Around the corner from Michigan Avenue, however, is **Oak Street**, Chicago's own Madison Avenue, Ginza, and Rodeo Drive all rolled up into one. Only one block long, it houses the most important designer boutiques (usually in beautiful brownstone settings), including Giorgio Armani, Sonia Rykiel, Betsey Johnson, Gianni Versace, Jil Sander, and Hermès, not to mention Barneys New York. (Prada is on the way.) You'll find a lot of the funkier boutiques, from vintage to fashion forward, as well as the hippest record stores, in **Lake View** and **Lincoln Park**. The main strolling streets there include Broadway, Clark Street, and Halsted Street. **State Street** in **The Loop** used to be the shopping mecca for Chicagoans, but no longer. Other than Marshall Field's—admittedly a big deal—a Crate & Barrel (not as good as Michigan Avenue's), Carson Pirie Scott & Co., and Carl Fischer (the city's best source for sheet music), there's not much there in the way of quality-time shopping, unless you like schlock shops.

Vertical Malls

For better or for worse, Chicago has perfected the urban

shopping mall. Michigan Avenue is lined with huge, generally pretentious marble monuments to the almighty dollar, ugly on the outside and, well, pretty ugly on the inside, too. But Chicago's towering malls at least are filled with scores of stores and restaurants that provide for a lot of good shopping—and great people watching. Built in 1976, **Water Tower Place** (tel 312/440–3165, 835 N. Michigan Ave. at Pearson St.) is the leader of the proverbial pack, with both Marshall Field's and Lord & Taylor weighing it down at its base, and the Ritz-Carlton Hotel (see Accommodations) perched on top. Walk into its impressive marble-walled, marble-floored lobby, go up the escalator past waterfalls and lush foliage to the mezzanine, and just wander. There's more than enough to see and do, whether you're a window-shopping kind of person, an inveterate bargain-hunter (yes, you will find some bargains here), or just a browser. With about 100 stores, the only limit is your budget. If you get bored shopping, there are six shoebox-size movie theaters, too. Across the street, **Bloomingdale's** anchors the **Atrium** at 900 North Michigan Avenue (tel 312/915–3916), a way upscale mall with Gucci, Christofle, Henri Bendel, and about 80 other stores, as well as direct access to the Four Seasons Hotel (see Accommodations). When the mall first opened it took a lot of guff for being too upscale and too controlling. For instance, the way the escalators were positioned

Auction action

The fun begins when Leslie Hindman steps up to the podium at Sothebys Chicago. Next to her, an assistant holds up a porcelain lamp. "Do I hear $1,000?" she asks. Dead silence. "Do I hear $900?" Another dead silence. "Oh come on, people. Think retail!" Paddles finally rise and the bidding begins, with Hindman increasing the price until she reaches $1,800. "Sold!" she shouts, banging the gavel. At the Midwest's premier auction house (tel 312/670–0100, 215 W. Ohio St.), savvy shoppers sit on rickety folding chairs, hoping to get for a song that pair of Frank Lloyd Wright leaded-glass windows or a painting that might be a Picasso. Admission's free, and exhibitions are held for three to five days before the actual auction (for dates, call 312/AUCTION). Don't worry—unless you arrange beforehand, no sneeze or mop of the brow will be misconstrued as a bid. And Hindman takes the fear out of bidding with her wise-cracking Eve Arden-like personality; during Bears games she even announces the scores. But novice buyers should beware: a 15% surcharge is added to each puchase. Hey, the lady's got to make money somehow.

forced shoppers to walk for what seemed like miles, passing store after store after store, to catch the next one going down. People balked (and didn't spend money), so eventually the owners of the mall installed more escalators, making it more user-friendly. One warning: if you suffer from vertigo, don't look down from the mall's walkways—it's a treacherous view. There is, however, a particularly good view of Michigan Avenue and beyond from the huge round window on the eastern side. Although eight-story **Chicago Place** (tel 312/642–4811, 700 N. Michigan Ave.) has a few good stores—such as Room and Board for furniture, The Real Nancy Drew for inventive children's clothes, Louis Vuitton, and a Williams-Sonoma—the place is sort of a low-energy bore. Even the Saks Fifth Avenue on the ground floor is a snooze.

Another washout is the **Shops at the Mart** at the **Merchandise Mart** (tel 312/527–4141, 450 N. Wells St.), which is crowded with secretaries, furniture and fabric reps, designers, and office workers during the week (mostly eating lunch in the greasy-smelling food court), but eerily empty on weekends. No wonder, either, since its selection of chain stores can all be found elsewhere. The Mart itself is a gargantuan and wonderful building, but most of it—in fact, the interesting parts—are off-limits to the hoi polloi unless they have card-carrying interior designers leading the way.

Lots of locals groan when the shopping mall at **North Pier Chicago** (tel 312/836–4300, 435 E. Illinois St.) gets mentioned—it was built expressly for tourists, after all—but don't pay attention to the fulminations of jaded Chicagoans. North Pier's setting along the scenic Ogden Slip alone is worth the trip; the building itself—a rehabbed commercial pier—is a terrific success. It's bright, light-filled, and designed to afford the best views of the outside. Granted, there's the cheesy Baja Beach Club dance club (see Nightlife), but there are almost 50 specialty and novelty stores, too, some of which are unique. Just don't expect to find Back-to-School sales, sensible shoes, or a Chanel suit.

Farther north, in Lake View, is the neon-frenzied **Century Shopping Center** (tel 773/929–8100, 2828 N. Clark St.), filled with fast-food joints, sunglasses stores, jeans, electronics, lingerie shops, and a health club on the top floor. The mall's advertisements claim it's where "progressive people shop," which says it all.

Money Matters

Chicago's merchants know they don't live by locals alone, so they are generally as accommodating as possible to out-of-towners. All the major department stores will hold merchandise for a reasonable amount of time and will ship your purchases home to you. Writing personal checks is an iffier proposition—and at some stores, especially department stores, it takes forever. But ask, and as long as you've got a driver's license or some other form of photo ID, most stores will accept your check. Haggling over prices in retail stores is pretty much frowned upon—after all, this isn't the Old Country. But, you've got nothing to lose by trying to get a better price at the various secondhand stores around town. Stores are not required to give refunds if you're not satisfied with your purchase—most will, however, though some will offer it only in the form of exchange credit. One of the best things about **Marshall Field's**, Chicago's most famous retail emporium, is that you can return things long after you've bought them (but, please, not long after you've worn them).

Hours of Business

Most stores, from the small boutiques to the large department stores, open around 10am and remain open until at least 5pm. On Thursdays, stores generally stay open until 9pm. Many bookstores stay open much later, some until 11pm. Many of the owners of vintage stores like to sleep in; hence, those stores often don't open until 11am, or even noon in some cases. Virtually all stores are open on Sunday.

Sales Tax

A state and county sales tax of 8.75 percent is added to every purchase in Chicago, except groceries and prescription drugs. Tax is waived, however, if you have goods shipped out of state, so have your expensive purchases sent home if you want to save a bundle.

The Lowdown

Landmarks... There are a few stores here whose names are instantly linked with Chicago. Of course, the main event is **Marshall Field's** department store—if nothing else here, you should buy a box of the store's famous Frango Mints, a consummately Chicago ritual practiced by natives as well as visitors. One hint, though: stick to the original flavor, no matter how exotic the lemon, raspberry, and others sound. The offerings at **Carson Pirie Scott & Co.** are nothing special, but the department store's flagship building itself is a don't-miss classic Louis Sullivan extravaganza. Make sure you see its main entrance on the northwest corner. A selection of pipes and other smoking accoutrements is sold in the Loop at **Iwan Ries & Co.**, as it has been since 1857—the second-story Pipe Museum is a hoot. **The Chicago Architecture Foundation Shop**, in the Loop, has beautiful posters and photos, books and, yes, even mugs, that will keep the city's skyline and history alive for you after you've returned home. **Carl Fischer of Chicago**, a huge dusty, musty place in the shadow of the el in the Loop, has one of the best selections of sheet music in the country. There are **Fannie May** candy stores all over town, and each one of them is an old-timey delight. **Crate & Barrel**, another quintessential Chicago success story, is responsible for more interiors than perhaps any other store in the city. Though it may connote middle-brow, mass taste elsewhere, Chicagoans still remember when it was just a funky little store in Old Town. And none can doubt that **Nike Town**, with its carnival atmosphere and huge selection of sporting goods, has become a retail landmark.

For pampered service... Stick to the Mag Mile/Oak Street nexus and you could hit all these shops in one extremely spoiled day. (Don't laugh—it's been done.) Standing in the handsome dressing rooms of **Barneys New York** while a tailor pins your hem and the saleshelp hurl flattering remarks your way can really help the ego, not to mention how the chic clothing (for both sexes) can help your fashion image. The staff at **Henri Bendel** will go out of their way, running back and forth fetching a different size or color, while ladies luxuriate in their lovely changing rooms, just like the women in *The Women*. The chic salespeople at **Hermés** will spend a surprising amount of time doting on you as well, even demonstrating how to tie one of their horsy-patterned silk scarves in that insouciant way French women seem to have perfected. (Men may have to figure out on their own what to do with the silk ties.) Chicagoans have long loved the attention they get paid at the **Hino & Malee** boutique, where the store's own label of eminently wearable but unique women's clothes are truly inspiring. Spend a few hours poring over the fancy cosmetics and perfumes at **Marilyn Miglin**—while you may not necessarily depart better-looking than when you entered, the staff is so fawning you'll definitely *feel* better. The well-dressed staff at the **Ultimo** boutique, for men's and women's clothes, is more accommodating than its snooty reputation allows. Buy something and you'll be their friend forever. On a much smaller scale, **June Blaker**, in River North, treats her male and female customers with respect by telling them, if necessary, they look lousy in that particular avant-garde Japanese concoction. After all, not everyone can wear Comme des Garçons.

Accessorize!... Quirky hats, funny slippers that make you look like a genie, sexy dresses and blouses, and unique hand-crafted jewelry are beautifully displayed at **Krivoy** in the Lincoln Park neighborhood. Whether it's a nighttime clutch or a major handbag in which you can schlepp everything but the kitchen sink, you're sure to find it at **Bottega Veneta**, the famous Italian leather-goods shop known for its woven butter-soft leather (and high prices). **Glove Me Tender** may be small in square footage, but then gloves and mittens don't take up much room; the store carries thousands of pairs. Adorning your head with a straw bonnet, pillbox hat, or sleek little cloche from **Raymond Hudd** may look like it would cost an arm and a leg, but the ladies' hats in this Lincoln Park boutique are actually quite reasonably priced. And when a button pops, please don't buy one of those little plastic things at Walgreen's—instead head to **Tender Buttons**, a teeny-tiny store with an enormous selection of buttons: new ones, old ones, square ones, round ones, wood, Bakelite, brass, mother-of-pearl, you name it.

Shopping scenes... Don't be surprised on a Saturday morning if housewares-and-furniture mecca **Crate & Barrel** is jammed with preppie-looking couples running around wielding clipboards and wedding registry forms. Things can get pretty hairy on Saturday mornings at **Filene's Basement**, too, with bargain-hunters free from

SHOPPING | THE LOWDOWN

weekday lunch-hour constraints battling over some of the best clothing bargains in town. Don't expect to find any cheap deals on the toys and stuffed animals at **F.A.O. Schwarz**, though there is the constant din of kids and parents duking it out over the latest Star Wars paraphernalia and Barbie couture dresses. It's a far more civilized scene at **Salvage One**, where do-it-yourselfers with "This Old House" complexes trek to shuffle through five vast floors, discussing the relative merits of this vintage toilet versus that one, these mahogany doors versus those doors in oak, etc., etc.

For foot fetishists... Up in Lake View, **Air Wair/Doc Martens Footwear and Clothing** is the place for what many consider the hippest shoes around. Doc Martens are generally clunky, often black, and usually hated by parents when worn by teenagers. In fact, when said parents were teenagers themselves they were probably running around in the comfy but odd looking sandals sold in Lincoln Park at **Hanig's Birkenstock Shop**, those stout-soled Nordic wonders that today come in all the colors of the rainbow. If you're trying to impress, though, head to **Cole-Haan** for beautifully crafted, sensible-yet-expensive leather shoes. There's nothing sensible about the spiky heels, square toes, and other shoes sold at **Stephane Kelian**, the biggest name in French footwear. **Lori's Discount Designer Shoes**, in Lincoln Park, peddles a wide, quickly changing array of bargain-priced designer shoes for women (20 to 40 percent off Kenneth Cole, Calvin, Joan & David, etc.). In-the-know customers arrive early in the day for the best selection.

For men with Cary Grant complexes... Plan your wardrobe for that deb ball at **Buy-A-Tux**, a south-of-the-Loop store where designer formalwear—including Joseph Abboud and Jhane Barnes—is about a third less than you'd pay anywhere else. Then, perhaps, stop into the gracious portal of the **Giorgio Armani** boutique for a formal black overcoat. Or maybe it's a day at Mummy's club you're planning. In that case, try **Sulka**, which sells the kind of clothes investment bankers might wear on their day off. At **Ermengildo Zegna** you'll find the most gorgeous (that's the only word that springs to mind) and expensive menswear this side of Milan. Then add a little James Bondish élan to your look with a gadget from **Hammacher Schlemmer**, which specializes in high-tech, and often wacky, wizardry. No self-respecting Cary Grant wannabe would appear without a pipe from **Iwan Ries & Co.**, a Loop shop with more than 25,000 pipes in stock, from wood to Meerschaum and everything in between.

For men who would rather resemble Lou Reed... Go to Lake View's **The Alley** and **99th Floor**, or Lincoln Park's **Urban Outfitters**—they all sell the kind of clothes that work well on the wild side, whether that means an all-nighter at the clubs, a gig with an alternative garage band, or just a few hours lolling around some see-and-be-seen outdoor cafe, leaning on your Harley.

Shopping bags to show off... The shiny black bags with white lettering from **Chanel** are a good start, since black goes with everything. The discreet, earth-toned bags from the **Giorgio Armani** or **Jil Sander** boutiques are also good choices, as they imply not only lots of money, but lots of taste. The brown-and-white-striped **Henri Bendel** bag connotes a youthful flair that few can match. If folks spy you walking down the street swinging a **Plaza Escada** bag, they may question your taste, but at least they'll know you've spent a lot of money. Gianni Versace, the man, may be gone, but **Versace**, the store, is still alive, kicking, and as expensive as ever. The **Ermenegildo Zegna** boutique for men may bankrupt you if you're not careful. At least, if that happens, you'll be a very, very fancy bag lady (or man).

Fashion forward... Chicago may not be known as the home of waif-thin models and ascot-wearing designers, but high fashion is alive and well here. **Blake**, in Lincoln Park, sells women's clothes by such on-the-edge designers as Dries van Noten, among others. At **June Blaker**, a store for both men and women, the eponymous personality-plus proprietor is usually on hand to offer you guidance through the hottest of the hot. It's a trip to the future for men and women at **Versace**, as well, where the designs tend toward the flamboyant, the metallic, and the hey-look-at-me mode (or should that be moda?). The city's power elite shop is **Ultimo**, where several men's and women's designers meet in a multilevel store. **Jil Sander**, which sells understated men's and women's clothes that have been called "architectural," was the German designer's first freestanding store in the United States. If you're interested in making a splash, but not the same splash as everyone else, it's not hard to find the unusual and sometimes one-of-a-kind at **Hino & Malee** or Lincoln Park's **Krivoy**, both of which are filled with their owners' designs for women. The tatami mats, shoji screens, and beautiful display cases at **Toshiro**, in Lake View, are an indication of the ease and simplicity of the clothes within, which generally come from young, hip designers. Boy-toy club kids do their shopping in Lake View at **Hardwear**, where the clothes are designed to show off those pecs, lats, and glutes they've been working lo, these many years. It's the only place in town to buy clothes by favorite gay-guy New York designer Raymond Dragon. At **Sugar Magnolia**, which caters to a youngish, hip crowd of women, you won't find weird hard-to-wear designs by Japanese designers or Belgians with hard-to-pronounce names, but sporty stuff by up-and-coming, mostly American designers.

Key notes... There's such an enormous selection of music available at Lincoln Park's **Tower Records** that you'll probably walk in planning to buy one CD and walk out with a dozen. It has particularly strong classical and show-tune departments and a staff that really knows its stuff, though no one is ever around when you need them. Also in Lincoln Park, the **Jazz Record Mart** not only sells CDs, tapes, and regular albums, but also has old, hard-to-find 45s and even 78s. **2nd Hand Tunes**, on the north side, is rife with collectors, from Judy, Barbra, and Bette fanatics to those seeking rare recordings by the not-forgotten Clash, Adam Ant, Blondie, and, well, you get the picture. No one over 21 has ever heard of any of the artists whose records are sold at **Wax Trax** in Bucktown.

Kid stuff, part one... There's often a human "toy soldier" standing in front of **F.A.O. Schwarz**, beckoning families into this frenzied toy palace. Lots of movie tie-in products, and a really kitschy Barbie boutique; but the best things here are the great stuffed animals, so cute they'll break your heart. For a calmer time, go up to Lincoln

Park to **Saturday's Child**, whose collection of educational, motivational, and creative toys (none of which are movie tie-ins) is culled from about 300 manufacturers around the world. Most boys and girls will go nuts in the **Chicago Cubs Sports Shop**, though parents might be put off by the high prices.

Kid stuff, part two... If you're looking for clothes that dress up your kids without making them look like baby Evangelistas, head to **All Our Children**, which sells a sophisticated yet charming collection in sizes infant through 7. **Oilily** carries its own line of bright, adorable kids clothes designed and made in Italy, with a hefty tariff to match.

Book nooks... Chicago is well stocked with major bookstore chains—notably your **Barnes & Noble** and **Borders** Megastores—but if you're reading needs are a bit more esoteric, try these specialty shops. On Wabash Avenue in the South Loop, the **Prairie Avenue Bookshop** specializes in books on architecture, design, and engineering, while the **Ginkgo Tree Book Shop** in suburban Oak Park sells books about that town's most famous past resident (not counting Ernest Hemingway), Frank Lloyd Wright. Like the name says, the **Abraham Lincoln Bookstore**, in River North, is devoted to books about Honest Abe, his life and times. At Andersonville's **Women and Children First** you'll find books on women's issues, as well as a good selection of children's books.

Used but not abused books... The Lincoln Park neighborhood is a target zone for secondhand book stores: You'll find thousands of high-quality used hardcover and paperback books at **Powell's** and **Aspidistra Bookshop** (which could use a good dusting). Even better, don't miss the wide selection of contemporary first editions sold at each.

Everything you always wanted to know about sex... Come to the **Pleasure Chest** in Lake View when your needs include sex toys, soft-core porn, skimpy maid's uniforms, and spiked leather dog collars. **Male Hide**, in Lincoln Park, is for leather lovers of all sexual orientations, with all sorts of paraphernalia including vests, chaps, harnesses, along with chains and other items that can turn any evening into a painfully good time. Yee-hah!

For aspiring Martha Stewarts... Given its important role in both the history of design and furniture manufacturing, Chicago is a good place to shop for furniture even if you're just visiting. The light-filled Michigan Avenue **Crate & Barrel** is filled with four-poster beds, big squishy floral-print sofas, club chairs, and all sorts of traditional furniture that, judging from the hordes roaming through the store, seems to appeal to everyone on earth, not just Chicagoans. The sprawling **Room & Board** nearby has similarly appealing furniture, most of it with a more contemporary feel. There are no mass-produced dining room tables, chairs, or sleigh beds at River North's **Sawbridge Studios**, where everything is hand-crafted by individual artisans across the country. Prices rise considerably when you start shopping at **Manifesto**, the city's prime source for architecturally inspired furniture. At **Mario Villa** the furniture design (all created by the store's New Orleans-based namesake) is less architectural than artful, while the overstuffed (and over-priced) sofas and chairs at **Shabby Chic** are so plush it's like sitting in a big bowl of pudding. In the old Saks Fifth Avenue building on Michigan Avenue, the **Sony Gallery** purveys all things electronic and high-tech. Though it looks off-putting, you really can try out everything—play to your heart's content with all that stereo and TV gadgetry. **Zepter International** sells the most expensive cookware in town—lovely to look at, ridiculous to buy.

Furnishing touches... If you're trying to re-create a home à la 16th arrondissement, or perhaps in the style of a sun-worn home in Provence, you might want to fill up on the charming French imported dishes, linen, stemware, etc. sold at **La Maison de Nicole**. Don't miss the Limoge. At **Elements**, you'll find very expensive cutting-edge designs, including artist-made lamps, picture frames, and some of the most creatively mixed-and-matched tableware in the city. Michigan Avenue's Showcase **Banana Republic** store sells swank and expensive home accessories—more like *The Thin Man* than *Casablanca*. The new **Pottery Barn** can't help but wow you, with its beautiful interior and equally beautiful interior home accessories. Dishes, flatware, frames, bedding, etc. For a casual but more rustic look, try **Jayson Home & Garden**, which will make you want to go home and plant bulbs. Everything's totally Italian at the appropriately named **Tutti Italia**, which sells the city's largest selection of hand-painted Paesanella ceramics. Both the Michigan Avenue **Crate & Barrel** and the **Crate & Barrel Outlet Store** up in Lincoln Park are filled with streamlined, contemporary-styled housewares, including dishes, glasses, bowls, picture frames, pots 'n' pans, and very handsome versions of such practical objects as salad spinners and apple corers. Also in Lincoln Park, **Lill Street Studios** offers one-of-a-kind hand-thrown ceramics—you can actually meet with the individual artists and help design your own tableware. Unspeakably beautiful stationery and paper, much of it imported or made by hand, is available at the **Paper Source**, where you'll no doubt spend more than you intended.

The sporting life... Hollywood might have movie stars and New York has fashion designers, but Chicago has sports gods, and everything and anything to do with them is available at the **Chicago Cubs Sports Shop**. It might look like a shrine to Michael Jordan, Scottie Pippin, and all the rest of the Bulls, but **Nike Town** is a real store selling almost everything the company sells—a cornucopia of footwear and sports clothing. Only tourists actually buy here—the prices tend to be as high as Jordan's jump shot (Nike gear is expensive, but hey, you can buy it for less almost anywhere else). There will be some things you can't get at Nike Town, but don't despair. There's always **Windward Sports**, in Lake View, which specializes in whatever you may need to cut quickly through the elements (i.e., skis, windsurfers, surfboards, snowboards, Rollerblades...).

The vintage vantage point... As you'd expect, funky Lake View is the neighborhood for equally funky vintage clothing stores. A recent addition to the used clothing scene, **Disgraceland** has a definite 1960s bent, selling kitschy vintage bellbottoms, chiffon beaded numbers, sandals, and lots of other stuff. It's all very Ann-

Margret. The 1960s are also alive just up the street at **Strange Cargo**, the place to come for vintage clothes à la Brady Bunch and campy lunch boxes from the Sixties and Seventies (Starsky and Hutch! Bobby Sherman! the Partridge family!). **Flashy Trash** is a bright shop that doesn't sell "used" clothing as much as truly vintage clothes and accessories, with a great selection of winter overcoats, shoes, and party dresses. Drag queens shop here.

Labels for less... The mundane atmosphere at **Buy-A-Tux**, south of the Loop, may not resemble the formal settings where these designer black-tie duds are eventually worn, but the prices are so good you'll be able to afford at least one more charity ball with the savings. You could shop at full-price retail establishments like Barneys New York and Henri Bendel, but if you search hard enough you'll find much of their private-label goods, as well as clothes by designers from Calvin Klein to Anne Klein, steeply discounted at **Filene's Basement**. Those same designers, as well as many others, are also represented at **Lori's Discount Designer Shoes**, a self-serve shoe store in Lincoln Park. For a preppie at-the-shore look for people whose budgets only allow for summer shares, the **Land's End** outlet on the north side is a good place to start. There's a certain timeless solidity in the casual clothes sold at the north side's the **Gap Factory Outlet**, where the discounts can be substantial. Though they claim that much of what's available here is seconds, the flaws are almost impossible to spot. And no outfit would be complete without a great pair of trendy shades from Ray Ban, Vuarnet, or other brand names, which can be found at a discount at **Sun King**.

When you need a sugar fix... Why waste your time or calories on fancy chocolates from Godiva when all over town there are **Fannie May** outlets selling indescribably good chocolate-covered peanuts, creams in all shades of the pastel rainbow, and turtles to die for? Skip the fudge, though, and instead head for the **Fudge Pot**, in Old Town, where the yummiest fudge around comes in many flavors. And don't forget those Frango Mints at **Marshall Field's**!

The Index

Abraham Lincoln Bookstore. Books and paraphernalia relating to the sixteenth president and the Civil War.... *Tel 312/944–3085. 357 W. Chicago Ave.* **(see p. 141)**

Air Wair/Doc Martens Footwear and Clothing. The place for combat boots and other thick-soled hip shoes.... *Tel 773/244–0099. 3240 N. Clark St.* **(see p. 138)**

All Our Children. Where the fashion-forward baby gets garbed.... *Tel 773/327–1868. 2217 N. Halsted St.* **(see p. 141)**

The Alley. Motorcycle jackets and all the accoutrements you could ever desire, plus lots of Dead Head paraphernalia.... *Tel 773/883–1800. 858 W. Belmont Ave.* **(see p. 139)**

Aspidistra Bookshop. An almost stereotypical-looking dusty old used-book store with an anything-but-stereotypical stock.... *Tel 773/549–3129. 2630 N. Clark St.* **(see p. 141)**

Banana Republic. Three-story mega-Banana sells the chain's entire attire collection, as well as jewelry and expensive home accessories.... *Tel 312/642–0020. 744 N. Michigan Ave.* **(see p. 142)**

Barnes & Noble. Book megastore sells almost everything at a 10 percent to 30 percent discount.... *Tel 773/971–9004. 659 W. Diversey Pkwy.* **(see p. 141)**

Barneys New York. If you're into Donna, Calvin, Giorgio, and all the rest, this clothing store is the place for you. Friendlier staff than you'd expect, too.... *Tel 312/587–1700. 25 E. Oak St.* **(see p. 136)**

Blake. This small discriminating women's boutique sells choice selections of white-hot trendy clothing.... *Tel 773/477–3364. 2448 N. Lincoln Ave.* **(see p. 139)**

Bloomingdale's. This six-story version of the famed Manhattan emporium sells trendy clothes, great housewares, and gallons of cosmetics.... *Tel 312/440–4460. 900 N. Michigan Ave.* **(see pp. 132, 133)**

Borders. Another three-story mega-bookstore across the street from the Water Tower Place shopping mall.... *Tel 312/573–0564. 830 N. Michigan Ave.* **(see p. 141)**

Bottega Veneta. Purses, briefcases, shoes, and other pricey Italian woven leather goods.... *Tel 312/664–3220. 107 E. Oak St.* **(see p. 137)**

Buy-A-Tux. Formalwear shop selling designer discounted tuxes and black-tie gear.... *Tel 312/243–5465. 615 W. Roosevelt Rd.* **(see pp. 138, 144)**

Carl Fischer of Chicago. Famous source for sheet music.... *Tel 312/427–6652. 312 S. Wabash Ave.* **(see p. 136)**

Carson Pirie Scott & Co. Once one of the Midwest's great department stores, it is today dreary and conventional.... *Tel 312/641–7000. 1 S. State St.* **(see p. 136)**

Chanel. Glamorous boutique for suits, little black dresses, and, of course, Chanel No. 5.... *Tel 312/787–5500. 935 N. Michigan Ave.* **(see p. 139)**

The Chicago Architecture Foundation Shop. A great selection of books, small architectural doodads, mugs, and T-shirts.... *Tel 312/922–8687. 224 S. Michigan Ave.* **(see p. 136)**

Chicago Cubs Sports Shop. This is the place downtown to get all the Cubs (and other sports team) memorabilia, plus tickets.... *Tel 312/321–9421. 445 N. Michigan Ave.* **(see pp. 141, 143)**

Cole-Haan. Expensive and stylishly conservative men's and women's shoes are sold in an unusually exquisite

store.... *Tel 312/642–8995. 645 N. Michigan Ave.*
(see p. 138)

Crate & Barrel. A homegrown Chicago institution, this store sells clean-lined, stylish furniture and kitchenware. The salespeople here are incredibly nice and helpful, even by Chicago standards.... *Tel 312/787–5900. 850 N. Michigan Ave.* **(see pp. 136, 137, 142, 143)**

Crate & Barrel Outlet Store. With savings anywhere from 20 to 70 percent off the prices at the regular store (see above), it's worth braving what is hands-down the worst parking lot in Chicago.... *Tel 312/787–4775. 800 W. North Ave.* **(see p. 143)**

Disgraceland. Secondhand clothes with a decided 1960s bent.... *Tel 773/281–5875. 3330a N. Clark St.*
(see p. 143)

Elements. One of the city's most cosmopolitan tchotchke shops.... *Tel 312/642-6574. 102 E. Oak St.*
(see p. 142)

Ermenegildo Zegna. Italian designer's gorgeous, and surprisingly colorful, sports coats, suits, and accessories.... *Tel 312/587–9660. 645 N. Michigan Ave.*
(see pp. 138, 139)

Fannie May. Old-fashioned hometown institution sells 100 types of chocolate candy, with names like pixies, Colonials, and turtles.... *Tel 312/664–0420. Water Tower Place, 835 N. Michigan Ave. (and many other locations).*
(see pp. 136, 144)

F.A.O. Schwarz. Over-the-top toy store.... *Tel 312/587–5000. 840 N. Michigan Ave.* **(see pp. 138, 140)**

Filene's Basement. Bargain-clothing-hunter's delight.... *Tel 312/553–1055. 1 N. State St.; and tel 312/482–8918, 830 N. Michigan Ave.* **(see pp. 137, 144)**

Flashy Trash. High-end vintage clothing store.... *Tel 773/ 327–6900. 3524 N. Halsted St.* **(see p. 144)**

Jayson Home & Garden. Two stores across the street from one another, both selling beautiful, (and way-overpriced) home and garden accessories.... *Tel 773/525–3100. 1901 & 1911 N. Clybourn Ave.* **(see p. 143)**

Jazz Record Mart. Featuring the world's largest selection of jazz recordings, this busting-at-its-seams store is a local hang-out. The staff really knows its stuff.... *Tel 312/222–1467. 444 N. Wabash Ave.* **(see p. 140)**

Jil Sander. Devoted to the austere but wearable women's clothes of this German designer.... *Tel 312/335–0006. 48 E. Oak St.* **(see pp. 139, 140)**

June Blaker. Known as an outpost of the avant-garde, this chic corner boutique sells European and Japanese designer clothes.... *Tel 312/751–9220. 200 W. Superior St.*
(see pp. 137, 139)

Krivoy. Most everything sold in this highly personal, quirky shop is designed by the owner.... *Tel 312/248–1466. 1145 W. Webster St.* **(see pp. 137, 140)**

Land's End. Overstocks from this well-known clothing catalogue are available at a 20 to 40 percent discount.... *Tel 312/281–0900. 2121 N. Clybourn Ave.* **(see p. 144)**

Lill Street Studios. A combination artists' commune, ceramics school, and pottery salesroom.... *Tel 773/477–6185. 1021 W. Lill St.* **(see p. 143)**

Lori's Discount Designer Shoes. Socks, hosiery, and handbags available, too.... *Tel 773/281–5655. 824 W. Armitage.* **(see pp. 138, 144)**

La Maison de Nicole. Graceful yet usable dishes, stemware, and table linen imported from France.... *Tel 312/943–3988. 66 E. Walton St.* **(see p. 142)**

Male Hide. Everything for the man or woman into leather and chains.... *Tel 773/929–0069. 2816 N. Lincoln Ave.*
(see p. 141)

Manifesto. This clever two-story furniture store sells original designs and exacting reproductions of 20th-century classics.... *Tel 312/664–0733. 200 W. Superior St.*

(see p. 142)

Marilyn Miglin. Expensive cosmetics and fragrances.... *Tel 312/943–1120. 112 E. Oak St. Closed Sun.* **(see p. 137)**

Mario Villa. Exquisite wrought-metal beds, lamps, tables, and chairs.... *Tel 312/923–0993. 500 N. Wells St.*

(see p. 142)

Marshall Field's. The legendary Chicago department store selling everything from clothing to housewares to furniture to antique cufflinks.... *Tel 312/781–1000. 111 N. State St.* **(see pp. 132, 135, 144)**

Neiman Marcus. A marble-clad tribute to all that's expensive and trendy—a one-stop couture-a-go-go.... *Tel 312/642–5900. 737 N. Michigan Ave.* **(see p. 132)**

Nike Town. This has to be the world's most extravagant sporting goods store, a shrine to professional athletes and their footwear.... *Tel 312/642–9525. 669 N. Michigan Ave.*

(see pp. 136, 143)

99th Floor. Leather and vinyl clothing for club kids and those who haven't realized heavy metal is passé.... *Tel 773/348–7781. 3406 N. Halsted St.* **(see p. 139)**

Oilily. Intensely colorful and creatively designed Italian clothes for junior.... *Tel 312/642–1166. 900 N. Michigan Ave.*

(see p. 141)

Paper Source. Handmade and machine-made paper, envelopes, and stationery, as well as a very large selection of rubber stamps.... *Tel 312/337–0798. 232 W. Chicago Ave.*

(see p. 143)

Plaza Escada. Bright, white-marbled, multi-level German-owned boutique, with playing clothes and accessories for trophy wives.... *Tel 312/915–0500. 840 N. Michigan Ave.*

(see p. 139)

Pleasure Chest. Sex-toy palace.... *Tel 773/525–7151. 3155 N. Broadway.* **(see p. 141)**

SHOPPING | THE INDEX

fortable it redefines the word.... *Tel 312/649–0080. 54 E. Walton St.* **(see p. 142)**

Sony Gallery. Severe-looking store displays high-tech Sony products, such as stereos, TVs, personal stereos, etc.... *Tel 312/943–3334. 663 N. Michigan Ave.* **(see p. 142)**

Stephane Kelian. Très bon women's shoes from one of the most prestigious French names in the business.... *Tel 312/951–2868. 121 E. Oak St.* **(see p. 138)**

Strange Cargo. In addition to used clothing, there's a wide selection of funky furniture and housewares for sale here.... *Tel 773/327–8090. 3448 N. Clark St.* **(see p. 144)**

Sugar Magnolia. Women's clothing from young, up-and-coming designers.... *Tel 312/944–0885. 34 E. Oak St.* **(see p. 140)**

Sulka. Elegantly tailored clothes, formalwear, leisure clothes, and even silk pajamas for men.... *Tel 312/951–9500. 55 E. Oak St.* **(see p. 138)**

Sun King. Cool shades from Ray Ban, Vuarnet, and others, all sold at a discount.... *Tel 312/649–9110. 44 E. Chicago Ave.* **(see p. 144)**

Tender Buttons. Scads of new and antique buttons.... *Tel 312/337–7033. 946 N. Rush St.* **(see p. 137)**

Toshiro. This dreamy three-story boutique sells simple women's clothes and farm-style antiques and housewares.... *Tel 773/248–1487. 3309 N. Clark St.* **(see p. 140)**

Tower Records. A vast tasteland where CDs of every conceivable musical type are for sale.... *Tel 773/477–5994. 2301 N. Clark St.* **(see p. 140)**

Tutti Italia. Everything Italian, from imported pastas and sauces to decorative tabletop accessories for the home.... *Tel 312/951–0510. 700 N. Michigan Ave.* **(see p. 143)**

Ultimo. The ultimate in designer boutiques, this handsome multilevel men's and women's clothing shop gets every-

thing first.... *Tel 312/787–0906. 114 E. Oak St.*
(see pp. 137, 139)

Urban Outfitters. Ersatz funkdom plying all the clothes, housewares, and shoes you need to be a hipster once again.... *Tel 773/549–1711. 2352 N. Clark St.* **(see p. 139)**

Versace. The late designer's often clingy but always flamboyant creations.... *Tel 312/337–1111. 101 E. Oak St.*
(see p. 139)

Wax Trax. The place to buy alternative music.... *Tel 773/252–1000. 1657 N. Damen Ave.* **(see p. 140)**

Windward Sports. Surfboards, snowboards, Rollerblades, sunglasses, bathing suits, and all other sleek modes of sports equipment.... *Tel 773/472–6868. 3317 N. Clark St.*
(see p. 143)

Women and Children First. Books and periodicals geared towards women.... *Tel 773/769–9299. 5233 N. Clark St.*
(see p. 141)

Zepter International. Expensive Italian pots and pans, displayed as if they're museum pieces—and priced that way, too.... *Tel 312/255–1900. 50 E. Oak St.* **(see p. 142)**

SHOPPING | THE INDEX

nigh

tlife

6

Chicago's bar
scene is organized
a lot like Disney-
land: You don't
really need to
have a specific
destination in

mind, just a theme, a mood, a lifestyle. Then hit the strip that suits those parameters. Conventioneers, suburbanites, and ill-informed visitors patronize the nearly indistinguishable pick-up bars radiating from State and Division streets, the traditional hub of the **Rush Street** area, which has been morphing into a dining and shopping scene in recent years. A few blocks of **Lincoln Avenue**, from Armitage to Fullerton, are populated by bars and live-music clubs pandering to clean-cut postcollegiate types. The crowd is basically the same farther north along **Clark Street** in Wrigleyville—a few reggae clubs and slacker-ish contingents mix things up a bit, but the sports bar rules here. Just a few blocks away, a passing parade of gays streams up and down **Halsted Street**. African-Americans congregate at a number of well-heeled nightclubs along **Michigan** and **Wabash avenues** in the South Loop. The spit-polished BMWs and motorcycles displayed outside a couple of bars on **Damen Avenue** north of North Avenue are a sign of the times: Lincoln Parkers have found a beachhead in too hip-for-its-own-good Wicker Park, though the neighborhood's arty types have managed to hang on to a few of their divey hide-outs. All this fragmentation doesn't mean clubbers don't cross boundaries: Choose carefully and you'll find a few places where there's plurality on the dance floor.

Sources

Head for Section 3 of the popular free weekly, *Reader*. Live music is listed according to genre, and there are plenty of ads to browse through in search of nightlife options. In its "Friday" entertainment tabloid, the *Chicago Tribune* publishes news of upcoming concerts and an "After hours" column profiling off-beat evening haunts. The *Sun-Times* provides hints about nocturnal goings-on in its "Friday Weekend Plus" pullout. *¡Exito!* keeps tabs on live music and happenings in the Latino community; *N'Digo*, a free black weekly tabloid, covers the African-American entertainment scene. The irreverent gay freebie *Gab*, available at many bars and stores in Lake View, chronicles the gay and lesbian party circuit. Get hip to the rave underground by studying the flyers and note cards dropped off at **Tower Records** (2301 N. Clark St.) or **Untitled** (2701 N. Clark St.), a hip-hop and rave boutique in Lincoln Park, or any trendy shop in Lake View or Wicker Park.

Liquor Laws and Drinking Hours

Chicago's drinking age is 21, and bars and nightclubs card practically everyone. The bar universe is divided into two constellations: those bars with 2am licenses, which allow the taps to flow until 3am on Saturday, and those late-night destinations with 4am licenses, which stay open until 5am Sunday morning and are welcome refuges after the others have called it quits. In the listings below, we note any place with a 4am license. And remember, Chicago may be home of the blues, but this ain't New Orleans, where revelers tote their beverages in the streets: Drink up before you continue your pub crawl.

The Lowdown

Where grown-ups can be grown-ups... When you want to get away from the kids (anyone five years younger than you are), Chicago offers plenty of places where a "mature" person who doesn't hit the hay by 9pm can enjoy a little civilized company. At the old-money Drake Hotel, the **Coq d'Or** offers a casual, clubby atmosphere with a buzzing crowd of Gold Coast regulars, out-of-towners, and loyalists of pianist Buddy Charles, who's charmed them here for years. **Seasons Lounge** in the posh Four Seasons Hotel is like a living room overlooking the Mag Mile—its upholstered divans are so cushy-comfy that you'll be excused if you nod off after a couple of cocktails. For a perch truly above it all, try the ninety-sixth floor of the John Hancock Center, where the **Signature Lounge** offers stunning views of the city from all sides. (Drink prices here are sky-high, too.) Sip a Scotch and stare out at the grid's streetlights disappearing in straight-arrow lines into the horizon. If you're in the neighborhood to ascend the Sears Tower, make it an evening by stopping next door at **Yvette Wintergarden**, a plush lower-level jazz room and French restaurant.

Calling all slackers... Artists, wannabe rock gods, and pierced-and-tattooed copy-shop employees have created their own exile community in the 'hoods of Wicker Park and Bucktown. At the epicenter is **Rainbo Club**, a former Polish social club where local hipsters and the occasional touring rocker hold forth in snug round booths along the wall. There's even a photo booth in back to accommodate tourists. If you can't be bothered with the chain-smoking crowd blocking the door, head over to **The Empty Bottle**, the reigning Ukrainian Village outpost of cool, where you'll find legions of purposefully disheveled twentysomething regulars roosting among the second-hand couches and bar stools. Even when live bands take over the stage, you can still converse comfortably over the noise with your buddies at the front of the bar or in the pool room. You've got a lot of seating options at **Danny's Tavern**, a warren of rooms in an old Victorian house that's been spiffed up with a recent re-do. The loafing vibe has been imported to Lake View at **Delilah's**, a dark, somewhat sinister bar where the bartender spins country classics on Wednesdays, and punk rock other nights. Follow the exposed electrical wiring upstairs for pinball and pool. A kinder, gentler breed packs the roomy beer garden with its outdoor pool table at **Sheffield's** in Lake View.

Dance fever... Flashy nightclubs open here every few years in spooky warehouses on the edge of downtown, and, yes, it is fun the first few months. The rest of the story is predictable: Carloads of suburbanites join the fun. Scenesters grow bored and flee. Fun is over. A line of anxious trendsters snakes down the street on weekends in front of **Crobar Night Club**, but the cavernous club's dark Gotham City decor and sprawling dance floor—one of the biggest around—makes the wait worth it. A pair of second-story lounges provide relief from the pounding house beat. You'll feel like you've stumbled into somebody's loft party at **Red Dog**, a Wicker Park dance club where a diverse aggregation of youngsters grooves to house and hip-hop music on the long, narrow dance floor. The lighting at the **Funky Buddha Lounge** is so low that you can't even *see* much of the dance floor. That's a shame, because the couples grooving to the DJ's deep-house spins are kind of an inspiration. Furnished with vintage sofas and kitschy-cool light fixtures, this slick new enterprise on a desolate stretch near downtown draws an interesting crowd, one you don't find at many Chicago clubs: sophisticated, racially mixed, slightly older than your typical club rats, with even a little sexual ambiguity. Things are more predictable at the bustling frat and sorority playpen known as **Drink**, an elaborately designed warehouse space with themed areas (take your pick: psychedelic, Moroccan, Mexican) and an overflowing dance floor propelled by the latest alternative and dance tunes. It's immensely popular, and it's easy to see why: Besides dancing, there are six bars, including a vodka station (look for the giant Absolut chandelier made of 336 empty bottles), late-night eats, and plenty of intimate hideaways. Sophisticated African-American patrons discoing at **The Clique** take the downtown club's upscale dress code to heart—if they don't, the tuxedoed bouncers will let them know. If the jammed upstairs discotheque isn't your style, you can seek refuge downstairs in a relaxed jazz lounge and comedy club. Don't be put off by **Neo**'s long alley entrance—you'll be surrounded by scrub-faced young professionals out for a nostalgic dose of early eighties tunes at this compact Lincoln Park dance den. Remember your black eyeliner for the weekly goth night. Those wild eighties nights when Chicago flirted with New York-style club life at the city's very own Limelight—housed in the fortress-like former Chicago Historical Society building—are long gone. But the same address now hosts the more subdued **Excalibur**, a sprawling for-the-masses amusement center crawling with suburbanites and tourists who *do* look like they're having fun. There are three dance spaces that include the adjacent "alternative" club, and the Dome Room. Happily, the gay disco **Berlin** has managed to retain its free-wheeling spirit after more than a decade in business, adding nongays and suburbanites to the mix on the weekends to a hospitable dance floor inexplicably able to absorb ever more spinning and twirling.

Where not to hear the blues

*For starters, the famed **Rush Street** nightlife zone really isn't Rush Street at all, but **Division Street** between Rush and Dearborn. Rush Street itself used to be home to a slew of great cabarets, bars, clubs, and restaurants—the center of Chicago's nightlife scene—which then spread to Division Street. Eventually the places on Rush closed as the street gentrified. The area is still referred to as Rush Street, but unless your idea of a good time is a keg party, there's no real rush to be found. Division is lined with the most hokey bars—crowded, loud, and obnoxious, with beefy bouncers manning most of the doorways. Wet T-shirt contests, hot legs contests, dollar nights, you name it, it's all depressingly here. But maybe Division Street is going the way of Rush Street—in the last few years a Starbucks coffee shop has opened, as has a huge Gap (the hundred millionth one in Chicago), and other stores that hopefully will squish out the bars. There are better bars to be found, believe me.*

NIGHTLIFE | THE LOWDOWN

Places to hear live rock... Local acts like Smashing Pumpkins, Liz Phair, and Veruca Salt, before they got too big for their britches, all played the stage at **Metro** (see Entertainment) in Wrigleyville, the city's preeminent rock venue. Owner Joe Shanahan has expanded his franchise into rocker haven Wicker Park at **Double Door**, a former biker bar with high pressed-tin ceilings, a beautiful long bar, and good acoustics for rock shows and more (acid jazzmeisters Liquid Soul are a Sunday night mainstay). The other major rock outlet in the area is **The Empty Bottle**, an arty club that usually books bands with impeccable indie credentials. **Lounge Ax** (see Entertainment) in the DePaul neighborhood still sells out for big-name alternative rock performers.

Places to hear live blues... Chicago's famous for smoky blues joints where legendary musicians jam seven nights a week, practically until dawn. At **Kingston Mines**, a fixture for three decades in Lincoln Park, two stages in a comfortably decrepit setting keep the music going without interruption. Female vocalists like Gloria Hardiman and Big Time Sarah are the specialty of **Blue Chicago**, a handsome forties-style room in River North with a die-hard crowd. On the southern edge of downtown, **Buddy Guy's Legends** welcomes both local talents and established stars (Dr. John, Koko Taylor, and Buddy Guy himself when he's in town) to a spacious room catering to tourists with its Hard-Rock-style displays of blues memorabilia. White college students and black locals share the ramshackle South Side digs of the legendary **Checkerboard Lounge**, where pros like Magic Slim and the Teardrops take the stage seven nights a week.

Places to hear live jazz... Get an early start at **Andy's Jazz Club**, a well-worn, friendly downtown jazz listening lounge where the first set kicks off at lunch. One of the city's most veteran jazz presenters, Joe Segal has moved his **Jazz Showcase** into a handsome new room in River North furnished with black-and-white photos of jazz legends who've played his clubs over the years. The caliber of music remains the same: a top-flight lineup of both national and local jazz acts. On the southern end of downtown, **The Cotton Club**, with a predominantly black clientele, is a classy white-walled jazz room that has boosted the careers of a number of talents (including saxophonist Art Porter and R&B superstar R. Kelly). The most intimate jazz room in town, the **Underground Wonder Bar** gets more interesting as the night wears on—it's a popular haunt of musicians looking for a pick-up gig on their way home for the night. Owner Lonie Walker sometimes takes the stage; watch for her Janis Joplin imitation. Bringing a little glamour to the local jazz scene, the **Green Dolphin Street** has converted an old autobody shop into a sophisticated forties-style nightclub with an attached restaurant that presents everything from big band to acid jazz. To hear jazz in a setting that hasn't much changed since jazz's golden age, nestle into a velvet booth at **The Green Mill**, a deco-ish uptown club once owned by one of Al Capone's henchmen. In its latest incarnation, the club has made a name for itself as one of the liveliest jazz venues in town, attracting a wildly eclectic crowd (all ages, classes, races) that keeps pouring in until the club's late-night closing. Some of the best jazz and cabaret vocalists show up at Lincoln Park's **Toulouse Cognac Bar**, a small romantic room done up in red velvet where the singers easily make eye contact with everybody in the room before the night is done.

Sports and suds... For starters, take your pick of most any place along North Clark Street near Wrigley Field, most notably **Cubby Bear**, which fills up with fans before and after Cubs games, or slick, pennant-festooned **Hi-Tops Cafe**, which overflows onto the sidewalk during Saturday afternoon gridiron games. The prototypical sports scene is **Gamekeepers**, a wood-paneled Lincoln Park bar with every game going on its multitudinous screens. For a more downtown crowd, try **The Hunt Club**, an upscale Rush Street saloon with wide-screen TVs and a large open bar in its airy main room.

Lesbian chic... The dearth of nightlife options for women (especially since the closing of Paris Dance) has made **Girlbar**, an out-and-proud dance bar located in straightsville Lincoln Park, a welcome and popular hangout for a young lipstick crowd. Pool tables and an outdoor deck make it as much of a hangout as a scene. No attitude or outfit is necessary to mix with the locals at **The Closet**, your standard-issue neighborhood dive with window-side stools and the famously bleached coif of the bartender.

NIGHTLIFE | THE LOWDOWN

Pinball and darts provide a few distractions, but the best seats in this basic black box are the bar stools peering onto Broadway. The windows really get steamed up on Bloody Mary Sundays and monthly heavy-metal nights.

Where the boys are... An evening stroll down a 10-block strip of North Halsted Street—the Main Street of the lakeside gay enclave known as Boys' Town—will keep any curious club crawler occupied late into the night. Excursions often start from **Roscoe's Tavern**, an inviting antique-laden saloon populated by a diverse mix of preppies, muscle boys, and tourists. Continue across the street to **Sidetrack**, a sleek video bar where the pretty-boy patrons ogle each other as much as the ubiquitous TV monitors showing Broadway musicals, Madonna tunes, and "Ab Fab" clips. On the Halsted strip, **Fusion** doesn't start pulsing until the festive Brazilian restaurant Rhumba clears its dining room for the night. Then the shirtless muscle boys start steaming up the large dance floor at this after-hours dance factory, which has a series of bars and also hosts touring disco divas. One of the only gay spots downtown is the friendly piano bar **Gentry**, a popular after-work stop with a cabaret room and a downstairs video lounge. Despite its name, **Big Chicks** has been overrun by a devoted clientele of gay misfits—a goateed, thrift-store-outfitted crowd drawn to the sparkling two-room Uptown bar by 50-cent midnight shots, a high-camp jukebox, free Sunday afternoon buffets, and an appreciative staff. The owner's idiosyncratic art collection alone makes it worth a visit. Way downtown from the gay ghetto, **The Generator** in River West lures a crowd to its sprawling wooden dance floor, packed with African-American men and a handful of women. Located below the Belmont el station, **Berlin** hasn't shown any signs of tiring as one of the city's reigning danceterias. Though it's a small room, really, Berlin maximizes its real estate with wall-to-wall stimuli: a mix of music from New Wave to techno, nonstop videos, go-go boys, and mirrors to check how the light is flattering you.

Neighborhood spots downtown and near North Side... If you're staying in the Loop, you'll have to venture a little farther afield if you don't want to spend the evening in a soulless hotel lobby bar. One downtown exception is **Kitty O'Shea's** at the Chicago Hilton and

Towers, a bar that manifests its Irish theme with imported Irish bartenders and traditional Irish music. An authentic spot that has weathered the onslaught of tourists pretty well is **Billy Goat Tavern** (see Dining), a legendary Chicago dive on lower North Michigan Avenue immortalized as the "cheezeburger, cheezeburger" joint on "Saturday Night Live." In the financial district, wheeler-dealers huddle at **Jesse Livermore's**, a comfortable downtown lounge with dark velvet curtains, brass chandeliers, and a fireplace that evokes the paneled study of some tycoon (perhaps the bar's namesake, a high-rolling New York trader of the 1920s). Look for the stainless steel door marking the entrance to **56 West**, a sleek underground lounge serving cocktails and a menu of eclectic eats to well-dressed patrons ensconced on leather banquettes. At this 1990s speakeasy, look out for a little attitude—it just seems to go with the territory wherever a doorman guards the portal. Thankfully the owners of the champagne and caviar bar **Narcisse** don't take themselves completely seriously. The new River North salon, resplendent in yards of draped fabric, gilded walls, and opulent chandeliers, even has cosmetic mirrors on the tables for people who take the bar's name to heart.

Neighborhood spots in Lincoln Park/Old Town... Just as its name suggests, **John Barleycorn Memorial Pub** is a generously proportioned English-style pub that exudes historic charm. The century-old building has functioned as a bar for much of its life, from twenties speakeasy to favored watering hole of John Dillinger. A longtime haunt of writers and actors, presided over by photographs of Irish literary lions (Yeats, Wilde, et al), **O'Rourke's** is a classic barroom devoted to conversation and the art of a well-poured Guinness—not a single TV in sight. It makes a good after-theater stop if you're seeing something at the Steppenwolf Theater nearby.

Neighborhood spots in Lake View/Wrigleyville... If you want to duck the army of dudes donning turned-back baseball caps on North Clark Street, the **Ginger Man Tavern** provides a sanctuary behind its big picture windows. A hipper, more laid-back clientele than you'll find in the rest of the neighborhood clusters around tightly packed tables and chairs up front or shoots pool in the larger back room. TVs are tuned to *Melrose Place* at **Hi-Tops Cafe**, where devotees of the Fox soap congregate. Even if you're not planning to take in one of the folkie/rock bands that are the mainstay of **Schubas Tavern**, the front bar is always a lively gathering place for fresh young neighborhood faces, and the attached Harmony Grill serves pretty good burgers and fries until late. An extensive beer list and an array of rooms to settle into with friends make **Sheffield's Wine and Beer Garden** a home-away-from-home for local twentysomethings. An important anchor on the gay scene is **Roscoe's Tavern**, a neighborhood haunt often disparaged by snobs who'll still buy a drink and survey the scene to see who's hanging out.

Neighborhood spots on the South Side... Travelers arriving at Midway Airport might consider stopping by **Baby Doll Polka Club**, where local polkaholics have been gathering for 40 years. The house band, the Merry Makers, play on weekends as middle-aged men spin their big-haired gals around the small dance floor. A Hyde Park institution, **Jimmy's Woodlawn Tap**, is a grungy grad student bar that hosts occasional improv performances and prose readings. Operated by the same family for generations, **Schaller's Pump** is the quintessential Bridgeport bar, where locals gather for dinner on vinyl red-checked tablecloths (there's a corned-beef-and-cabbage special on Thursdays) and sit around watching the Sox or the ten o'clock news. Check out the peephole on a side door for signs of the Prohibition past. One of the last vestiges of a vibrant South Side blues scene is the **Checkerboard Lounge**, where regulars sit in the ramshackle chairs alongside college students.

For people who wouldn't be caught dead drinking a Bud... The chalkboard menu at **Sheffield's Wine and Beer Garden** boasts 60-plus offerings, most of them regional microbrews. This Lake View tavern guides your choice with one recommended and one "bad" beer of the month and a free glossary of beer terms (from aftertaste to wheat beer). Take a peek at the brewing equipment on your way into **Goose Island Brewery**, the city's original microbrewery, which features a fermented repertoire of 40 rotating microbrews including its flagship Honker's Ale, which you'll find sold all over town. They're always ready for a special occasion at **Pops for Champagne**: The elegant Lake View music room stocks more than 125 kinds of sparkling wines. You can buy vino by the glass, or you can train your palate by sampling flights of Merlot, Chardonnay, and Pinot Noir at casual, cozy **Webster's Wine Bar** in Lincoln Park, which provides place mats labeled with the names of each of the four or five samples. Retro crazes converge at **Liquid Kitty**, a stylized seventies lounge (red and orange geometric-patterned walls, soul-funk soundtrack, leopard-print carpet) shaking up 40 different martinis (try the Dreamsicle). It was fleetingly the place of the moment when the trendies descended here in 1997; it's still far trendier than the neighboring dive bars and diners on the strip, though the upscale mid-twenty types who come here now aren't quite as cool as the room itself.

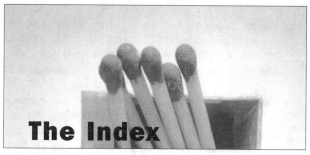

The Index

Andy's Jazz Club. A solid downtown place to while away the afternoon or evening listening to hard-working players.... *Tel 312/642–6805. 11 E. Hubbard St., Grand and State el stop. $3–10 cover.* **(see p. 160)**

Baby Doll Polka Club. It's across the road from Midway Airport—you can listen to "Roll Out the Barrel" while planes roll down the runway.... *Tel 773/582–9706. 6102 S. Central Ave. Midway el stop, transfer to #63 W bus.* **(see p. 164)**

Berlin. Veteran gay disco with a freaky pansexual crowd.... *Tel 773/348–4975. 954 W. Belmont Ave., Belmont el stop. Until 4am. $5 cover Fri–Sat.* **(see pp. 159, 162)**

Big Chicks. An out-of-the-way gay alternative to the Halsted Street party parade.... *Tel 773/728–5511. 5024 N. Sheridan Rd., Argyle el stop.* **(see p. 162)**

Blue Chicago. This lively blues club in the heart of the River North tourist zone offers two clubs for one cover.... *Tel 312/642–*

6261, 736 N. Clark St., Chicago and State el stop; closed Sun. Tel 312/661–0100, 536 N. Clark St., Grand and State el stop; closed Mon. $6–8 cover. **(see p. 160)**

Buddy Guy's Legends. The Grammy-winning Chicago guitarist owns this simple, acoustically superb blues hall that also serves up Louisiana-style soul food.... Tel 312/427–0333. 754 S. Wabash Ave., Harrison el stop. $6–15 cover. **(see p. 160)**

Checkerboard Lounge. A blues mecca for locals, tourists, and rock stars alike. Music begins nightly at 9:30pm. A secure parking lot is available across the street for minimal or no charge.... Tel 773/624–3240. 423 E. 43rd St. $5–7 cover. **(see pp. 160, 164)**

The Clique. Something for everyone at this African-American entertainment complex.... Tel 312/326–0274. 2347 S. Michigan Ave., Cermak el stop. Until midnight weeknights, 4am weekends with $10 cover. **(see p. 159)**

The Closet. Lesbians in the neighborhood call this unpretentious video bar home, but gay men and straights mix here too, especially after hours.... Tel 773/477–8533. 3325 N. Broadway, Belmont el stop. Until 4am. **(see p. 161)**

Coq d'Or. Late nights, customers settle into the wood-paneled bar's red Naughahyde banquettes or crowd around the small piano.... Tel 312/787–2200. 140 E. Walton St. (Drake Hotel), Chicago and State el stop. **(see p. 157)**

The Cotton Club. Named for the renowned Harlem club, this downtown jazz spot has an upscale African-American following. The Monday open mike draws big crowds. Dance club in back.... Tel 312/341–9787. 1710 S. Michigan Ave., Roosevelt Rd. el stop. Until 4am. $7–10 cover weekends. **(see p. 160)**

Crobar Night Club. This multilevel dance factory gets crowded with a roiling sea of bodies on the dance floor—adventure-seeking yuppies and suburbanites disguised in their best alternative rags.... Tel 773/413–7000. 1543 N. Kingsbury St., North and Clybourn el stop. Until 4am. Open Wed, Fri–Sun. $4–15 cover. **(see p. 158)**

Cubby Bear. One of Wrigleyville's bigger clubs, this spacious, multifloor-space keeps customers busy with pool, darts, and rock bands.... *Tel 773/327–1662. 1059 W. Addison St., Addison el stop. $5–10 cover* **(see p. 161)**

Danny's Tavern. A candle-lit Bucktown bar in a two-story house. Good beer selection.... *Tel 773/489–6457. 1951 W. Dickens St., Damen el stop.* **(see p. 158)**

Delilah's. Dark and alternative. Find your way to the bar and you'll be greeted with a choice of 50 beers and twice as much whiskey. On Saturdays the Psychotronic Film Society screens locally produced indie films.... *Tel 773/472–2771. 2771 N. Lincoln Ave., Diversey el stop.* **(see p. 158)**

Double Door. Wicker Park rock club for the obscure, the offbeat, and the up-and-coming (even the establishment: the Rolling Stones have played here). Pool tables downstairs in the Dirt Room.... *Tel 773/489–3160. 1572 N. Milwaukee Ave., Damen el stop. $6–10 cover.* **(see p. 160)**

Drink. Flavored vodkas and beverages served in buckets help this mega-club live up to its name. Live 70s-tribute band once a week.... *Tel 312/733–7800. 702 W. Fulton St., Clinton and Lake el stop. Until 4am. Closed Sun. $5 cover after 9pm Thur–Sat.* **(see p. 158)**

The Empty Bottle. A grunge clubhouse for twentysomethings in Ukrainian Village. Try the pasta at the attached late-night diner, Bite.... *Tel 773/276–3600. 1035 N. Western Ave.; Western el stop, transfer to #49 Western bus. $5–10 cover.* **(see pp. 157, 160)**

Excalibur. This River North mega-club offers a million things to do—a dance floor, huge game room, pool hall, and down-home restaurant.... *Tel 312/266–1944. 632 N. Dearborn St., Chicago and State el stop. $5–10 cover.* **(see p. 159)**

56 West. This sophisticated new late-night lounge aims for a jet-set crowd. The owners are sticklers for their dress code.... *Tel 312/527–5600. 56 W. Illinois St., Grand and State el stop. Closed Sun–Mon. Until 4am Thurs–Sat.* **(see p. 163)**

Funky Buddha Lounge. This dimly-lit dance-and-drink lair is a hot scene with high cover prices. Call ahead to reserve VIP

seating, which will cost you extra.... *Tel 312/666–1695. 728 W. Grand Ave., Chicago el stop. $15–20 cover.*
(see p. 158)

Fusion. The biggest dance floor on Halsted Street makes this a popular late-night destination for young multicultural party-ers.... *Tel 773/975–6622. 3631 N. Halsted St., Addison el stop. Until 4am. $8–15 cover.* **(see p. 162)**

Gamekeepers. Television monitors never leave your field of vision at this Lincoln Park sports bar. Kitchen snacks until midnight.... *Tel 773/549–0400. 345 W. Armitage Ave., Armitage el stop. Until 4am. $3 cover for occasional bands.*
(see p. 161)

The Generator. Nonstop infusions of house music keep the big dance floor at this black gay disco busy.... *Tel 312/243–8889. 306 N. Halsted St., Clinton el stop. Until 4am. Open Wed–Sun. $2–5 cover.* **(see p. 162)**

Gentry. You don't have to go far for your showtunes: This friend-ly gay cabaret has both a downtown and Halsted Street presence. Music starts at 5:30pm weeknights.... *Tel 312/664–1033, 440 N. State St., Grand and State el stop. Tel 773/348–1053, 3320 N. Halsted St., Belmont el stop.*
(see p. 162)

Ginger Man Tavern. This unpretentious Wrigleyville bar offers a huge selection of mircobrews on tap.... *Tel 773/549–2050. 3740 N. Clark St., Addison el stop.* **(see p. 163)**

Girlbar. The name says it all. Wednesday is "Boy Bar."... *Tel 773/871–4210. 2625 N. Halsted St., Fullerton el stop. Closed Mon. Cover $5 after 9pm.* **(see p. 161)**

Goose Island Brewery. Brew-pub restaurant with a handsome rectangular front bar.... *Tel 312/915–0071. 1800 N. Clybourn Ave., North and Clybourn el stop.* **(see p. 164)**

Green Dolphin Street. This retro-cool nightclub is an out-of-the-way place to catch a range of musical styles.... *Tel 773/395–0066. 2200 N. Ashland Ave., Armitage el stop. Main room closed Sun–Mon. $5–10 cover.* **(see p. 161)**

The Green Mill. This movie-set-perfect Uptown jazz club draws an eclectic crowd to nestle into cozy velvet booths to listen to swing, big band, and torch singers.... *Tel 312/878–5552. 4802 N. Broadway, Lawrence el stop. Until 4am. $3–7 cover.* **(see p. 161)**

Hi-Tops Cafe. This popular Wrigleyville saloon has a large bar up front, leading to an airy raftered room dominated by a big-screen TV. Cigar lounge upstairs.... *Tel 773/348–0009. 3551 N. Sheffield Ave., Addison el stop. $5 cover after 9pm Fri–Sat.* **(see pp. 161, 163)**

The Hunt Club. Upscale sports bar attracts a youngish crowd with a dance floor, pool, and cigar lounge.... *Tel 312/988–7887. 1100 N. State St., Chicago and State el stop. Until 4am. $3 cover weekends.* **(see p. 161)**

Jazz Showcase. A tuxedoed staff attends to you at one of the city's leading jazz clubs.... *Tel 312/670–BIRD. 59 W. Grand St., Grand and State el stop. $10–20 cover.* **(see p. 160)**

Jesse Livermore's. Clubby downtown bar across from the Chicago Board of Trade.... *Tel 312/786–5272. 401 W. LaSalle St., Van Buren and LaSalle el stop. Open until 10pm. Closed Sat–Sun.* **(see p. 163)**

Jimmy's Woodlawn Tap. A gritty University of Chicago hangout for smoking, drinking, and intellectualizing.... *Tel 773/643–5516. 1172 E. 55th St.* **(see p. 164)**

John Barleycorn Memorial Pub. Stately Lincoln Park saloon decorated with antique sailing vessels.... *Tel 773/348–8899. 658 W. Belden St., Fullerton el stop.* **(see p. 163)**

Kingston Mines. With two large rooms, this Chicago institution on the blues scene heats up with capacity crowds.... *Tel 773/477–4646. 2548 N. Halsted St., Fullerton el stop. Until 4am. $9–12 cover.* **(see p. 160)**

Kitty O'Shea's. Traditional Irish duos and trios perform every night at this hotel bar.... *Tel 312/922–4400, ext 4454. 720 S. Michigan Ave., Harrison and State el stop.* **(see p. 162)**

Liquid Kitty. This hipster martini bar in Ukrainian Village bombards you with grooviness. Attached is Celluloid Moviebar, showing second-run films.... *Tel 773/489–2700. 1807 W.*

NIGHTLIFE | THE INDEX

Division St., Division el stop. $7 cover Fri–Sat after 9pm.
(see p. 165)

Narcisse. This swank-o-rama scene in River North is a magnet for model-ish types and those who want to bask in the glow of their clear skin..... *Tel 312/787–2675. 710 N. Clark St., Chicago and State el stop.* **(see p. 163)**

Neo. Dependable dance den for college kids, clean-cut New Wave nostalgists, and leather-clad freaks.... *Tel 773/528–2622. 2350 N. Clark St., Fullerton el stop. Until 4am. Closed Wed–Thur and Sun. $2–5 cover.* **(see p. 159)**

O'Rourke's. Charming Irish pub.... *Tel 312/335–1806. 1625 N. Halsted St., North and Clybourn el stop.* **(see p. 163)**

Pops for Champagne. This sophisticated Lake View boîte features pages and pages of champagnes, as well as an array of wines and spirits.... *Tel 773/472–1000. 2934 N. Sheffield Ave., Belmont el stop. Most nights $5–9.50 cover.*
(see p. 164)

Rainbo Club. The art students clear out on Fridays to make way for slumming yuppies checking out the Wicker Park scene.... *Tel 773/489–5999. 1150 N. Damen Ave., Damen el stop.*
(see p. 157)

Red Dog. Get ready to sweat to the house beat at this urban dance pad overlooking the nightlife scene at North, Damen, and Milwaukee.... *Tel 773/278–1009. 1958 W. North Ave. (entrance in alley), Damen el stop. Until 4am. Closed Sun, Tues, Thurs. $6–10 cover.* **(see p. 158)**

Roscoe's Tavern. There's something for everyone at this popular gay bar: antique-filled front room with a large flowing bar; billiard area; a dark dance floor in back, outdoor patio.... *Tel 773/281–3355. 3356 N. Halsted St., Belmont el stop. $2 cover Sat after 10pm.* **(see pp. 162, 164)**

Schaller's Pump. This century-old South Side bar serves a menu of burgers and steaks.... *Tel 773/847–9378. 3714 S. Halsted St., 35th St. el stop.* **(see p. 164)**

Schubas Tavern. Live folk and country music is the focus of this old Schlitz saloon.... *Tel 773/525–2508. 3159 N.*

Southport Ave., Belmont el stop. $4–15 for live music.
(see p. 164)

Seasons Lounge. The large bar area at the Four Seasons Hotel is a restful oasis with a huge fireplace and plush furnishings.... Tel 312/280–8800. 120 Delaware Place, Chicago and State el stop. **(see p. 157)**

Sheffield's Wine and Beer Garden. It doesn't look like much from the street, but this Lake View corner bar draws a friendly postcollege crowd.... Tel 773/281–4989. 3258 N. Sheffield Ave., Belmont el stop. $1 cover weekends for beer garden. **(see p. 164)**

Sidetrack. This high-tech gay bar baby-sits some of the city's best-looking men with endless video clips. Rooftop deck open in warmer months.... Tel 773/477–9189. 3349 N. Halsted St., Belmont el stop. **(see p. 162)**

Signature Lounge. Sky-scraping view atop the John Hancock Center.... Tel 312/787–7230. 875 N. Michigan Ave., Chicago and State el stop. Until 12:30am Sun–Thur, 1:30am Fri–Sat. **(see p. 157)**

Toulouse Cognac Bar. Intimate cabaret, one of the city's premiere venues for homegrown and touring vocalists.... Tel 773/665–9071. 2140 N. Lincoln Park W., Armitage el stop or no. 151 Sheridan bus. Closed Sun. $5–15 cover with 2-drink min. **(see p. 161)**

Underground Wonder Bar. It's clear that everybody really loves music in this funky little jazz club with three performances a night.... Tel 312/266–7761. 10 E. Walton St., Chicago and State el stop. Until 4am. $3–6 cover. **(see p. 161)**

Webster's Wine Bar. This Lincoln Park bar caters to both the wine connoisseur and neophyte. The back library is a cigar lounge.... Tel 773/868–0608. 1480 W. Webster Ave., Fullerton el stop. **(see p. 165)**

Yvette Wintergarden. A mature, well-dressed crowd shows up at this French restaurant to see local jazz trios and occasional special guests.... Tel 312/408–1242. 311 S. Wacker Dr., Quincy el stop. Until 8pm weekdays, 11pm Fri–Sat. Closed Sun. **(see p. 157)**

NIGHTLIFE | THE INDEX

enterta

inment

Forget any
notions you may
have about the
Midwest as hope-
lessly square—
there are plenty of
boundary-pushing

artists in Chicago. The stock of creative folk is constantly renewed by students coming out of the universities and emigrants from all over the Midwest, and not everybody who makes it big here immediately jets off to the coasts—plenty of actors, musicians, and dancers, like regular nonartistic newcomers, find it such a *manageable* place to live that they end up staying. Though big Broadway imports often run for months, Chicagoans don't hold their breath for out of towners to grace their stages: the city hosts enough home-grown shows to keep more than 300 theater companies busy. In fact, many of the smaller offbeat theaters serve as a late-night alternative to the bar scene: some shows often don't start until 10:30pm (or later), and some even allow alcoholic beverages, if they don't happen to sell it themselves. Five professional sports teams also confer a certain kind of prestige on the city, while highbrow, world-class institutions like the Lyric Opera and the Chicago Symphony have given Chicago the serious outside validation it craves as the perennial second (now third) city.

Sources

The city's main alternative paper, the *Reader*, gets much of its heft from voluminous reviews, listings, and advertisements for concerts and performing arts. Published on Thursdays, the tabloid prides itself on providing the most complete theater coverage in the city, reviewing even the most obscure productions. More extensive profiles and analyses are carried in the *Chicago Tribune's* daily arts section and its "Friday" entertainment pullout. The competing *Sun-Times* is worth a look in its Friday "Weekend Plus" and Sunday "Showcase" sections. Look to the entertainment section in *N'Digo*, a free weekly tabloid, for an African-American perspective; *¡Exito!* is a Spanish-language free weekly that offers a weekly calendar of events of Latino-related events; and the city's predominant lesbian and gay newspaper, *Windy City Times*, offers its own spin on both gay and non-gay events. Tune into **WBEZ** (91.5 FM), the local National Public Radio affiliate, for erudite discussions of the latest cultural happenings. A few other comprehensive sources on the web are the *Chicago Tribune's* **Digital City** (http://chicago.digitalcity.com) and Microsoft's **Chicago Sidewalk** (http://chicago.sidewalk.com).

Getting Tickets

We're not sure what bothers us more about **Ticketmaster**:

175

the teeth-gnashing service charges or the way the telephone ticket reps repeat the logistics of your event ad nauseum. But if you're looking for tickets to concerts, Broadway imports, or sporting events, the monolithic ticket agent is still the only game in town. You can charge tickets on a credit card by calling 312/559–1212, or pay with cash only at one of their outlets at **Carson Pirie Scott & Co.** (1 S. State St.), **Tower Records** (2301 N. Clark St.), or several **Hot Tix** locations (see below). If you're willing to pay even bigger bucks, you can get tickets to just about any event by thumbing through the Yellow Pages for one of more than 40 ticket brokers (all must be licensed by the state). Two reputable ones are **Tower Ticket Service** (tel 312/454–1300) and **Gold Coast Tickets** (tel 312/644–6446). They take credit card orders by phone and deliver overnight or the same day (of course, adding various commissions based on availability, demand, etc.). Less legitimate, and a misdemeanor in Illinois, is selling scalped tickets. But take a walk around Wrigley Field or the United Center on a game day and you'll see that the law hasn't exactly driven the illegal ticket trade underground. Be wary of what you buy on the

Chicago in the movies, part 3—The Suburbs

Director/writer/producer John Hughes was responsible for a raft of movies that immortalized the lakeshore Chicago suburbs: Sixteen Candles (1984), The Breakfast Club (1985), Home Alone (1990); in Ferris Bueller's Day Off (1986), an impish Matthew Broderick borrowed his pal's dad's Porsche for a joy ride into the city. The great Ordinary People (1980), directed by Robert Redford and starring Mary Tyler Moore, Judd Hirsch, and Timothy Hutton, was filmed mostly in affluent Lake Forest. Then, of course, there's Risky Business (1983), in which Tom Cruise popularized parading around in your underwear (gay bars in Chicago now have underwear parties where everyone wears nothing but their skivvies). Mike Myers and Dana Carvey played pubescent public-access heroes in Wayne's World (1992), but to Chicagoans the real star was former Blackhawks hockey star Stan Mikita, who made a cameo appearance as the owner of a donut shop.

ENTERTAINMENT | INTRODUCTION

street: you don't want to find that you've bought a ticket to last week's game. You don't always have to resort to such desperate measures, especially if a theater outing is on your agenda. Besides full price Ticketmaster events, **Hot Tix** (tel 312/977–1755), run by the nonprofit **League of Chicago Theatres**, also sells half-price, day-of-show tickets to many theatrical productions, concerts, and dance performances in the city and suburbs. Available by credit card, check, or cash, tickets can be purchased only *in person* at several outlets: the Chicago Visitor Center inside the Historic Water Tower, at Michigan and Chicago Avenues, across from Marshall Field's in the **Loop** (108 N. State St.), Tower Records, and at the **City Parking Garage** in **Evanston** (1616 Sherman Ave.). Getting there early always helps ensure that you get to choose from the widest selection of shows; ticket availability varies from day to day, but most don't sell out until later in the day. The outlets are open daily, and tickets to many weekend performances are sold on Friday. If you want to pay a little extra, you can call the **Hot Tix info line** (tel 900/225–2225 or 888/225–8844) for tickets available that day; calls are $1 a minute, and they say the average call will cost you $3. In general, it's pretty easy to see smaller off-Loop shows simply by leaving your name on the theater's answering machine; your place usually will be guaranteed if you show up at least 15 minutes before showtime, and someone will return your call if they're already sold out. Larger theaters guarantee seats by using plastic over the phone, though you might want to save on the minimal service charge by stopping by the box office. A few theaters, including the biggest ones in town, offer discount or half-price tickets at the box office the night of the performance. Many others reguarly reduce the price of admission for students and seniors.

The Lowdown

The theater establishment... Every year, scads of theater grads dream of following the trajectory of the highly regarded **Steppenwolf Theatre Company**, which was born out of a North Shore church basement in the seventies and has settled down into its own $8 million theater complex in Lincoln Park. While these days Steppenwolf ensemble members—Gary Sinise, John Malkovich, Joan Allen, and Laurie Metcalf, among them—show up everywhere from film to TV, they remain vested in the theater that launched their careers, and have in recent seasons returned to Chicago to help drum up ticket sales and audience interest (notably Sinise in a recent revival of *A Streetcar Named Desire*).

Steppenwolf continues to be a major presence in the city, with world premieres and inventive adaptations marked by visual pyrotechnics; their latest production is always the subject of much scrutiny. Of course, risk-taking is, well, risky, and these perpetrators of the in-your-face Chicago acting school still occasionally prove too daring for audiences. The other biggie in town is the **Goodman Theatre**, the city's oldest and largest resident theater, which offers a season of crowd-pleasing plays and musicals; often premieres by the likes of David Mamet, director Frank Galati, and Edward Albee—with edgier works in its smaller studio theater. Lavish Broadway musicals trucking into town put up their tents at the **Auditorium Theatre**, a Louis Sullivan-designed architectural gem with wonderful acoustics; a 1906 vaudeville house, the **Shubert Theatre**; a refurbished 1921 movie palace, the **Chicago Theatre**, which the Disney organization runs as a showcase for its musical stage shows; and, around the corner in what's really starting to look like a Loop theater district, the freshly rehabilitated Oriental Theater, which has been re-christened the **Ford Center for the Performing Arts**, reopening in October 1998 with the new musical *Ragtime*. For the works of an Englishman with more impeccable theater credentials, check out **Shakespeare Repertory**, which mounts three solid productions a year; in 1999, its new digs at Navy Pier should really help to bring the Bard to the masses.

On the fringes... The Chicago theater scene really came alive during the eighties—you can hardly walk a block on the North Side without stumbling across a storefront theater. On any given night, a small production is guaranteed an audience of, say, eight people: actors' moms, actors' friends who are also actors, and perhaps even a few nonacting innocent bystanders. Though some of the stuff can be raw or amateurish, a few of the more original, exciting shows in town toil for months in modest, out-of-the-way theaters until a word-of-mouth buzz attracts the notice of the downtown critics and vaults the show onto a higher-profile stage. Among the next generation, **Lookingglass Theatre Company**, an ensemble of twenty-something Northwestern theater grads, has earned its media-darling status with highly physical, lyrically staged productions of literary works, as well as original works rooted in company members' personal obsessions. They even have a certified star in their founding ranks: sensitive guy David Schwimmer of NBC's sitcom "Friends." Another promising Northwestern-spawned company is **Roadworks Productions**, a more recent crop of graduates who produced some critical smashes in the last few seasons; their lineup includes daring adaptations and Chicago premieres. Tired of Hollywood's pillaging of old TV shows? Blame the scandalous improvisers at **Annoyance Theatre**, who still haven't lived up to (or lived down) the runaway success of their *The Real Live Brady Bunch* a few years back. One of our favorite things about this Wrigleyville theater is its goofy show names (*Shake, Shake, Shake, Shake, Shake, Shake, Shake Your Ass, Brainwarp, the Baby Eater*). They claim the city's longest-running musical, *Coed Prison Sluts*, a sophomoric parody of jailhouse films—introduced as being "just like *Annie*, except she's in prison and she's a whore"—that's chockful of anal-sex jokes and other naughty pranks guaranteed to get the frat boys in the audience laughing. Much easier on delicate ears is the late-night hit *Too Much Light Makes the Baby Go Blind*, performed by the **Neo-Futurists**. They promise "30 plays in 60 minutes," an entertaining evening (Friday and Saturday at 11:30pm or 7pm Sunday) with much left to chance: audience members pay $4 plus the roll of a six-sided die (therefore, $5–$10) and determine the random order of short skits by shouting out their assigned numbers to performers. The group has written more than 3,000 plays, so no evening is ever the same. Also in the neighborhood is **Bailiwick Repertory**, a busy theater space that gives young companies a chance to develop their craft and produces a summer gay pride series. Next door is the **Theatre Building**, another rental complex that's always worth checking out to see what's playing. Chicago's only gay theater, **About Face**, has quickly built a solid reputation in only a few years with fresh, ambitious productions of gay-themed works, such as a recent revival of *Boys in the Band*. In 1998 About Face moved into its own space in the heart of the gay ghetto, Boystown. It's a hike down to 75th Street for the city's most prominent African-American theater, **ETA Creative Arts Foundation**, well-respected for its top-notch staging of serious dramas by black playwrights.

Classical sounds... It's easy to slip into hyperbole when referring to the **Chicago Symphony Orchestra**, but we'll do it anyway: The 110-member body, now under the baton of musical director Daniel Barenboim, is one of the country's top orchestras, in large measure because of a peerless brass section chaired by one of the world's finest trumpeters, Adolph Herseth, and its principal horn player, Dale Clevenger. A traditionally strong wind section also makes the CSO popular among fans of Strauss, Mahler, and late Beethoven. Even when concerts are sold out, it's worth stopping by the night of the performance to nab turned-back tickets from subscribers. Their home base, **Orchestra Hall**, reopened in 1997 after a $105-million renovation that sharpened the auditorium's less-than-perfect acoustics (local legend claims that CSO founder Theodore Thomas died a few weeks after Daniel Burnham's concert hall debuted in 1905, so horrified was he by the acoustics). It's now the centerpiece of **Symphony Center,** an expanded cultural center with a new recital hall, an education center, and a fine restaurant, Rhapsody (see Dining). Along with the CSO, the Symphony Center hosts a series of jazz, classical, and chamber music concerts, piano recitals, and the occasional vocalist. Also playing at the Symphony Center, the **Chicago Civic Orchestra**, the CSO's "farm team" of students and semiprofessional musicians, has a similar repertoire, but experiments more with new works by young composers—it's easier for them to do that, since their tickets are free. The CSO shares its summer home, the pastoral North Shore music venue **Ravinia**, with visiting orchestras, chamber music ensembles, and soloists. Though the music ostensibly draws people to this idyllic, tree-covered park, there's also the competition to out-Martha-Stewart everyone else with your outdoor concert accoutrements: to bring the china or not to bring the china? Right in the city's front yard, the **Grant Park Music Festival**, the last free classical concert series in the country, offers summer concerts five nights a week at the **Petrillo Music Shell** by the **Grant Park Symphony Orchestra** and the **Grant Park Symphony Chorus**, composed of members of the **Lyric Opera** and other vacationing musicians. Here's a tip: Skip the grass and move up front to avoid the amplified version of events on stage. Empty seats in the season ticket-holders' section are released 15 minutes before each performance.

What's opera, doc?... Chicago may be a sports-mad town, but passes to the **Lyric Opera of Chicago** compete with Bulls seats for being the toughest ticket in town. Over the last couple of decades, the Lyric has vaulted into the ranks of the opera world's heavy hitters with a string of financially successful *and* artistically ambitious seasons. Much of the credit goes to the late Ardis Krainik, the longtime Lyric boss who presided over the opera's ascendancy until her death in 1997. Along with the usual sturdy museum pieces from the opera canon, the Lyric also stages 20th-century works, including a few experimental pieces, just to keep audiences on their toes. It may not have the cachet of the Lyric, but the **Chicago Opera Theater** makes opera accessible to the masses. For starters, all of the works (mostly American operas) are sung in English; what the company saves on supertitles it can spend on professional singer-actors, costumes, and sets, often coming up with creative reinterpretations of classic operas. While opera snobs may be disappointed here, tickets are less pricey and an easier buy, and a smaller venue gives audiences a degree of intimacy you won't find at the Civic Opera House (unless you've got floor seats).

Men in tights... Using a variety of venues around town for its shows and festivals, Chicago dance often gets lost in the shuffle among other performing arts. Dance flowers in the spring when many of the city's major companies come together for the Spring Festival of Dance, a six-week series of performances at the downtown **Auditorium Theatre** and other venues around the city. Classical ballet had long struggled for a foothold in Chicago, but that's changed since the **Joffrey Ballet of Chicago** moved here from Manhattan in 1995. The company, which continues to be led by its cofounder Gerald Arpino, performs regularly in the city, during the Spring Festival of Dance and around the holidays with its Victorian American staging of *The Nutcracker*. The other classical troupe, **Ballet Chicago**, is a mere blip on the cultural radar, with no permanent corps of dancers and one annual full-length ballet in the spring. An exciting local company with national aspirations is **Hubbard Street Dance Chicago**, a 22-member ensemble guided by Broadway veteran Lou Conte. Its technical mastery has earned it star status, though its blend of jazz, ballet, and modern dance is crowd-pleasingly safe. Hubbard Street dancers often make the leap from the **River North Dance Company**, a younger, hipper troupe strong on jazz, that performs commercial, though highly skilled, MTV-inspired choreography. Vibrant tribal costumes, energetic drumming, and traditional dance stress the African and African-American experience in performances by the widely touring Muntu Dance Theater of Chicago. The center for modern dance in the city, the **Dance Center-Columbia College Chicago**, provides a venue for a lot of hometown performers as well as touring guest artists from around the world including DanceAfrica, a celebration of African and African-American dance and music. If you enjoy getting close enough to feel dancers sweat, tiny **Links Hall** presents experimental, often raw performances by young dancers and choreographers, as well as returning veterans.

In concert... New World Music Theatre is your basic theater-under-the-stars—it's fine when you feel like driving a million miles out to the suburbs and indulging in a rock concert spectacle with 30,000 other people. Teenagers make out in the grass plots in back. More rarefied is **Ravinia Park**, summer home of the Chicago Symphony and an eclectic menu of dance, opera, jazz, and entertainers from Mel Torme to Mary Chapin Carpenter. A mix of music, dance, and theater moves front and center at the **Skyline Stage**, a 1,500-seat open-air theater under a pristine white canopy on Navy Pier. The name **House of Blues** is a bit of a misnomer, since this venue books musical acts that span the musical scale, from alternative rock to swing to reggae. Performers take the stage in an ornate faux—European opera house exuberantly embellished with owner Isaac Tigrett's sprawling collection of Mississippi Delta folk art (check out the first-balcony bar, created by local outsider artist Mr. Imagination). Co-owned by Dan Aykroyd—yes, Elwood Blues himself, who smashed up hundreds of police cars in Daley Plaza in the first *Blues Brothers* movie—the House of Blues complex also encompasses a Southern-style restaurant

ENTERTAINMENT | THE LOWDOWN

(with live blues daily) and a new blues-themed hotel, all carved out of the base of the corncob-shaped Marina City on the north side of the Chicago River. Before they hit stadiums (or perhaps on the long slide down), a lot of testosterone-infused rock acts come through **The Vic**, a Lake View theater dating to the teens that doubles as a second-run movie house. Another mid-size venue, **Park West**, is a more upscale nightclub that brings in an assortment of alternative rock, reggae, and jazz acts; there's not a bad seat in the house. Right up the street from Wrigley Field, **Metro** is the granddaddy of rock clubs, a former theater that's a good grungy place to see many touring acts before they're booked into bigger venues. Get there early to claim a seat in the balcony, unless you want to join the mosh pit at center stage. The creative booking of **Lounge Ax**'s owners has made this DePaul rock club a place to check out upcoming acts, both local bands and touring artists, though popular shows pack the narrow rock room so tight that it's tough to see much of anything if you're not ensconced up front. The bands are slightly more obscure at **The Empty Bottle** (see Nightlife), a Ukrainian Village club that attempts to expand the musical palate of its alt.rock regulars with a couple of experimental jazz nights and a dance-hall DJ party. With a reputation as an adventurous presenter of international and local music, the not-for-profit **HotHouse**, which closed its Wicker Park club two years ago, has brought eclectic musical life to the Loop since it reopened in 1998 in a spacious downtown location. You can practically make eye contact with singer-songwriters from the Austin-Nashville axis that appear on stage at **Schubas Tavern**, a former Schlitz beerhall (see Nightlife). You'll find a mix of folk, country, bluegrass, and other traditional forms at concerts sponsored by the **Old Town School of Folk Music**, the oldest training ground for folk music in the country. The school long ago outgrew its original home in Lincoln Park, and by the fall of 1998 should be settled into larger quarters, a 1930s art deco library out in the Lincoln Square neighborhood that is being outfitted with what promises to be an intimate, acoustically superb 420-seat auditorium. (Children's programs will continue at the old location, 909 W. Armitage Avenue.)

Comedy tonight... Improvisational comedy has spawned a bit of a cottage industry in Chicago. Of course, tourist magnet **Second City** looms large over the burgeoning scene, with its comedy revues skewering local politics and pop culture, capped each night by improvised sketches. The show's format—sketch, blackout, sketch—had gone stale in recent years, until the company shook things up by hiring away some of the city's best improvisers and borrowing a few tricks from other improv groups. But you'll often find more experimental stuff from a number of quick-witted newcomers. Training ground for funny guys like Mike Myers and the late Chris Farley, **ImprovOlympic** has energized the improv scene with long-form productions—wholesome, clean-cut twenty-somethings taking improv workshops invent full-length plays from single audience suggestions. Enterprising graduates of the group often turn up with their own spin-off projects at **Annoyance Theatre** (a midnight show called Screw Puppies). Another group taking up the long form is **The Free Associates**, an ensemble that hilariously sends up anything from Tennessee Williams plays *(Cast on a Hot Tin Roof)* and Brontë novels *(Blithering Heights)* to detective mysteries and TV hospital melodramas. While the standup comedy rage has (blessedly) ebbed, Raymond Lambert figured there was still something missing from the scene: he opened **All Jokes Aside** to showcase some very funny African-American and Latino comics who weren't getting gigs at other clubs in town. In Old Town, **Zanies** reigns as the big professional comedy club in town by hosting marquee-name comedians from TV.

The spoken word... The thriving performance and poetry scene here is noted for the number of women doing one-woman shows. Since the demise of a legendary club called Lower Links a few years ago, performers have scattered across a number of theater spaces and clubs. If you have a pen, a crisp cocktail napkin, and an urge to share your pain, that's all you need to participate in the long-running Sunday-night "Poetry Slam" at **The Green Mill** (see Nightlife), a vintage jazz club. The raucous evening features an open mike, followed by a competition pitting street poets against each other. Former champs have gone on to performance careers, but many in this democratic show go back to their drinks after the judges are through with them. **Guild Complex** sponsors a weekly poetry performance every Wednesday in Wicker Park, as well as a wide range of readings and workshops. The auditorium at the **Museum of Contemporary Art** (see Diversions) is also a venue to watch for cutting-edge performance art.

Da sports... "Saturday Night Live" has made sure that Chicago will forever be linked in popular imagination with rib-eating, beer-slurping, linguistically challenged sports fans. Of course, come to think of it, in a lot of cases SNL wasn't too far off the mark. (Just try making your way through one of the brats and Old Style tailgate parties in Soldier Field's parking lot before a Bears game.) Chicago fans are indulging in citywide denial over the inevitable disassembling of the five-time world champion **Chicago Bulls**; most obstinately refuse to face the fact that someday soon Mike will hang up his Air Jordans for real. So while you can, try to get a seat inside the spanking-new **United Center**, the successor to the famously ear-splitting Chicago Stadium, which now rests in stadium heaven along with the old Comiskey Park, former home of the **Chicago White Sox** baseball team. Now in a new mall-like stadium, also called **Comiskey Park** ("Sox Park" to locals), the Sox tradition-ally attract blue-collar, South Side, and south-suburban fans. Saturday-night fireworks and Monday-night half-price tickets are good incentives to keep in mind. Sox fans tend to be hardcore baseball lovers, who often deride the North Side's **Chicago Cubs** as a yuppie team. But the Cubs and **Wrigley Field**, one of baseball's oldest parks, occupy a special place in people's hearts, not only in Chicago but all over the country (thanks to cable transmitted WGN-TV). The lovable losers haven't made it to the World Series since before the second World War (even then they lost the Series), but ducking work to sit in the bleachers for an afternoon game is a summer ritual. Wrigley's ivy-covered outfield and manu-ally-operated scoreboard are throwbacks to baseball as it used to be—back when the late Harry Caray, longtime "voice of the Cubs," was just a cub himself. While base-ball divides the city, football brings it together: the **Chicago Bears** still enjoy the goodwill brought by NFL founder and former owner George Halas Sr.; his son, coach George "Papa Bear" Halas Jr.; and a tradition of big-name players from Dick Butkus to William "Refrigerator" Perry. It's been a few years since he led the team, but Mike Ditka, the prototype for the SNL gag, still retains the moniker "Da Coach." You practically have to inherit Bears season tickets these days, and most games are sold out (single tickets go on sale, and get snapped up, in early summer). If you must see the Bears, prepare to use a broker or a scalper, or pack a parka for a frigid late-season game when saner fans stay home by the TV. And then there is the cult of **Chicago Blackhawks** hockey fans—hard-working people from factory workers to CEOs—who with their impassioned vocalizing made the old Chicago Stadium a death-defyingly loud place for visiting teams. The larger United Center has diluted things a bit, but you should still observe three rules at a Blackhawks game: 1) Hate the long-time owners, the Wirtz family, and never, *never* forgive them for trading away Bobby Hull more than two decades ago; 2) When the players set up for a power play, shout "SHOOT! SHOOT!" at the top of your lungs; and 3) No matter how much the team sucks, stick by the hard-working players, knowing that you love hockey and no one else in town really cares.

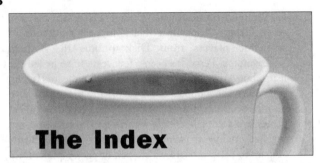

The Index

About Face Theatre. A company dedicated to gay-themed drama—original works, adaptations, and revivals.... *Tel 312/409–4863. 3212 N. Broadway, Belmont stop. $12–18.* **(see p. 178)**

All Jokes Aside. This comedy club on the Near South Side features a predominantly African-American roster. Phone reservations are accepted, or stop by the box office after 6pm; jeans and gym shoes are frowned upon.... *Tel 312/ 922–0577. 1000 S. Wabash St., Roosevelt el stop. $5.75–12.75 and two-drink minimum. Wed–Sun.*
(see p. 183)

Annoyance Theatre. Wide-open warehouse theater with gross-out antics onstage.... *Tel 773/929–6200. 3747 N. Clark St., Addison el stop. Tickets $5–12 (no reservations).*
(see pp. 178, 183)

Auditorium Theatre. The original home of the symphony and the opera, Adler and Sullivan's 4,000-seat masterpiece offers the finest acoustics in the city.... *Tel 312/902–1500 (Ticketmaster Arts Line). 50 E. Congress Pkwy., Harrison el stop. Tickets $15–57.50.* **(see pp. 177, 180)**

Bailiwick Repertory. The stage lights rarely go dark in the complex's three theater spaces, with a constant stream of adventurous plays.... *Tel 773/883–1090. 1229 W. Belmont Ave., Belmont el stop. $15–20.* **(see p. 178)**

Ballet Chicago. A small classical ballet company that presents an annual full-length production during the Spring Festival of Dance.... *Tel 312/251–8838. Offices at 185 N. Wabash Ave., suite 2300. Tickets $16–46.* **(see p. 180)**

Chicago Bears. Season tickets passed down through the generations have contributed to years of sold-out games at Soldier Field. If you miss the early summer offering of single tickets, your best bets are going through a ticket broker, showing up at the game hoping to find a few (scalped) extras, or packing a parka for a frigid late-season game when saner fans stay home by the TV.... *Tel 847/615–2327. Soldier Field, Lake Shore Dr. and 16th St., Roosevelt el stop. $33–52. Aug–Dec.* **(see p. 184)**

Chicago Blackhawks. The defense-oriented hockey team has made the playoffs several times in recent years but a poor draft over the last decade has kept the team in the NHL's second tier. Still, don't think of showing up to root for the other team. Just don't.... *Tel 312/559–1212 (Ticketmaster) or 312/455–7000 (offices). United Center, 1901 W. Madison St. $15–75. Sept–Apr.* **(see p. 185)**

Chicago Bulls. Just another NBA team with a forward named Mike and a bunch of other guys who've won the championship two or three times. Tickets are nearly impossible to get.... *Tel 312/455–4000. United Center, 1901 W. Madison St. $20–140 ($425 courtside). Oct–June.*
(see p. 184)

Chicago Civic Orchestra. This training body of the Chicago Symphony Orchestra performs in frequent sold-out concerts at Orchestra Hall. Tickets are free, but must be reserved for a small handling fee in advance.... *Tel 800/223–7114 or 312/294–3000. 220 W. Michigan Ave., Jackson el stop. Sept–June.* **(see p. 179)**

Chicago Cubs. They've pretty much been in a slump for the last half-century, but no matter—the bleachers are filled every game, day or night, with fans drawn by Wrigley Field's ivy-covered outfield, manually operated scoreboard.... *Tel 800/347–CUBS (outside Illinois) or 773/831–CUBS (Ticketmaster). Wrigley Field, 1060 W. Addison St., Addison el stop. $6–21. Apr–Oct.* **(see p. 184)**

Chicago Opera Theater. Opera for the rest of us. The company emphasizes American performers and composers and uses a mid-size theater with the goal of making the genre inviting to the non-black-tie crowd.... *Tel 773/292–7578.*

60 E. Balbo Ave. Tickets $25–55. June, Nov, April.
(see p. 180)

Chicago Symphony Orchestra. This top-ranked orchestra has a devoted audience that follows them from their downtown home at the Symphony Center to their summer residence at north-suburban Ravinia. Students and seniors get a discount.... *Tel 312/294–3000. 220 W. Michigan Ave., Jackson el stop. $10–91 ($165 box seats). Sept–June (Orchestra Hall); June–Sept (Ravinia).* **(see p. 179)**

Chicago Theatre. Restored 4,000-seat house at the head of State Street.... *Tel 312/902–1500 (Ticketmaster). 175 N. State St., Washington el stop. Tickets $18–55.*
(see p. 177)

Chicago White Sox. The city's South Side team has played consistently better than the Cubs over the years, but even Saturday night fireworks can't compete with the devotion Chicagoans hold for the crosstown ball club. That said, Sox fans show up to watch *the game*, so it's beside the point that they've been saddled with a soulless ballpark.... *Tel 312/831–1769 (Ticketmaster) or 312/924–1000 (office). Comiskey Park, 333 W. 35th St., Sox/35th el stop. $10–22. Apr–Oct.* **(see p. 184)**

Cominsky Park. See Chicago White Sox above.

Dance Center-Columbia College Chicago. This hub for modern dance in the city keeps a busy year-round schedule. The uptown setting is a bit edgy, but there's a paid parking lot across the street.... *Tel 773/989–3310. 4730 N. Sheridan Rd., Lawrence el stop. $10–25. Sept–May.*
(see p. 181)

ETA Creative Arts Foundation. This highly regarded African-American company stages serious drama in its 200-seat theater.... *Tel 773/752–3955. 7558 S. Chicago Ave. $20 mainstage.* **(see p. 178)**

Ford Center for the Performing Arts (Oriental Theatre). Scheduled to open in October 1998, this 2,000-seat former movie palace has been restored as a Broadway musical venue.... *Tel 312/902–1500 (Ticketmaster). 24 W.*

Randolph St., Washington and State el stop. $32.50–67.50. **(see p. 177)**

The Free Associates. Practitioners of long-form improvisational comedy.... *Tel 773/975-7171. Ivanhoe Theater, 750 W. Wellington St., Belmont el stop. $10–12.* **(see p. 183)**

Goodman Theatre. Goodman doesn't seem afraid to take a few risks even on its mainstage, a comfy 683-seat theater with pleasing sightlines and a proscenium-arch stage. Half-price, day-of-performance tickets (students $10). The theater begins selling extra tickets at 1pm for matinees and 6pm for evening shows. Rarely is anyone turned away.... *Tel 312/443-3800. 200 S. Columbus Dr. (eastern side of the Art Institute), Monroe el stop. Tickets $28–40 mainstage, $19–25 studio.* **(see p. 177)**

Grant Park Music Festival. The Chicago Park District's free summer concert festival. Concerts are Wed–Sun at 7:30pm.... *Tel 312/742-4763. Petrillo Music Shell, Grant Park, Columbus and Jackson drives, Jackson el stop. June–Aug.* **(see p. 179)**

Guild Complex. This not-for-profit literary organization hosts poetry readings, open-mike nights, and writing workshops.... *Tel 773/278-2210. Chopin Theater, 1543 W. Division St., Division el stop. $3–10.* **(see p. 184)**

HotHouse. This downtown venue features an eclectic brew of local and world music in an 8,000-square-foot downtown loft.... *Tel 773/235-2334. 31 E. Balbo Ave., Harrison el stop. $5–25.* **(see p. 182)**

House of Blues. The Chicago flagship of the chain is anchored by a gilded music hall, plus a restaurant, hotel, and, of course, a gift shop. Gospel brunch on Sundays.... *Tel 312/923-2000 or 312/559-1212 (Ticketmaster). 329 N. Dearborn St., Grand and State el stop. $5–75.*
(see p. 181)

Hubbard Street Dance Chicago. One of the only companies in the country to perform Twyla Tharp's pieces, the city's premiere dance troupe, founded in 1978, will be based at the Chicago Music and Dance Theatre when it opens in

ENTERTAINMENT | THE INDEX

1997; until then it performs at various sites around town.... *Tel 312/850–9744. $16–46. Apr–May.*

(see p. 181)

ImprovOlympic. This theater hosts Chicago's top improvisers together on Monday nights, as well as more structured shows staged upstairs in a 100-seat space.... *Tel 773/880–0199. 3541 N. Clark St., Addison el stop. $8.*

(see p. 183)

Joffrey Ballet of Chicago. This 33-dancer classical ballet troupe incorporates members of the former New York company and a few dancers stolen from Ballet Chicago (see above).... *Tel 312/739–0120. Offices at 70 E. Lake St., suite 1300. $17–50.* (see p. 180)

Links Hall. An intimate second-floor studio in Lake View is a popular venue for modern dance, experimental choreography, and performance art.... *Tel 773/281–0824. 3435 N. Sheefield Ave., Addison el stop. $5–10.* (see p. 181)

Lookingglass Theatre Company. Original, highly physical, intellectually curious theater is performed in three big shows a year at a variety of venues. There are a limited number of $10 tickets available before performances.... *Tel 773/477–9257. Offices at 2936 N. Southport Ave. $16–21. Sept–May.* (see p. 177)

Lounge Ax. A dependable neighborhood club that's the place to hear bands only you and your coolest friends have heard of. Tickets are occasionally sold in advance.... *Tel 773/525–6620. 2438 N. Lincoln Ave., Fullerton el stop. $3–10.* (see p. 182)

Lyric Opera of Chicago. A-list singers, spectacular sets, and the regal Civic Opera House make the Lyric one of the toughest-to-find tickets in town. Check with the box office for turned-back tickets the day of performance.... *Tel 312/332–2244. 20 N. Wacker Dr., Randolph and Wells el stop. $27–125. Sept–Feb.* (see pp. 179, 180)

Metro. A Chicago institution, this sturdy old theater can be crowded, sweaty, and smoky when you pack in throngs of alterative-rock fans. Save on Ticketmaster fees by buying advance tickets at the club's box office in the adjacent record shop (no phone orders). Shows sell out quickly.... *Tel 773/549–0203. 3730 N. Clark St., Addison el stop. $5–20.* **(see p. 182)**

Neo-Futurists. Located above the Nelson Funeral Home, this theater group offers one-acts and other experimental stuff. They don't take reservations, so show up early.... *Tel 773/275–5255. 5153 N. Ashland Ave., Montrose el stop, walk to #9 Ashland bus. $5–10. Fri–Sun.* **(see p. 178)**

New World Music Theatre. Well, at least you're outside. The view from the pavilion seats isn't all that bad, while the cheaper grass plots in back offer close-ups of teenagers making out while big-name rockers take the stage.... *Tel 312/559–1212 (Ticketmaster). 19100 S. Ridgeland Ave., Tinley Park. $15–50. May–Sept.* **(see p. 181)**

Old Town School of Folk Music. This long-established school has welcomed all the major players, from Peter Seeger to Alison Krauss, to its 300-seat concert hall and other venues in the city. The offerings now also embrace jazz, world music, Native American, Celtic, Latin, and Cajun. A Sunday showcase series introduces emerging artists.... *Tel 773/525–7793. 4544 N. Lincoln Ave., Western el stop. $8–18.* **(see p. 182)**

Orchestra Hall. Centerpiece of the new Symphony Center, this sublime 1905 hall designed by Daniel Burnham is home to the Chicago Symphony Orchestra, the Chicago Civic Orchestra, and visiting jazz, classical, and chamber artists.... *Tel 312/435–6666. 220 S. Michigan Ave., Jackson el stop.* **(see p. 179)**

Park West. Intimate nightclub graced with good sightlines and acoustics. Call ahead to reserve a table for an extra 20 bucks.... *Tel 773/929–5959. 322 W. Armitage Ave., #151 bus from Michigan Ave. or State St. $5–40.*
(see p. 182)

Ravinia. This tree-covered music idyll is a romantic spot to relax on the lawn on a summer evening. Rent a pair of lawn chairs and a side table ($8) and pick up a boxed meal at the well-stocked concession area. During the rest of the year, recitals featuring young "rising stars" are held in the park's **Bennett Hall** ($15).... *Tel 847/266–5100. Lake-Cook and Green Bay roads, Highland Park; Metra train to Ravinia Park stop. $8–10 for lawn seats, $15–45 for covered pavilion seats. June–Sept.* **(see pp. 179, 181)**

River North Dance Company. Performing at various venues, this 14-member jazz-oriented company gives a lot of local artists a shot at choreographing.... *Tel 312/944–2888. Offices at 1016 N. Dearborn Pkwy, $20–25. Oct–May.*
(see p. 181)

Roadworks Productions. Acclaimed upstart theater company that burst onto the scene in 1992, with three to five shows a year. Highlights include the Chicago premiere of Eric Bogosian's *Suburbia* and Mike Leigh's *Esctasy*.... *Tel 773/489–7623. Most shows at Victory Gardens Theater, 2257 N. Lincoln Ave. (Lincoln Park); offices at 1532 N. Milwaukee Ave. Tickets $15–20.* **(see p. 178)**

Second City. The Old Town institution has been a launching pad for comedic careers from Ed Asner to Gilda Radner to the voice of Homer Simpson (Dan Castellaneta).... *Tel 312/337–3992, 642–8189. 1616 W. Wells St., Sedgwick el stop. $6–16.* **(see p. 183)**

Shakespeare Repertory. The Bard is all this acclaimed company does and they do him well.... *Tel 312/642–2273. Ruth Page Theater, 1016 N. Dearborn Pkwy. Tickets $22–34. Oct–May.* **(see p. 177)**

Shubert Theatre. This grand old 2,000-seat theater keeps a busy schedule of Broadway-style crowd-pleasers, from *Rent* to *Peter Pan*. Avoid the second balcony and some obstructed seats.... *Tel 312/902–1500 (Ticketmaster Arts Line). 22 W. Monroe St., Monroe el stop. $15–67.50.*
(see p. 177)

Skyline Stage. Part of the reinvigorated Navy Pier entertainment complex, this open-air hall hosts a variety of fun summer concerts.... *Tel 312/595–7437. www.navypier. com. Grand Ave. at Lake Michigan, Grand el stop, transfer to #65 Grand or #29 State buses. $20–30 tickets for concerts.* **(see p. 181)**

Steppenwolf Theatre Company. Seriously grown-up after years as an intinerant young company, the city's acclaimed off-Loop theater operates from a rather austere Lincoln Park compound containing a 500-seat mainstage and upstairs studio space.... *Tel 312/335–1888. 1650 N. Halsted St., North and Clybourn el stop. $24.50–36.50 mainstage; $14.50–19.50 studio. Year-round.* **(see p. 176)**

Symphony Center. A combination of mostly classical and jazz music concerts.... *Tel 312/294–3000. 220 S. Michigan Ave., Jackson el stop. Call for ticket prices.* **(see p. 179)**

Theatre Building. Shows sometimes gravitate to this beehive of play-making after finding audiences in smaller houses around town. More than a dozen theater companies, including some promising young upstarts, use the three spaces.... *Tel 773/327–5252. 1225 W. Belmont Ave., Belmont el stop. $5–20.* **(see p. 178)**

The Vic. Teen rock fans stand outside for hours waiting to get the best seats for the occasional general-admission show. You'll practically have to shoehorn yourself into the tight cabaret seating.... *Tel 773/472–0366. 3145 N. Sheffield Ave., Belmont el stop. $12–20.* **(see p. 182)**

Wrigley Field. See Chicago Cubs above.

Zanies. Big name talent and suburbanites' birthday parties fill the room at this Old Town comedy club, which hits you with a standard two-drink minimum.... *Tel 312/337–4027. 1548 N. Wells St., Sedgwick el stop. Closed Mon. $13–16.* **(see p. 183)**

ENTERTAINMENT | THE INDEX

hotlines &
other basics

Airports... **O'Hare Airport**, as everybody knows, is the world's busiest airport. And though technically located in the city of Chicago, it's actually 17 miles northwest of the Loop, tethered to the city by a narrow corridor of land. Much of the airport has been refurbished since it was originally built, or totally built new in recent years—there's even a Starbucks out there now. The international terminal is a high-tech addition; the United terminal, designed by Helmut Jahn, has a great light show and an eerie sound system that makes you feel like you're on your way to Pluto, even if you're just heading to Dayton. The city's other airport is the small **Midway Airport**, 10 miles southwest of the Loop, off the Stephenson Expressway on South Cicero Avenue. In some ways it's more convenient to deal with than O'Hare, and it's serviced by a lot of smaller airlines such as KIWI and MarkAir.

Airport transport to downtown... While both airports are jammed with cabs vying for your business, Chicago is blessed with a subway system that allows travelers to get to and from both O'Hare and Midway for only $1.50 (a cab from O'Hare to downtown will run about $35, including a $1 surcharge, while from downtown to Midway it can cost up to $20). From O'Hare, the O'Hare/Congress/Douglas line runs 24 hours a day and transports you directly to the North Side and into the Loop. (If you're heading to Lincoln Park, Lake View, or another neighborhood, you can get off at any point along the way and take a bus or cab either east toward the lake or west away from it; just make sure you get a transfer for an extra 30¢ when you pay your fare at O'Hare.) The trip can take about a half hour but it's still faster than any other mode of transport. At O'Hare, follow the signs that look like the front of a subway car to get to the station. The line that runs to Midway is less convenient because once you get to the airport the walk to the terminal is a long one and there are no moving sidewalks as there are at O'Hare. The Midway line only runs until 11pm. Other modes of transportation include **Continental Airport Express** (tel 312/454–7799), which offers door-to-door bus service from either airport to most downtown hotels. From O'Hare it costs $15.50, or $28 round trip; from Midway it's $11, $20 round trip. In addition, all the major car rental agencies are available at both airports, with courtesy buses running between the terminals and lots.

American Express... Travel service offices are located at 122 S. Michigan (tel 312/435–2595) and 625 N. Michigan (tel 312/435–2570). Both are open Mon–Fri 9–5.

Baby-sitters... In the mood to dump the kids and trip the night fantastic? **The American Registry for Nurses & Sitters** (tel 773/248–8100), a state-licensed service that's been around since 1950, may be able to help. All sitters have passed background checks, must have at least three references, and must be certified in child and infant CPR. You're responsible for the sitter's transportation home if it's after 10pm. Cost varies.

Buses... The **Chicago Transit Authority** operates more than 100 bus routes in the city; the fare is $1.50. Transfers cost 30¢ extra and must be used within two hours of purchase; they must be purchased *as you board the bus*—the drivers are sticklers about this and no amount of whining will get them to back down. There's generally a bus stop every other block along each individual route, marked by a blue-and-white sign illustrating the route itself. If it says there's "night owl service," that route runs 24 hours. Many don't, though, so always check (and frankly, for safety's sake, you probably shouldn't ride the buses late at night anyhow).

Car rental... All major car rental agencies are represented in Chicago, with outlets throughout the city and at both airports. Prices vary widely, so ask in advance. And take note, the city of Chicago levies an 18 percent tax on car rentals. Call for locations; here are the phone numbers: **Alamo** (tel 800/327–9633); **Avis** (tel 800/331–1212); **Budget** (tel 800/527–0700); **Dollar** (tel 312/686–2030); **Hertz** (tel 800/654–3131); **National** (tel 800/227–7368); **Rent-a-Wreck** (tel 800/535–1391); **Thrifty** (tel 800/367–2277).

Chicago Office of Tourism... Tel 312/744–2400, 800/ ITS–CHGO. The office staffs a visitor information desk at the Water Tower Pumping Station, 163 E. Pearson Street (at North Michigan Ave.), open Mon–Fri 9–5.

Chicago Park District... Tel 312/747–2200.

Chicago Transit Authority (CTA)... Call the **CTA** (tel 312/836–7000) for information on how to take the subway from where you are to where you want to go.

Children's Emergency Services... Internationally recognized as one of the finest—if not *the* finest—children's hospital in the country, **Children's Memorial Hospital** (tel 312/880–4000, Fullerton and Lincoln Aves.) operates the city's only emergency room geared toward children.

Convention centers... **McCormick Place** (tel 312/791–7000, 2300 S. Lake Shore Dr.) is one of the biggest and most important convention complexes in the country; it has 63 meeting rooms and over 2.2 million square feet of exhibition space.

Doctors... The **Chicago Medical Society** (tel 312/670–2550) makes free referrals weekdays, 8:30am to 4:30pm.

El... see Subways, below.

Emergencies... Most Chicago hospitals have 24-hour emergency rooms. Call **911** for ambulance, paramedics, and police, or to report a fire or an animal bite. **Northwestern Memorial Hospital** (tel 312/908–2000, 233 E. Superior St.), generally considered the best emergency room in the city, is near many Magnificent Mile hotels. Other vital numbers: **Children's Memorial Hospital Emergency Room** (tel 773/880–4000); **Coast Guard Search and Rescue** (tel 312/768–4093); **Poison Control** (tel 312/906–6194).

Events hotlines... Desperate for something to do? Call the **City of Chicago Events Hotline** (tel 312/744–3370); **Jazz Hotline** (tel 312/427–3300); **Dance Hotline** (tel 312/419–8383); **Classical Music Alliance** (tel 312/987–9296) for classical music and opera information; **Hot Tix**

Hotline (tel 312/977–1755) for a recorded message listing all shows for which tickets are available on that day (calls on Friday also receive weekend information).

Festivals and special events...

January: **Chicago Boat, Sports, and RV Show** (tel 312/567–8500, McCormick Place); **Sports, Fishing, and Outdoor Show** (O'Hare Expo Center, tel 843/318–6666).

February: **Chicago Cubs Fans Convention** (tel 773/477–8173); **Azalea Flower Show** (tel 312/742–7737, Lincoln Park Conservatory); **Camellia Flower Show** (tel 773/746–5100, Garfield Park Conservatory); **Chinese New Year Parade** (tel 312/326–5329, Wentworth and Cermak Aves.); **Chicago International Auto Show** (tel 312/692–2220, McCormick Place).

March: **St. Patrick's Day Parade**, March 17 (Dearborn St. at Wacker Dr.).

April: **Cubs Opening Day**, Wrigley Field (tel 773/404–CUBS, see Entertainment); **White Sox Opening Day** (tel 312/674–1000, Comiskey Park, see Entertainment); **Spring and Easter Flower Show** (tel 312/742–7736, Lincoln Park Conservatory); **International Kennel Dog Show** (tel 312/237–5100, McCormick Place).

May: **Buckingham Fountain Color Light Show**, runs through September (Grant Park at Congress St. and Lake Shore Dr.); **Polish Day Parade** (tel 312/744–3315, Clark St. at Wacker Dr.); **Greek-American Parade** (tel 312/744–3315, Michigan Ave. at Wacker Dr.).

June: **Gay and Lesbian Pride Week Parade** (tel 773/348–8243, Halsted St. at Belmont St.); **Chicago Blues Festival** (tel 312/744–3315, Petrillo Music Shell, Grant Park); **57th Street Art Fair** (tel 773/684–8383, Hyde Park); **Old Town Art Fair** (tel 312/337–1938 or 312/744–3315, Lincoln Park W at Orleans St.); **Puerto Rican Day Parade** (tel 312/744–3315, Clark St. at Wacker Dr.); **Andersonville Midsummerfest** (tel 773/728–2995, Clark St., between Foster and Catalpa Aves.); **Printer's Row Book Fair** (tel 312/987–1980, Dearborn St. at Harrison St.).

July: **Chicago Country Music Festival** (tel 312/744–3370, Petrillo Music Shell, Grant Park); **Chinatown Summer Fair** (tel 312/225–6198, Wentworth Ave. at 22nd St.); **Sheffield Garden Walk and Festival** (tel 773/929–9255, Webster and Sheffield Aves.); **Halsted Street**

Market Days (tel 773/868–3010, Halsted St. at Belmont Ave.); **Taste of Chicago** (tel 312/744–3315, Grant Park); **Fourth of July Celebration**, July 3 (Grant Park).

August: **Medieval Fair** (tel 773/880–5200, Oz Park, at Webster, Larrabee, and Lincoln Aves.); **Sandcastle Competition** (tel 312/670–7770, North Ave. Beach); **Gold Coast Art Fair** (tel 312/787–2677, River North); **Venetian Night** (tel 312/744–3315, Monroe Harbor); **Bud Billiken Parade**, the largest African-American parade in the country, celebrating the beginning of the school year (tel 312/225–2400, 39th St. and King Dr.); **Air and Water Show** (tel 312/744–3315, North Ave. Beach).

September: **Chicago Jazz Festival** (tel 312/744–3315, Petrillo Music Shell, Grant Park); **"Viva! Chicago" Latin Music Festival** (tel 312/744–3315, Petrillo Music Shell, Grant Park); **Octoberfest** (tel 312/427–3170, Adams St. between Dearborn and State Sts.); **Mexican Independence Day Parade** (tel 312/744–3315, Michigan Ave. at Wacker Dr.).

October: **Chicago Marathon** (tel 312/744–3315), which starts in Grant Park and runs throughout the city; **Columbus Day Parade** (tel 312/828–0010, Dearborn St. at Wacker Dr.); **Chicago International Film Festival** (tel 312/425–9400); **Chicago International Antique Show** (tel 312/787–6858, Navy Pier).

November: **Chrysanthemum Show** (tel 312/746–5100, Garfield Park Conservatory, and tel 312/742–7737, Lincoln Park Conservatory); **Veterans' Day Parade** (tel 312/744–3315, the Loop); **Christmas Tree Lighting** (tel 312/744–3315, Daley Plaza, the Loop).

December: **Christmas Flower Show** (tel 312/746–5100, Garfield Park Conservatory, and tel 312/742–7737, Lincoln Park Conservatory).

Gay guys and lesbians... Important local organizations include the **Illinois Federation for Human Rights** (tel 773/477–7173); **Queer Nation** (tel 773/202–5482); **Gay & Lesbian Physicians of Chicago** (tel 312/670–9630); **Anti-Violence Project/Horizons Community Services** (tel 773/871–CARE); **Chicago Black Lesbians & Gays** (tel 312/409–4917); **Rainbow Bridge** for disabled gays and lesbians, (tel 773/539–1240); **Men of All Colors Together** (tel 312/409–6916); and **Parents and Friends**

of Lesbians & Gays (tel 773/472–3079). Three churches with especially strong gay outreach programs are **Metropolitan Community Church** (tel 773/262–0099); **Unity Church of Chicago** (tel 773/973–0007); and the **Wellington Avenue Church** (tel 773/935–0642). For gay-oriented social activities, contact **Chi-Town Squares** for square dancing (tel 312/357–3100); **Chicago Smelts**, the "mostly" gay swim club (tel 312/409–4974); **Cafe Pride** for underage lesbians and gays (tel 773/278–2438); **Women's Sports Association** (tel 773/334–2100); **Frontrunners/Frontwalkers**, the gay running club (tel 312/409–2790); **Gay/Lesbian Yacht Club** (tel 773/327–6092); the **Metropolitan Sports Association** (tel 312/409–7932); and the organizers of the **International Mr. Leather Weekend** (tel 773/878–6360). Health-oriented resources include **AIDS Alternative Health Project** (tel 773/561–2800); the **AIDS Foundation of Chicago** (tel 312/922–2322); **AIDS Hotline** (tel 800/AID–AIDS); **AIDS Walk Chicago** (tel 312/422–8200); the **Lesbian Community Cancer Project** (tel 773/561–4662); and the **Jewish AIDS Network of Chicago** (tel 773/275–2626).

Hearing-impaired services... City of Chicago Events Hotline TDD number for the hearing impaired (tel 312/744–8599).

Newspapers and magazines... The big kahuna is the *Chicago Tribune*, for which the city's biggest journalistic embarrassment, Bob Greene, writes. The daily paper costs 50¢; the Sunday edition is $1.50. The "Friday" section is good for nightlife and entertainment listings. The *Chicago Sun-Times* has equally good Friday listings and, since it's a tabloid, is easier to read on the el. It's cheaper than the *Trib*, too, at 35¢ for the daily and $1.25 on Sunday. Both have a fairly conservative political slant. If you still can't decide on which paper to read, remember Gene Siskel writes for the *Trib*, while his full-figured counterpart, Roger Ebert, flips his thumb at the *Sun-Times*. The *Chicago Reader*, which comes out on Thursdays, has the city's most comprehensive nightlife listings; it's available, free, at bookstores and other stores throughout the North Side. Another freebie, upstart *New City*, is a terrific blend of service information, listings, reviews, and in-your-face journalism. *Chicago* magazine ($2.50) carries 120 or so restaurant reviews every month; though its reviewers don't dish the restaurants as much as merely list the dishes, they still hold a lot of sway among the foodie cognoscenti. The magazine's also a good resource for dozens of theater reviews, gallery listings, and special events. For the Muffie and Chads amongst you, go to **Chicago Social** for complete listings of benefits, black tie galas, and fashion shows, not to mention the best big-bucks real estate ads in the city.

Parking... If you're willing to pay for it, there is parking galore in Chicago. Municipal lots, where the rates are comparatively low ($5.50 for each 24-hour period, believe it or not), are generally located downtown; privately owned lots are sprinkled throughout the city. Municipal lots include: **East Monroe Underground** (tel 312/294–4740, 350 E. Monroe St.); **Grant Park Underground North** (tel 312/294–2437, N. Michigan Ave. at Monroe St.); **Grant Park Underground South** (tel 312/294–4593, S. Michigan Ave. at Congress); **Midcontinental Parking Garage** (tel 312/986–6821, 55 E. Monroe St.); **Navy Pier Parking** (tel 312/791–7437, 600 E. Grand Ave.); **Soldier Field** (tel 312/294–2437, 14th St. and Lake Shore Dr.).

Pharmacies... **Walgreens** has more than 100 branches throughout the city, with 17 of them open 24 hours a day. The 24–hour branch at 757 N. Michigan Ave. (tel 312/664–8686) holds claim to being one of the world's busiest pharmacies, for whatever that's worth. Another big chain, **Osco** (tel 773/477–3333), has a number of 24-hour branches, too.

Pro sports... The **Chicago Bears** NFL football team (tel 312/976–9600); the **Chicago Blackhawks** hockey team (tel 312/455–7000); the **Chicago Bulls** NBA basketball team (tel 312/455–4000); and the **Chicago Cubs** (tel 312/404–2827) and the **Chicago White Sox** (tel 312/674–1000) for baseball. For more details on these teams, see Entertainment.

Radio stations... WBEZ (91.5 FM), local National Public Radio; WFMT (98.7 FM), classical music; WLUP (97.9 FM and 1000 AM), rock; WXRT (93 FM), traditional and alternative rock.

Restrooms... Plenty of clean bathrooms exist if you know where to look. Try department stores, from **Marshall Field's** to **Neiman Marcus**, even **Crate & Barrel** on Michigan Avenue, or scout out the bathrooms off the lobbies of any of the downtown hotels. The **Starbucks** coffee bar on Rush Street is another handy pit-stop spot. You can generally disregard signs in restaurant and bar windows that say "restrooms for patrons only." There are public restrooms at the **Water Tower Pumping Station**, at the corner of Michigan Avenue and Pearson Street.

Subways... Four subway lines are operated by the **Chicago Transit Authority (CTA)**, though the entire system, whether below-ground or above, is generally referred to as the "el." Most trains run 24 hours a day, though some stations are closed at night and some routes run limited hours on Sundays (it's always wise to check first). Stations generally alternate "A" and "B," with the major stations being both; still, it's a good idea to check your map when making plans. There's nothing worse than being on a train that only makes "A" stops when you want to get off at a "B." The city claims the trains run every 5 to 15 minutes, and that's probably true during the morning and evening rush hours, but at other times the wait can be a drag. Fortunately, many of the outdoor el platforms have heat lamps that actually work, a real lifesaver in winter. You must use tokens to ride the system—buy them at any station. Most stations are unmanned. As in any big city, there's the constant threat of raising the fare, but tokens are currently $1.50, with a 30¢ transfer available if you want to switch to any bus route (the transfer must be used within two hours). There are reduced fares for children under 11 and seniors over 65. Always check maps to make sure you can find transfer points between lines; most el stations have maps posted. Call the surprisingly useful **CTA hotline** (tel 312/836-7000) for information on how to get from where you are to where you want to go.

Taxes... Chicago sales tax is 8.75% on everything but groceries and prescription drugs, for which there is, thankfully, no tax at all.

Taxis... A necessary evil, Chicago taxis are often dirty, unpleasantly aromatic, and driven by men and women who neither know the city well nor care to learn. It's not unheard-of to get in a cab, give your destination, and have the driver ask *you* for directions. Supposedly, a light on the top of a cab indicates that the cab is available, but lit cabs zoom by with riders all the time, while dark ones roam the streets with no fares. You might as well hail any cab you see coming—the worst that can happen is that it passes you by. The farther you go away from the Loop and the Michigan Avenue area, the more difficult it becomes to get a cab; in many neighborhoods you simply have to phone ahead (tel 312/TAXICAB). As with the public transportation system, cab fees are in constant flux. Currently they're fixed at $1.20 as the meter starts, $1.50 for each additional mile. There's a surcharge (or rip-off, depending on your attitude) of 50¢ for each additional person in the cab.

Ticketmaster... Tel 312/559–1212 for tickets to theater, music, and sports events.

Time... Tel 312/976–1616.

Trains... Train service to Chicago's suburbs is fast and relatively convenient. **METRA** (tel 312/836–7000) operates commuter lines to almost all of them, departing from various stations in the city, including the Northwestern Station (Madison St. and Canal St.), Union Station (Adams St. and Canal St.), LaSalle Street Station (LaSalle St. and Van Buren St.), and the Randolph Street Station (Randolph St. and Michigan Ave.). **The Illinois Central-Gulf Railroad**, or IC (tel 312/755–7500), commutes to Hyde Park. **Amtrak** (tel 800/872–7245) trains use grand old Union Station, which just happens to have a nifty children's playroom to help make long waits a little more bearable for train-traveling families.

Travelers with disabilities... For information, (tel 312/744–4016).

TV stations... The networks: CBS is channel 2, NBC is channel 5, and ABC is channel 7. Local stations: Chicagoland Television (local 24-hour news) is on channel 10, Fox-WFLD is on channel 32, WGN is on channel 9. The PBS affiliate, WTTW, is on channel 13. For channel-surfers, the Chicago area is wired with the usual host of cable-TV options.

Visitor information... Chicago Convention and Tourism Bureau, tel 312/567–8500; **Chicago Office of Tourism**, tel 312/744–2400; **Illinois Bureau of Tourism**, tel 800/223–0121.

Weather... Tel 312/976–1212.

Western Union... Tel 800/325–6000.